BAREFOOT REPORTER

**The best of the Richard Hughes columns from the
Far Eastern Economic Review, 1971-83**

Edited by
Mike MacLachlan

ISBN 962-7010-19-7

Published by Far Eastern Economic Review, Ltd.,
6th Floor, Centre Point, 181 Gloucester Road,
G.P.O. Box 160, Hongkong.

Printed by Yee Tin Tong Printing Press, Ltd.,
Morning Post Building, Tong Chong Street,
G.P.O. Box 47, Hongkong.

Contents

Page

Foreword 5

1971: The Mystery of the Missing March 7

1972: The Year of the Rat; The Old Shadow Master; Prisoners in China; A Dialogue with Mao; Tbilisi on the Trans-Siberian; The Emperor's Horse; The Aussie Asians; A Roll of Honour; The Wise Judge of Japan; Cambodia's Naughty Elephant; Australian Espionage; In Search of Anzac 9

1973: Japan's Man to Watch; Sing-Song in Taiwan; The Hijacked Tourists; Return to Shanghai; Suzhou's Leaning Tower; A Foreign Field; Death of a Jungle Fighter; Cow-Cake in Victoria 30

1974: The Enigma of Laos; Holmes the Revisionist; Morin Meets his Deadline; The Slopes of Mt Fuji; An Audience of Eggs; The Third China; An Embarrassing Incident; In Praise of Ginseng; The Disputed Temple; Hughes the Hangman 42

1975: The Horn Harvest; An Actor's Death; Clampdown on the Ginza; Homage to Two Martyrs; Good Neighbours; Snippets from 1949; Strongman Shareholders; Incident in a Lift; 'Demon' Hyde of Delmonte's; The Changing Triads 56

1976: Zhou's Last Bow; A Tribute to Deng Yingchao; Death of a Mate; The Cult of Kim; Sad News from Saigon; Up Stumps in Hongkong; The Other Richard Hughes; Captive Koreans; Of Drink and Drugs 71

1977: Salute to the Constellation; The Blind Bonze; Old Whampoa; A Haunting Mystery; RIP Memories; Blacktrackers in the Jungle; The People's Army; Kim's Kidnappers; Tokyo Revisited; The Old Homestead 83

1978: Frazer's Australia; Suzie Who?; Wine in China; Travels with 007; Gallantry and Gullibility; Hope in Quemoy; Pearls Before Greyhounds; Occupation Babies; The Murdered Generals; Sihanouk and his Princess; Catholics in China 97

1979: Memories of Xinjiang; Boxers and Boxing; The Beer Championships; Holy Hotline; The Kanto Disaster; Missing Millions; Operation Flying Elephant; The Perils of Shouting 113

1980: A Rogues' Gallery; The Teikoku Poisoner; Sealing the Peace; Lost, Stolen or Strayed; A Tourist in Russia; New Peking Opera; The Shin Factory; Slave Children of Shanghai; A Foreign Saint; Australia Looks North *125*

1981: Return of a Communist; Landmarks No More; The Year of the Cocked Pistol; Who Lost Singapore?; No. 1 Shimbun Alley; The Prince Charles Tapes; Teach Yourself Strine; The Past in Print *141*

1982: The Vanishing Colonel; 'Ivan the Chain-Puller'; North Korea's Class System; Asean or Anzus?; The New Australians; What's in a Name?; Ayo Gorkhali; The Case of the Kert; 1839 and all That *155*

1983: A Great Newspaperman; Death of a Spy; The Wind of the Gods; Talking to the Re-educated; Confucius and Christ; The Horse Traders; Anzac Rejected; Protecting the Pandas; Crime and Punishment; The Holt Affair *169*

Foreword

The sense of loss which follows the deaths of most of our friends dwindles quickly into occasional twinges of sorrow. When, somewhat apprehensively, the Falstaffian soul of Richard Hughes went to meet its Maker on 4 January 1984, it left his earthly friends burdened with an acute and permanent personal bereavement. His usual haunts — Hongkong's Foreign Correspondents Club and his favourite corner (it bore his name) in the Hilton Hotel Grill — are duller places today because he is not there. His name still crops up with extraordinary frequency whenever pressmen and other mortals of wit and benevolence foregather.

His soul had reason to be nervous as it approached the Pearly Gates, for Dick, a true Australian, had extravagantly lapsed from the Catholicism of his Irish mother in which he had been raised, and the Calvinism of his Welsh father. Lurching between the two stools, he fondly imagined a God created in the Hughes image — a Rabelesian figure sipping wine on a heavenly couch, slapping his naked thigh with understanding mirth as he contemplated the antics of humans below. I, for one, hope the Archbishop (his friends all accorded him episcopalian authority and unfailingly addressed him as "Your Grace") was right.

He was always a pressman. Although he started work on the Victorian Railways, it was a writing job in the public-relations department, and he soon joined the Melbourne *Star* (inspiring the crack, "Leaving PR for journalism is like running away from sea to go to school"). From there he went on to Sydney's *Daily Telegraph*, which sent him to Tokyo whence he penned warnings to Australia about the challenges to come. After reporting World War II, he returned to a defeated Japan and began again his long journey to the doyenship of correspondents in Asia via the Korean War, the lamented death of two wives, a rumbustious spell as manager of the Tokyo press club, work for the London

Economist and *The Sunday Times*, several scoops (the best known being an exclusive interview in Moscow with British traitors Burgess and MacLean), a shift of base from Tokyo to Hongkong, a third happy marriage to a gentle Chinese matron, Ann, and the beginning — in 1972 — of his weekly columns in the *Far Eastern Economic Review*.

But he was always more than just a pressman. He was a towering personality, never less than the best of company. Two writers as different as Ian Fleming (who, while writing his James Bond thrillers, was Dick's foreign editor) and John le Carré wrote him into their books. Dick was "Dikko" Henderson of the Australian Secret Service in Fleming's *You Only Live Twice* and more memorably Old Craw in Le Carré's *The Honourable Schoolboy*. Le Carré wrote: "Some people, once met, simply elbow their way into a novel and sit there until the writer finds them a place. Dick is one. I am only sorry I could not obey his urgent exhortation to libel him to the hilt. My cruellest efforts could not prevail against the affectionate nature of the original."

Generous too: the only times Dick lost his temper were when his guests, which included many a visiting bludger, attempted to reach for the bill. He would hear no slander even against the least admirable types, particularly if they were fellow pressmen. He reserved his anger for communists, and the mark of the beginning of a convivial evening in his company, when Dick had hoisted in a vodka or three, came with his traditional toast: "Death to the commy dogs!" Even that was theatrical, soon to be replaced by increasingly crowded memories of those who had gone before: "To absent friends!"

This book is by way of being a memorial for a man-mountain of wit and magnanimity. It contains some of the best columns he wrote for the REVIEW, in which he combined the best of Hughes the pressman and Hughes the man, as a raconteur with memories of Asia stretching back over six decades. We present it with pride — and with sympathy for those who never had the pleasure and the honour of his company. And we dedicate it to Ann.

Hongkong, October 1984   DEREK DAVIES

1971 October

Even the appetite of hungry watchers of China-watchers has become sated by the orgy of speculation over The Case of the Missing March — the unexplained cancellation of the October 1 National Day military parade — which merged with the Mystery of the Dying Chairman (or should it now be the Chairman's Dying Most Trusted Comrade-In-Arms?). But there are still some tasty morsels to be found — and indirect lessons to be learned.

The China-watcher for whom I have the most reverence — a conservative and a sceptic — told me brusquely: "It is a capital mistake to theorise before you have all the evidence." I forebore from the malicious observation that he had lifted this Thought, unattributed, from the Master. (By The Master, of course, I mean Sherlock Holmes, not Chairman Mao. But the quote came, appropriately, from *A Study in Scarlet*.)

The hard evidence, after all, appears to have been a last-minute refusal or reluctance to parade a protocol muster of party brass on the reviewing dais for The Missing March. As in Moscow, this ceremonial muster reveals party status or disgrace by literally a step down or a step up, by physical presence or absence.

All the surmise — wild or sceptical — derives, in fact, from that vexing but common weakness in both communist and fascist regimes: an inability to arrange a decorous, non-lethal, popular succession in leadership. In these circumstances, the health and appearance of Chairman Mao Zedong's appointed and annointed heir-apparent, Lin Biao, and the rating of his army boys, would have been more significant, blasphemously but realistically, than another illness of the Chairman.

The North Vietnam Workers' Party demonstrated with dignity, reverence and affection, when their Mao, Ho Chi Minh, "ascended the dragon," that an agonising war, wider doubts about succession, and expedient dependence upon the "destructible friendship" of Moscow and Peking, need not provoke a shabby masquerade to delay or deny a father-figure's passing. (Of course, it may plausibly be submitted that the Hanoi comrades, historically anti-Peking anyway, are more Vietnamese than communist. Certainly — as all foreign correspondents know — they are more polite and correct than the Peking mandarins in their acknowledgment (even if they refuse to grant them) of polite and correct applications for visas.

However, six indirect lessons of the Peking uproar, as my revered Hongkong mentor severely insisted, are now rewarding if marginal:

● Peking does not give a damn about astute, imaginary or concocted foreign speculation on Peking happenings. Chairman Mao, the old hero, and Premier Zhou Enlai, the old "adjuster," must have spared a belly-rumble or a scrutable chuckle for "the sparks that started a prairie fire." (Mao this time, not Holmes.)

● Zhou, durable and indispensable, shows no aspiration to raise himself above his No. 2 posting, whatever the struggle or intrigue around him.

At 73, he accepts his party — and now army — role of being always the bridesmaid and never the bride. He once held higher rank nominally in the party than Mao. As a young, and then ambitious, leader of the sophisticated "international clique" in the confused and divided party of the Thirties, he was indeed opposed to both Mao and his "Chinese clique" and Wang Ming and his "Russian clique." He was an intimate of Li Lisan but managed to escape the disgrace and exile which that faded hero suffered when Mao and his indomitable peasants overcame. He has had remarkable luck (and the party, the Chinese and the world have also gained from that luck) in switching sides safely and unobtrusively in top party controversies. He can afford now to smile at those old labels: The Great Dissembler, The Elastic Bolshevik, The Chinese Talleyrand, The Confucian Communist.

Perhaps he remains durable and indispensable because he prefers to remain No. 2. He was manifestly happy last week publicly to pass the credit — or responsibility — for the Nixon kowtow to Chairman Mao himself.

● Whatever the health of long-ailing Lin Biao, and whatever the military support for chief-of-staff Huang Yongsheng, the army continues to run China, and the official party remnants, "reformed and reformed," are still running-dogs — rather limping-dogs — for the soldiers.

● The Soviet Union will not provoke "incidents" on the old Khabarovsk eastern Siberian frontier, if only because its forces there are more vulnerable and exposed than in the Mongolian and Xinjiang sectors.

● Chairman Mao had wanted himself to de-fuse the "Mao cult." He surely made this clear enough to his own Dr Watson, Edgar Snow, who also hinted to a then unspeculative world that Peking was waiting for a Nixon sunrise.

The sixth and final lesson is irrefutable and perhaps more disquieting for the world than for China:

● Mao's high command is now an Old Men's Brigade, and the new Chinese leader for the next decade has not yet been sighted — inside or outside the army.

"Old men live too long," Mao once told Andre Malraux. Taiwan-watchers in Peking, though as quick and reckless on the draw as some China-watchers, have refrained, not surprisingly, from developing that plausible line against another "old man."

The first Richard Hughes column, published on 16 October 1971.

1972 January

T he year 1972, all readers will instantly recall, is the Year of the Rat, which — appropriately in these days of change and betrayal — ushers in the new cycle of 12 years in the Oriental zodiac.

The 12 years, in star-destined order and zoological omen, are the Years of the Rat, Ox, Tiger, Hare, Dragon, Serpent, Horse, Ram, Monkey, Cock, Dog and Wild Boar (1971). The late Comrade Marx may not have heard of this celestial law of the animal calendar, and Chairman Mao himself does not refer to it in any of his manifestos; but stubbornly it persists, real and abiding, if non-ideological (and now, indeed, in China officially heretical).

Felicitously, as it happens, the traditional animal attributes of this Year of the Rat coincide with the coldly logical anticipations of leading Asia-watchers in London, whose judgment I have been humbly soliciting.

My favourite Chinese soothsayer, Chow, veteran expatriate and glib barber at China Hair-Dressers (8 Gerrard Street, W1), reminded me severely that the ruling attributes of those born in the Year of the Rat, and which also shape the course of national events, are: "Ambition and cunning, but surface reasonableness, persistence, compromise and a preference for cautious talk until new action has been planned."

Even the most sceptical will concede that this superstitious blueprint for 1972 is persuasively foreshadowed by the projected visits of President Nixon to Peking and Moscow, by the anguished re-thinking of policies by Japan and Southeast Asian states, and by the advent of Peking in the UN. Diplomat Asian-watchers in London expect no swift, firm or dramatic changes during the coming year, but predict rather a breathing — or talking — spell of pragmatic negotiation and expedient realignment.

"President Nixon's eyes, reasonably enough, are on the White House rather than the Imperial Palace of the UN Assembly," one Foreign Office authority said. "As a formidable and realistic politician, he naturally doesn't expect international

miracles or serious communist changes of heart."

"Premier Zhou Enlai was born in the Year of the Monkey." Chow observed later. (He did not sit in with the FO man and myself.) "And he is splendidly true to his zodiac type: quick, highly observant, curious and searching; a retentive memory and well-informed; agile enough to swing away from adversity; great capacity for survival — but chattering and jumping, rather than in command.

"President Nixon was born in the Year of the Ox, whose adherents, despite normal unemotional behaviourism, can anger easily and be rash and petty. You will recall

9

that the equivocal former foreign minister, Chen Yi, was an Ox-man."

"Whether he initiated it or not, Mao is of course pushing the new Zhou line of realistic adjustment, surrendering nothing while labouring to restore internal Party influence and authority over the still dominant army," the FO man argued.

"Chairman Mao was born in the Year of the Serpent," Chow resumed, picking his teeth. "That means flexibility and longevity; great wisdom but indifferent organisation; dexterity in avoiding, foiling and despatching a strong enemy from the rear; venomous striking reaction when protecting its young or its hole; a fondness for the night time." (Which, I gather, means a talent for conspiracy.)

Chow was surprised when I produced a copy of that hardy perennial of Chinese superstition, *The Kitchen God's Almanac*, which I had picked up in the Arts and Crafts of China Emporium (89 Baker Street). Although ideologically banned in China, the Almanac, which is an unbroken link with the great astrological Emperor Yao, is obviously still being printed in revisionist provinces (my copy came from Sichuan) and exported for sale to Overseas Chinese.

It forecasts harvest output — "very promising" for 1972 — gives advice on how to propitiate the non-Politburo gods in the heavens and names lucky days for personal, non-communal endeavour.

Chow pointed out that the historic portrait of Grand Marshal T'ai Sui, the Spirit of Jupiter, who has acted as China's Minister of Time since 1000 BC, had been censored from my errant copy of the Almanac, though his name was still reverently invoked as celestial commissar charged with protection of livestock from distemper, children from smallpox and crops from flood. Also, some faithful party cadres had stamped my Sichuan Rat-Year edition with orthodox slogans: "Beware of the Liu Shaoqi type political swindlers," "Peoples of the world, unite," and "Beat down the US invaders and their running-dogs."

"I am confident that Chairman Mao still reads this *Kitchen God's Almanac*," said Chow (a reactionary, I fear). "After all, he was born a farmer and, as a Serpent, he understands the farmers better than any of his advisers do — whether they adapt to the expedient 'reasonableness' of the Rat, or are endowed with the mental agility of the Monkey. There will always be rats in the Chinese farmers' kitchens."

February

Only an old shadow master like Sir Robert Thompson could have made such a stealthy — nay, underground — encore visit to Thailand at this time of belated counter-insurgency operations in the north, northeast and along the Cambodian and Malaysian borders. A Thai officer tried to prevent an alert Thai newspaperman from approaching him at Bangkok's appalling airport on his surprise return. His subsequent movements, consultations and recommendations remain a closed secret, I gather, but it is known at least that he and Richard Noone, that other tough and smooth British veteran of the Malayan

"Emergency," together toured the north and northeast . . . old men like myself recall that the real authority on the disappearance of another Thompson — silken Jim — was, and is, Dick Noone.

It is no secret that both Seato and Thailand's National Executive Council would like to recruit Sir Thompson's services full-time. But he declines. (Thais, like Japanese, tend to call him "Sir Thompson.")

However, his influence and advice fortunately linger still in Thailand, as in South Vietnam where his shadowy presence, I well remember, mystified occasional visiting pressmen because it was always a murmured apology: "I am not really an 'adviser.' I just like to keep in touch with the changing tactics of subversive operations." He was, I know, pushing this line, deadpan, on his encore visit to Bangkok.

The Thanom Kittikachorn "Revolutionary" National Council is at last striking back confidently and "according to plan," against the Peking-backed Siamese version of the Vietcong: the Thai People's Liberation Armed Forces (carrying Mao badges like St Christopher medals).

The known outline of these countermeasures follows the familiar basic pattern of recovery in Thompson Malaya and Thompson-CIA South Vietnam: resettlement and protection of displaced or anti-insurgent villagers; isolation and surveillance of suspected villages; construction of strategic roads in vulnerable areas; transfer of combat-toughened troops from South Vietnam to northern Thailand, but top priority against infiltration, underground organisation, terrorism and arms-stock-piling in northeastern Thailand;

expedient and flexible border alliance with Malaysia and Cambodia; and — to quote Malaysian Home Affairs Minister Tun Ismail (which means re-quoting "Sir Thompson") — "the only defence against communist subversion is a socially just and united society." Thailand has another non-secret weapon: the king.

Perhaps it is not indiscreet to record other recurrent whispers in Bangkok because they have been confirmed by testimony from recent disillusioned defectors to the Thai Communist Suppression Operations Command. That old Thompson ploy — which the CIA also employed in the South Vietnam Delta area and Central Highlands — is now paying off, with heavier dividends to come, in Thailand:

You seed "volunteers" for the seducers in areas which are open to infiltration; they secretly and eagerly approach the first enemy agents, are fraternally recruited, suspiciously "screened" of course, and then despatched, with Mao visas, to the commie training camps. Elementary, my dear 007.

It may well and happily transpire that Bangkok's tardy recognition militarily of the harsh communist facts of life, revolution and the pursuit of slavery, while permitting initial and deadly infiltration, will reap a more rewarding harvest on this 007 front because that evil Bondian-Thompson line was promulgated earlier in Thailand than in Malaysia or South Vietnam.

The first "screened" Thai traitors passed through Hanoi camps. The later cadres-to-be have been smilingly, and contemptuously, handled in Laos camps. The Hanoi bosses are now deeply — and rightly —

suspicious of some of these Laos-trained recruits: hence, the defectors agree independently, a current witch-hunt.

And how sure can they be of new "converts" in Thai villages — and perhaps, in retrospect, of earlier suspect Hanoi-trained double-agents, whose performances have not justified party hopes?

It is a nice Thompson conundrum which, delightfully, will amuse Moscow as much as it distracts Hanoi and encourages Bangkok. It is always fun when rogues — I mean, comrades — fall out.

March

In Peking's early springtime mood, it seems a reasonable presumption that John Thomas Downey, 42-year-old CIA agent, will be at last sprung from his prison cell. His original life-term was quietly reduced to 25 years last year. He and another agent, 45-year-old Richard Fecteau — who was freed in December — were jailed in 1952, when they were found guilty of espionage after their plane was shot down over China or North Korea.

Two other US Air Force men, Capt. Philip Eldon Smith and Lieut Robert Flynn, have not been heard of since they were captured, in 1966 and 1967, when their planes strayed from Vietnam into China. Unlike Downey, they were honest strayers, but they have probably since been shipped to Hanoi.

Peking's Party indulgence is certainly not reflected by the Catholic renegades who still posture disgustingly as "priests"

in China, with the little red bible inside their brevaries. One such fearless Judas, "Bishop" Shin Yu-kin of Peking's betrayed St Mary's Church, last week lyingly repeated the preposterous charge that Bishop James Edward Walsh of Shanghai had been guilty of "espionage" and "sabotage." That real bishop was framed in 1960 and sentenced to 20 years. By coincidence, he was visiting Hongkong, still broken in health, when the creature Shin waited for the cock to crow outside St Mary's.

I still believe, with a respectful genuflection, that Vatican miscalculation was primarily responsible for Bishop Walsh's ordeal. As a good Christian Brothers' boy from St Kilda, I had the temerity to ask Bishop Walsh, whom I had the honour of meeting in Shanghai in 1957, why he was imprudently remaining in the diocese, after his Chinese superior had quit, running hard from Peking. The bishop replied simply that he would naturally remain at his post until His Holiness directed him to depart.

Then, all-advisedly, the Vatican posted the bishop's superior to Taiwan as a cardinal of "China." And so the enraged party struck back at Bishop Walsh. Politically, the Church is not always infallible.

One wonders naturally about other foreign-devil prisoners in China. There is another American: the scholarly ex-Brooklynite, Izzy Epstein, an idealistic Party-member, I thought, with a good sense of humour — one of those "contradictions." He and his handsome statuesque English wife — a Cholomondely, who, most aliens in Peking agreed, should have been more at home at a fox hunt than in the Forbidden City — disappeared during the "cultural revolution."

Other resident English victims of that witch-hunt are Michael Shapiro, friendly host to all visitors; David Crook, and Mrs Gladys Yang. She was a Cambridge intellectual who married a Chinese graduate; the Chinese mission in London, alas, rejected a respectful petition for her release last week.

Comrade Rewi Alley, that doughty Kiwi, managed to escape the "cultural" dragnet. His adroit adaptability and durability have won him the envious label: "The poor man's Zhou Enlai."

Until this week, the unhappiest forgotten foreign devil was Francis James, a notable Australian eccentric, who vanished in December 1969 after his unaccountable return to China. He had written a controversial article about China's nuclear installations on an earlier approved visit; this was denounced as a "fabrication" by the Chinese Foreign Ministry; one can only guess why he rashly returned.

Now we hear from a "ministerial source" that his release can be expected. Let us all pray devoutly that this does not prove to be yet another premature leak from the Australian cabinet which could cause Peking to think again.

James is a liberal journalist of great courage, with a pawkish sense of humour and a discerning darning-needle for the *derrières* of the pompous and pretentious. He even tolerates the friendship of such stony reactionaries as myself. We first met in Peking in 1956, when he was accompanying the then Anglican Archbishop of Sydney, Dr Mowll, on a tour of foreign missions. I suspect that he may well have gone back under the fatal delusion that he could discover some high Party officials who shared his good humour.

He was, of all things, a "religious" journalist. But he adheres to the Anglican heresy, so at least he was not vulnerable to the calumnies of those despicable "Catholic" masqueraders in Peking. Needless to add, not one of his ultra-leftist "friends" in Australia had raised a single picket to demand his release. After all, he was seized in China — not Taiwan or Greece or Spain or Russia.

April

Premier Zhou Enlai: May I invite your attention, Chairman, to alarm and despondency in the US Senate Foreign Relations Committee over the Paris talks between us and the United States?

Chairman Mao: Despondency? Fair enough. Alarm? Don't tell me it's serious. Anyway that foreign devil Kissinger will soothe them. He's a good, round turtle's egg; we could use him in the Party.

Zhou: It is a question of drunkenness, Chairman. *Drunkenness*. Not any suggestion of a confidence breach between the People's Republic and the White House.

Mao (*halting his half-raised glass of maotai in midair and slapping it on a fat, dusty file marked "Liu Shaoqi, Lin Biao, et al"*): What do you mean? I can drink what I like. If the foreign devils object — (*Hunanese obscenity*).

Zhou *(eyes rolling)*: I apologise for the misunderstanding, Chairman. The US senators are alarmed and despondent because their new Ambassador in Paris, who opened the negotiations, is reported to have been drunken and abusive in public on an international flight to Washington.

Mao *(gulping with a snort of laughter)*: Good on him. What's his name?

Zhou *(consulting his file)*: Someone called Watson.

Mao *(surprised and suspicious)*: Watson? Wasn't he a running dog for that London CIA fellow Sherlock Holmes? I thought he was dead. He is older than I am.

Zhou *(patiently)*: No, Chairman. This is an Arthur Watson, a recent personal appointment by President Nixon himself to the post of ambassador in Paris. There has been some high-level agitation in Washington — expressed chiefly by Senator Fulbright, whom we have invited to China, and by Secretary of State William Rogers, who has already visited us, you remember . . .

Mao *(mystified)*: Never heard of him.

Zhou *(a cough)*: To continue, Chairman; these admirable, cooperative, senatorial Americans are alarmed because they do not believe that we would welcome negotiations with an envoy who was "flagrantly drunk in public." They fear that we have no respect for drunkards. A Senator Church —

Mao *(a hiccough)*: Trust the Church to spoil things.

Zhou: A Senator *Frank* Church has referred to "the disdain of the Chinese for flagrant drunkenness in public."

Mao *(refilling his mao-tai cup)*: I have never heard such — *(Hunanese)* nonsense. I'd have liked Nixon more if he had had more to drink. Wasn't that turtle's egg, Doster Fulles or Foster Dulles, a teetotaller? Our old comrade, Chen Yi, certainly wasn't. May his ascent of the dragon have been well-lubricated and comfortable. I went to his funeral, didn't I? I reckon he was one of our best Foreign Ministry negotiators. No reflection on you, of course, Comrade Chou, as you well know. Sure you wouldn't like a shot? *(Extends the mao-tai tin.)*

Zhou *(with a bow)*: No, thank you, Chairman. Pray excuse me; I have a working schedule until 0400 tomorrow; some American students are arriving. But I second your fraternal toast . . .

To resume, should we transmit a discreet cable to the White House? Assuring them that our hopes for world peace, presidential re-election and Soviet rebuff from these continuing negotiations in Paris are unaffected by the fleeting indisposition of this man Watson — which might have been corrected by acupuncture? I should add that Secretary of State Rogers has said that Watson, anyway, was "never intended" to be the continuing Paris negotiator.

Mao: Now I am the one who is alarmed and despondent. I would rather have had a drunken negotiator. I dislike the cold sober Americans. You remember, comrade, what that old foreign-devil — Quincey or Quancey, who ate opium — said: "Men are not disguised in liquor but by sobriety." I say, let us have around us enemies who are fat and not disguised. *(Beginning to ramble.)* Remember the good old Yenan Caves? I wonder whatever happened to that old distillery up there. Did Zhu Deh put any Party money into it? I wouldn't put it past him. And of course *(an old gleam in his eye)* that was where I first met —

Zhou *(swiftly)*: Chairman, your warm human sentiments are always the foundation of the People's Republic and mean certain victory for world revolution. But, to close this minor incident, may I suggest that we "indicate" to the White House that the man Watson's excesses — if proven — do not decrease our cautious confidence in — nor increase our "tensions" over — the promises extended in Peking?

Mao *(relaxed)*: Fair enough. And tell them we'll provide the *mao-tai* for the Paris talks. What's that Ambassador drink? Gibson? But isn't that his name? Oh, *Watson*. Queer lingo. Let's give them the old *mao-tai*. What about one for you for the Long March, comrade? *(A tucket sounds. Zhou exits. Madam Mao enters. Curtain.)*

May

President Nixon, rallying from his Chinese *mao-tai*, would be well advised to begin sampling discreetly some Soviet "champagne" in wine-tasting preparation for his Moscow mission.

This week, my own Moscow and Siberian memories of the heady, yeast-fortified Georgian bubbly subterfuge were revived by a well-timed gift from an old non-party friend in Moscow: a formidable rocket-stoppered bottle of *Tbilisi* (non-vintage) from what is called, with brutal Stalin frankness, "a champagne factory." The party vignerons force-feed this "champagne" through steel vats, accelerating the French process of randy hand-rolling seduction, which should take two years, to two weeks by computerisers.

The Chinese comrades, we know, have their own Maoist version of "champagne," which was available in an alleged "nightclub" in a *hutung* behind the old Peking market as late as 1957; but the less said about that bastardised product the better for the Washington-Peking detente.

Myself, I discovered on my old Russian sallies that *Tbilisi* was a pleasant and prudent alternative to vodka with a *peever* (beer) chaser — what the Russkies, sincere drinkers, call "a ton-truck and a trailer." I was accustomed to indulge, with Irv Levine and Welles Hangen, in a hospitable if improbable supermarket bar opposite the Gorky Street cable office. But my real *Tbilisi* blooding came later on the 5,800-mile, eight-day, six-night trans-Siberian rail trek from Nahodka, with vodka stopovers at Khabarovsk and Irkutsk (Lake Baikal), to Moscow. That was mid-1963, when Khruschev and Kennedy were getting together more rewardingly than, I fear, Brehznev and Nixon will next week.

If a foreigner is lonely on the trans-Siberian express, it is his own fault. Language is not a real barrier; lively passengers drift from compartment to compartment, carrying their own refreshment, but never propaganda; and the dining-car is always a gregarious rendezvous. There, unfailingly, were lashings of the rough, sweet *Tbilisi* in large bottles fitted with clamped stoppers which exploded like pocket mortar-shells and which, effectively aimed, could raise a bruise at a distance of two tables.

Outside Irkutsk, I had fallen into pleasant sign-doggerel with two young Russian technicians and an East German. (You could always tell the East Germans on the train: they never shaved.) I blenched when my exhilarated chance companions reciprocated my initial offering with three bottles of *Tbilisi*. I blenched even more when one of the Russians laughingly pointed his unopened bottle at the bullet head of the severe, one-eyed colonel who, with a silent, massive, gluttonous wife, shared my soft-seat sleeping compartment, and who was then seated at a table to starboard, with his broad back incautiously turned towards us. In alarm, I diverted my companion's trajectory by jiggling the champagne nozzle at the last minute, so that the stopper smacked against the swaying ceiling and splashed harmlessly into the unruffled colonel's borshch.

I do not know what transpired in the diner after I bade the flushed table goodnight and repaired with quiet dignity to my compartment, where the one-eyed colonel and his lady were already relaxing. The colonel, as was his fascinating custom after each meal, had removed his glass eye and was substituting another, which he fastidiously selected from a collection of spares in his wife's reticule.

Then, alas, the technician lurched in, resentful and truculent on "ton-truck-and-trailer" chasers to his *Tbilisi*. I guess the waitress — and maybe other diners — had rebuked him, after I left, for alarming a stranger. I tried in pidgin-Russian to clarify and mollify his indictment, while

Trans-Siberian at Krasnoyarsk.

other curious passengers — sympathising with me — crowded outside, and the outraged colonel, still fumbling with his spare eye, explained to me in halting English that the intruder was drunken.

I felt (and still believe) that the technician had a legitimate grievance, and that my dining-car trepidation had been distorted; but when he seized my lapels I lost patience, thrust him back, and cried: "Knock it off!" For some strange Russian reason, this remonstrance delighted the jostling passengers in the corridor. "Knockitoff!" they chanted in chorus, beating one another on the back. The colonel, having at last settled the glass replacement in his empty Leningrad eyesocket, arose menacingly, pointed to the door, and, in a Red Square parade voice, roared: "Knockitoff!" The poor technician slunk out.

For the rest of the trip, I was always addressed as "Gospodin Knockitoff" — no longer "Mister Hoojis." My favourite waitress — who kept the best dining-car steaks for me — adopted the new name eagerly and with a certain pride, perhaps believing that I had undergone a baptismal naturalisation or had suddenly revealed a remote Georgian ancestry . . .

This is, I agree, an irrelevant drunken anecdote. But it might be a warning — nay, an encouragement — to President Nixon, when he toasts the Russians with *Tbilisi* in the Kremlin and welcomes another "week that changed the world." Neither *Tbilisi* nor *mao-tai* is, of course, a substitute for champagne. But *Tbilisi* is certainly more agreeable and does not affect articulation at state banquets as imprudently as either *mao-tai* or "a ton-truck and a trailer" will. Without doubt, Nixon and Brehznev will be shouting "Knockitoff!" at each other.

● **Nixon, having recently visited Peking was due to visit Moscow.**

July

By happy coincidence a Japanese-owned racehorse — with the non-*kabuki* name of Erimo Hawk and a bog-Irish jockey aboard — won the Royal Ascot Gold Cup last week, when Emperor Hirohito, 71, became Japan's longest-reigning monarch and the world's longest-ruling sovereign. True, the Japanese grey won the English classic only after disqualification of a locally-owned nag, Rock Roi. But the stewards' decision is final, even if the Emperor is no longer divine, and plenty of *sake* was drunk in Tokyo to celebrate the honourable and well-timed victory on barbarian turf.

Because of a further coincidence affecting stables, this is perhaps an appropriate time to lift the veil on one of the amusing secrets of the Occupation, which involved a far more famous Japanese horse than Erimo Hawk — none other than White Snow, the Emperor's own noble Arab, which US Adm. Halsey, in an expansive moment, had once threatened to ride bareback down the Ginza after Japan had been defeated. Following surrender, the chivalrous Admiral preferred not to be reminded of his vow.

Urbane Shigeru Ozu, then chief of the Horse Administration Bureau of the Imperial Household, told me the curious sequel of Japanese guile and Western gullibility, in confidence, over a couple of beers in the old Press Club in Tokyo's Shimbun Alley in 1947.

On 11 November 1945, tens of thousands of US Occupation troops at a Victory Rodeo in Meiji sports arena, Tokyo, enthusiastically cheered a Lieut Dick Ryan as he proudly cantered around the ground on a spirited white charger, while the loudspeakers hailed him as "the first American to ride Emperor Hirohito's favourite horse, White Snow."

Alas, it was an unfortunate error, which Ozu-*san* explained with proper Japanese regret and apologies. Lieut Ryan, described as "a cowboy officer," arrived in Japan in October 1945 after having staged rodeo shows for the Allied forces in Australia, New Guinea and the Philippines. He made persistent approaches to government officials and the Imperial Household, insisting on his right to ride the Emperor's horse at the Meiji rodeo.

The Japanese, though pledged and anxious to cooperate sincerely with all Occupation personnel, were reluctant to sanction this sacrilege. They had, in fact, secretly whisked White Snow out of the Palace stables to rural Sanrizuka because of fears that the salty old admiral might show up at the Palace gates in riding breeches and brandishing a riding crop.

Ozu-*san*, bowing and hissing, tactfully promised "inquiries," and then escorted Ryan to the jockey training grounds at Setagaya, ostensibly to requisition unbroken horses also needed in the rodeo.

Here, by artful contrivance, a white Arab was "accidentally" discovered. This was First Frost — high, white and handsome, but only an import from Korea. It had been a failure at stud and was serving as a hack for jockeys.

"Why," shouted the delighted Ryan, "this is the Emperor's horse here, isn't it?" Ozu-*san* was decently embarrassed by the unhappy misunderstanding. He assured me earnestly that one of the Setagaya officials tried to tell Ryan that the horse was only a rejected stud Arab and that the Emperor had never ridden it. But the interpreter — no doubt confused — did say it was "the Emperor's horse."

"Lieutenant Ryan," Ozu-*san* told me ruefully, "demanded possession of First Frost then and there, turned a deaf ear to all our further explanations that it was only a stud and not the one he was seeking, and refused to leave until a military truck was summoned to convey First Frost to Meiji."

Hence the mistaken identity. (White Snow was to die at Sanrizuka in democratic retirement — untouched by *gaijin* buttocks — in 1947.)

Ozu-*san* observed magnificently: "Although we Japanese naturally regretted any misunderstanding, we were all sincerely delighted that the Allied forces were, in the outcome, happy and satisfied and grateful."

That last observation could surely be an ironic epitaph for the whole Occupation.

I am increasingly in personal debt to Singapore's formidable and percipient Premier Lee Kuan Yew. He is, justifiably, no admirer of Australian initiative on the international scene, and he once coined a most incisive reprimand in that field (in an interview with my evil old friend, Jim Cameron) when he referred to "the strange reluctance of Australia to accept promotion above the rank of deputy sheriff."

Now, out of the cool blue, he has revealed that over the years since *merdeka* he has been selecting known communist students for higher education in Australian universities. Why? Because they were then persuasively brainwashed into "fairly middle-class and comfortable armchair critics." True, he mentioned New

Zealand and Canada as similar sugar-coated penitentiaries for potential anarchists, but the devious and subtle Australian reindoctrination methods obviously lead most decisively from the barricades to the armchairs.

This handsome backhand compliment to the great conservative south-land is reported to have "rocked" Australia and to have "shocked" Prime Minister William McMahon. As a senile expatriate who manages to return regularly and gratefully to the old homeland, my own reaction was only one of delayed self-revelation and self-reproach. Over the years I have maintained happy and rewarding contacts with many students from Singapore, Kuala Lumpur, Hongkong and Taipei who had ventured into Australian halls of learning under the benevolent Colombo Plan. But I had blindly overlooked political or ideological influences, and had detected — sometimes with an old exile's regret — only uniform and all-too-familiar reflections of Australian proselytising social standards and habits.

For example, the brainwashed Asian students, returning from Australia, all drank beer with relish, mispronounced "a" as "eye," peppered their conversation with each Australian idiom as "bloody," "bastard" (in no literal sense), "bludger," "dunny" and "mug." If they had conducted their studies in Melbourne, Adelaide, Hobart, Brisbane or Perth, they were fanatical followers of Australian-Rules football. (If from Sydney, they preferred rugby to soccer when they returned to their home towns.) They were accustomed to men and women drinking in segregated groups. They preferred cricket to baseball.

Now, in the wake of Premier Lee's televised revelation, I tardily discover that, of course, their youthful political and ideological instincts and aspirations were similarly remoulded in the sunburned Australian tradition. Over the years since the convict fleets arrived, the Aussies have always been magnificent, intolerant and deceptive "absorbers" and provincial missionaries. "Australia is a suburb in search of another goldrush" was an appropriate comment made, I think, by a Pommie scholar. The world's best con-men — Sherlock Holmes, Scotland Yard and the FBI agreed over the years — are Australians.

After the convicts took over, and following the Eureka Stockade civil war (with a revolutionary flag which Peking has copied), the Australian mores and standards, inhibitions and adjustments, have prevailed over the civilised but maverick foreign habits of constant surges of migrants. What was useful or convenient was adopted or adapted. What was too alien — "too bloody-Pommie" or "the hell with the dagoes, mate" — was suppressed.

Minorities may rattle or picket, but the mob sticks. A policeman is still "a mug copper," not "a pig." The term "bastard" can be a compliment — though not always. When some Sydney demonstrators harassed President Johnson in 1966, the New South Wales premier exhorted "a mug copper": "Drive over the bastards!" When strikers were agitating in Melbourne, the Victorian premier told the press: "The bastards can march up and down until they're bloody footsore."

This Australian conservatism, which occasionally and indulgently surrenders the government benches in Canberra to the Labor Party, has been no encouragement to the pathetic alien communist factional movements — or stirrings — in some unions. The card-carrying strength of the once-united Communist Party in Australia was 20,000 at the end of the Japanese war. Today, counting dispirited and desperate "parties" and factions, there are probably 4,000 communists (including planted security agents).

One now realises, shamefacedly, that Premier Lee had taken careful note of this fraternal frustration and "she'll-be-right-mate" parochialism.

The curious fact about the continuing "White Australia" policy is that no Chinese or Asian students who have been admitted to Australia, and whom I have met, were conscious of any racial feeling. The local Chinese minority, it seems to me, is now more popular than the Poms. Migrants are unwelcome at the moment because of unemployment; the local hostility to new arrivals stems mainly from the latest assisted migrants, now being indoctrinated — like the putative anarchists from Singapore — by the remorseless Australian legend. After all, according to the 1966 census almost one Australian in five was either a post-war settler or the child of one. And over 60% of the 2-million-odd new settlers are of non-Pommie stock. But only 1.7% are Asian or African. So the "White Australia" policy still operates, mate.

I sometimes brood over what would have happened in Australia if Lee Kuan Yew had been born and assimilated there.

August

"**B**loody war correspondents!" sneered the young marine at Hué. "They can go whenever they want to."

"Yes," replied the sergeant, "but they didn't *have* to come."

They were both right, of course. Most reporters and photographers who go to the wars have pushed their way there, but they push their luck by sticking around. Few, it seems, want to go and, if they are reassigned, most become bored or restless and push to get back to the grapeshot.

One of the latest Vietnam casualties, brilliant young Terence Khoo, ABC staff cameraman, was killed on the eve of his departure after nearly a decade of combat coverage. Born in Singapore, he was due for marriage and reassignment to West Germany. An out-giving comrade, in the honourable tradition of (say) Larry Burrows and Damien Parer and Carl Mydans, he had told friends that he was glad to be getting out. But I would bet that, after a year or two in dull Bonn, he would have been aching for action again.

That casual line-up of his predecessors, by the way, is instructive. Larry was English, Damien was Australian, Carl was American. (Carl is the only one who survived, and after the Pacific, Korean and Vietnam wars, he was restless in his peaceful days in Tokyo.) Recalling their varying origins and backgrounds, the sentimentalist will brood over their common heritage in human values, generous instincts and camera talent.

That obsession with, or itch for, highly

competitive excitement persists so often. Without danger, for so many, the game grows cold, even if the luck runs out. I know at least one agency chief in Japan who lost his top-brass post because he preferred to file from the Korean front rather than direct and edit coverage from Radio Tokyo. Jack Belden escaped with Stilwell, covered the Rommel war, was machine-gunned at Salerno, and returned to the China war as soon as the Nazis surrendered. Denis Warner should have been killed as an AIF (Australian Infantry Forces) commando at Alamein; he lived to report the Pacific and Korean wars and still covers the Vietnam war. Keyes Beech misses the Montagnards more than he now pretends. Frank Robertson, transferred to Fleet Street, and Pat Burgess, turned back from Vietnam, both elected to go, of all places, to Ulster. Jim Cameron is lucky to be alive after a jeep smash when he sallied, without direct assignment, into Bangladesh.

Less lucky men were Ian Morrison and Christopher Buckley, who survived so many perils, only to die together when their jeep ran over a mine behind the lines in Korea. Their driver, tragically, was gallant Col Unni Nayar, nine-lived veteran from the Indian Division in the Western Desert (who still owes me a bottle of champagne). A sardonic footnote: There was another reporter in that doomed jeep, modest Derek Pearcy, covering his first war as a Reuter-AAP man; but he was too young to be remembered, though both Morrison and Buckley reckoned that he was another Alan Moorehead in the making.

The "enemy" must be included, too. The late "Tiger" Saito, ace war correspondent for the *Asahi*, who refused to wear uniform, covered the Japanese war in China, the invasion of Hongkong and the occupation of Singapore, and got out of Manila in the last Japanese fighter — strapped precariously in a surplus seat. "That was a very hard experience," he ruminated with relish in occupied Tokyo. His words and nostalgia typify the eager compulsion of the average war reporter.

In the Rommel war — the last of the gentlemen's wars — the Russians posted an alleged Tass correspondent with the 8th Army. His despatches were read with keen interest by British military intelligence as well as the press censors because he was known to be a colonel in the Red Army and his reports were designed for Kremlin superiors rather than communist editors. He was "Solly" Solodovnyk, a good bloke with a Slav sense of humour. At a press conference after the first blunted frontal assault against the Mareth Line, the very-Sandhurst briefing officer explained with a cough that the halt was due to failure of some of the tanks to haul guns to forward positions. "The general," inquired "Solly," raising a respectful hand, "has he been shot yet?"

"Solly" was particularly intrigued by the ingenuity of Fleet Street's Paul Bewsher who had a habit of creasing and crumpling his despatches and rubbing sand across the first take before handing them over for air delivery to the censors in Algiers or Cairo. "It makes them feel a bit guilty sitting behind the lines there when they get rough soiled copy from the front," he argued. "I reckon they push my dirty copy through far more quickly."

"Solly" proved that he was a professional soldier and not a war correspondent — a distinction that must be constantly repeated — by deciding to return to Moscow after the breakthrough at Medjez-el-Bab, and not deigning to wait for the German surrender at Cape Bon. "Why should I remain?" he asked. "I now know that the Americans have learned how to use their tanks on hills. There is no more news here." He was sighted later by correspondents in Europe in a general's uniform. I hope he is still around (I still owe him a bottle of vodka).

War reporters — East or West — have a common weakness: they reminisce tediously and wait impatiently to cap each other's stories. A Vietnam reporter grits his teeth, crouched, as a Korean or Pacific war veteran relates anecdotes and, of course, vice versa. But, rivals in the field, they all close superior ranks against pretentious outsiders. And their shared memories are spiritually masonic, essentially personal and seldom respectful.

Chester Morrison wrote limericks, between battles, about all his colleagues. A printable offering:

There was a young girl from Benghazi
Who slept with a frog and a Nazi,
*   A goat and a wog,*
*   And a razor-back hog,*
But she still drew the line at Gervasi.

Dear Chet died — not in battle; I have lost touch with Frank Gervasi, who rightly cherished that tribute.

If there's any justice, the shades of all war reporters will be welcoming Terence Khoo at some appropriate bar somewhere, all still happily boring one another with their "that-reminds-me."

Blow wind, come wrack!
At least we'll die with harness on
*   our back.*

— W. Shakespeare, *not* Chet Morrison.

A wise Australian, who presided unhappily over one of the more equivocal events of the Allied Occupation of Japan, died at 85 in Brisbane last week. I wonder if his passing was noted in the Tokyo press. I don't think he wrote his memoirs, and he never got credit for his characteristic but futile attempt to temper doubtful justice with mercy.

He was Sir William Webb, one of Australia's top jurists, who was chairman of the International Tribunal which tried Japan's "major war criminals." Originally, 28 leaders were arraigned, but only 25 stood trial. The tragic Prince Konoye escaped certain hanging by taking poison the night before he was to be arrested. Former Foreign Minister Matsuoka and Adm. Nagane, naval chief of staff who approved the Pearl Harbour attack, beat hanging by dying. Shumei Okawa, a Black Dragon boss, enlivened the proceedings at an early stage by rising, giggling and slapping the bullet-head of Gen. Tojo, in the row of the crowded deck below him; he was declared to be insane.

The trial, which dragged on for two and a half years, was a stale and anti-climatic encore of Nuremberg. It never achieved its aim of impressing the Japanese people with the evil of their defeated leaders and the wisdom and justice of their conquerors. They were fed up with the performance after six months; they had got the point — and they had got bored. "We lost the war" — how often we heard this summation — "and these *bakayaro* [bloody fools] were to blame as our leaders. All right, so you won. Shoot or hang them."

The artificial trial would have lasted another year without the drive and impatience of Sir William Webb, who was undoubtedly the leading man in the cast. His fleshy nose, black eyebrows, silver hair, heavy jowls and rasping voice dominated the rest of the performers, as he called defence and prosecuting counsel alike to heel: "Sit down! . . . You are not helping the court . . . I have warned you before . . . Objection overruled . . . Sit *down!*" His harsh Australian accent whistled and cracked about the wretched heads of lawyers and witnesses like a tireless stockwhip.

Yet, away from the theatrical courtroom, Sir William was a man who combined generosity and urbanity with a bawdy wit. One could only guess at the ordeal which he endured in trying to compose the bitter arguments behind the scenes with fellow-judges, whose judgments were based on majority votes. The implacable judge was the Soviet Army witch-hunter, who was resolved that no prisoner should escape. Of course he represented Soviet policy. Russia had come in at the kill, breaking technically the same kind of expedient Stalin "non-aggression pact" with Japan which had cynically given the green light for Hitler's attack on Poland, and manifesting then in Tokyo the same blind retribution that keeps the ancient lunatic Hess in solitary confinement in Berlin.

The allied judges: bitter arguments.

Sir William had the agonising task of delivering the majority judgments — with most of which he disagreed. The crowded court was for once profoundly shocked when the crumpled old figure of Koki Hirota, the aged political chameleon who had tried to be all things to all Japanese, swayed with closed eyes against the box as he was sentenced to hang.

Of course the death sentences grabbed the headlines. Gen. Douglas MacArthur refused to intervene. And so Sir William's historic humanitarian personal rider was brushed aside and forgotten: "It might prove revolting to hang or shoot such old men as several of the accused." He hinted that the death sentence could be reduced to exile on a Japanese island — a classic Japanese punishment for errant ministers of state and advisers to the emperor.

The Japanese press did not play up that ignored rider, which would have restored some Western dignity and mercy to the shabby masquerade. Nor did the press stress the fact that the death sentences were imposed by a vote of six to five in some cases, but in no case by a vote of more than seven.

Some of us raised these points when bidding Sir William goodbye. "The court's decision is final, gentlemen," he replied — unhappily. R. I. P.

September

Comrade-Prince Sihanouk of Cambodia, bravely wearing his hairshirt in Peking, has written a book exposing the alleged fatal corruption of his homeland by US aid. It will be published this year — perhaps coinciding with Peking's expected attempt to seat his Royal Government of National Union in the UN. In an interview with Dr Mo Teitelbaum in last week's *Sunday Times* of London, he runs a prepublication trailer, claiming the Americans were "concerned neither with the safeguarding of Cambodia's neutrality nor with the feelings of the Khmer nation, but only with their own aims."

"As soon as the US funds began to flow," he declares, "a veritable dollar party was created, a certain greed, a certain lifestyle, the American way of life which profoundly perverted our society."

This, of course, is utter nonsense — however expedient and unsurprising because of the Peking dateline. I have never known an objective foreign-devil correspondent from the old days who did not have affection and sympathy for the gay, tragic Prince, confronted with his desperate dilemma as the communists set up their blackmailing sanctuary-bases inside his kingdom. At his morning champagne briefings at Phnom Penh Palace, he talked frankly and freely, obsessed only by selfless personal anxiety for the peace and safety of his people.

He made no secret of the fact that he rightly feared and distrusted the communists and the Vietnamese — Hanoi and Saigon alike — more than he feared or distrusted the Americans and the West. He managed to keep deferring the inevitable showdown by a skilful policy of circumventing alien internal influences while exacting maximum aid tribute from all alien bidders for their share of Cambodian "neutrality." If the Sihanouk book concentrates only on US aid and its alleged corruption, it will denigrate both the facts of life of all Cambodian aid and Sihanouk's own adroit international manoeuvring.

An envious Burmese diplomat once pointed out to me, with drunken pencil and notebook at the old Raja Hotel bar, at the height of Sihanouk's ambivalent foreign-aid programmes, that it would have been theoretically possible for a Cambodian pedestrian, who had been accidentally knocked down by a Polish steam locomotive, travelling to a brand-new seaport constructed by the French on a railway line built by the Chinese, to be rushed in an East German ambulance, chauffeured by a Japanese-trained driver and fuelled by US oil, along a highway laid down by the Americans, to a hospital built by the Russians and staffed by nurses (using Czech medical equipment) who had been educated under the Colombo Plan — the accident, meanwhile, being reported to Phnom Penh citizenry, listening on US radio sets through a broadcasting station provided as a gift by Zhou Enlai.

I still think that a formidable white elephant was the living and intransient symbol of unchanging Cambodia, unaffected by the persuasive lures and bribes of all alien intruders and their alien customs. It was a darkish pink elephant with a broken tusk and evil eye, and, as it fretted at large around the emerald gardens of the golden-roofed palace on the banks of the broad Mekong, it sometimes rubbed an itchy backside against the palm trees, and it sometimes lumbered with a blast of hate into the outside boulevards. By West veterinary judgment, the wretched animal clearly was suffering from a form of mange which had produced the pinkish (white) pigmentation. But, by Buddhist belief, it was a sacred white elephant — perhaps Lord Buddha incarnate.

During one early visit, when I was trying to assess the effect of foreign aid, the elephant, in a rogue mood, charged a neat, tiny, red bus (a gift from Peking) in which six neat, tiny, Red acrobats (travelling on a Peking cultural mission) were impassively sardined. The elephant worried and butted the bus against a temple wall, furiously trying to overturn and trample it. The terrified acrobats hammered in a frenzy against the closed doors of the teetering bus, while an agitated Court musician played a sweet Khmer flute to pacify the animal. The incident, which happily terminated without fatalities, embarrassed the palace officials, not because the elephant had been aggressive but because they feared that there had been a culpable breach of neutralism by the sacred beast in its selection of a Chinese communist target for attack. To the outside world, might this not suggest "Americanisation" of Cambodia?

By fortuitous chance, however, the elephant ran amok again that week and, with a cunning Mao-like flank attack, trapped and tossed an elderly visitor over the same wall into the temple compound. I say fortuitous because this second unwary victim, only bruised and shaken, proved to be a technician serving with the US aid mission. The delicate neutral balance which Prince Sihanouk was seeking to maintain between East and West was, accordingly, restored. No "Americanisation" here.

Later, the elephant's behaviour became more violent and erratic. It began to pursue Cambodians. This was an unacceptable non-Cambodian deviation. On my last visit to Phnom Penh, I rediscovered the elephant, tethered by the ankles, in a pagoda alongside the southern walls of the Palace, sullenly munching choice hay and glaring at a bilingual sign outside his comfortable prison: THE NAUGHTY ELEPHANT; *L'ELEPHANT MECHANT*. (There was no Chinese or Russian translation; unfair to the West?)

This story, it seems to me, admirably illustrates the flexible and realistic imperviousness of true Asians to foreign influences, whether American, non-American, or anti-American. Asians select, consider and adapt Western customs, gimmicks and systems, but they never surrender their own traditions. The evidence proffered by The Naughty Elephant was climaxed decisively when I asked a Cambodian friend whether the elephant's hay had been enriched by foreign-aid fertiliser from the United States, Russia, Scandinavia or Japan.

"None of these," he replied stiffly. "It was cultivated by our own pure natural manure — far superior to any artificial foreign substitute."

An affectionate and respectful pro-Khmer salute to you, Prince Sihanouk.

November

Only the naive, surely, were surprised at last week's headlined "revelation" in the Sydney public prints that the cunning Australians have been operating an "es-pionage service" in their embassies in Southeast Asia. It would be a curious foreign embassy anywhere which lacked its "intelligence" set-up (sounds much better than "espionage") masquerading by convention as "cultural" or "consular" services.

True, an instructive detail was the allegation that these Australian James Bonds, after graduating at home, are given sophisticated training with MI6 in London. And there was a mystifying incidental claim that, in addition to mastering normal cloak-and-dagger technique, unarmed combat and parachuting, the Aussie 007s are being taught, of all things, "canoeing." Bonds's boss M. (Sir Miles Messervy) was a rasping seadog, but I'm damned if I can imagine him paddling a canoe down the Thames or up the Kwai.

Australia, of course, boasts a highly efficient internal security organ (ASIO), which has had spectacular successes: e.g., the Petrov defection (1954) and the double-agent unmasking of Ivan Scripov (1963). It has also castrated by skilful infiltration the numerically diminished and schism-wracked local Party.

In their routine involvement in Asia, the Australians, the British and the CIA confront two separate Soviet espionage and intelligence bodies: the KGB and the 4th Bureau of the Red Army (the latter reputedly the more effective). This Far Eastern network suffered a grievous blow in the groin earlier this year when a top agent defected in Jakarta.

The Chinese, however, invented espionage and "intelligence" four centuries before Christ, when the superstitious West was preoccupied with Delphic oracles, myths and astrology. In his *Art Of War*, the Chinese sage Sun Tzu demanded "foreknowledge for the wise general, which cannot be elicited from spirits, nor from gods, nor by analogy with past events, nor from calculations, but which must be obtained from men who know the enemy situation."

Sun Tzu, whose classic opus influenced Chairman Mao's military tactics, was the first man to list the original and abiding five varieties of James Bonds: native, inside, double, expendable and living. The "expendables" are agents who fool the enemy with false reports and who eventually will be discovered and liquidated. The "living" are the spies whom Allen Dulles of the CIA called "penetration agents" (with or without expertise in canoeing). Sun Tzu's poetic non-Marxist title for his five varieties of agents was "The Divine Skein."

Chinese and Russian espionage agents worked together in the dear dead days of revolutionary fraternalism and mutual trust. Before the 1959 breach, the Russians sent advisers to China and young Chinese were selected for intelligence training in Moscow. But even then the Chinese manifested their basic and enduring Chinese assurance of mental superiority over alien barbarians.

I recall a joke going the diplomatic rounds in Peking in early 1957 during the giant confidence-trick known as the Dance of the Hundred Flowers. A Chinese security official proudly reported to a comrade the arrival of a Soviet "adviser" on espionage: "He is as tall as a pagoda, with a chest like a water-buffalo, feet like temple stones and a fist like the Great Wall." "But how is he here?" inquired the comrade, tapping his forehead. "Well, he is, after all," the official conceded reasonably, "a Russian."

Before they ousted Taiwan and entered Geneva, the Chinese maintained — and still maintain — "intelligence"-swollen missions in Bern and Vienna, and now they are purposefully moving into the UN, Canada and South America. They have had only one serious defection: the disappearance of security chief Chao Fu in Stockholm, 10 years ago.

So the Australians would have been even more parochial than is their normal wont had they piously held aloof from the challenge and responsibilities of "foreknowledge" in their near north. But I still brood over that "canoeing."

December

So the fearless Anzacs — not the Anzuks — are together again. Comrades Norman Kirk in New Zealand and Gough Whitlam in Australia at least restore, with upstanding Siamese-twin tread, the blurring image of the sunburned Anzac: both big, fair-dinkum blokes. Kirk evokes memories of Australia's last Labor prime minister, the great and good, modest and human Ben Chifley. Both drove railway steam locomotives in their formative years. (You can always trust the footplate, mate.)

I asked my anonymous Peking contact in

Hongkong — Comrade Chow (shall we say?) — what would be the Chinese reaction to the overthrow of the evil conservative régimes on both sides of the Tasman. He was on guard (as always): "We are naturally gratified at the restoration of socialist principles and anti-imperialist policies in Canberra and Wellington. We welcome the prospect of exchanging friendly views and diplomatic recognition with both your free and independent colonial — I mean Commonwealth — states." He then hung up abruptly.

We must now prepare for the passage of poor-men's Kissingers to Peking from the two old Anzac partners. I have no information on the identity of the likely kowtowing Kiwi emissary — though I have no doubt who should unquestionably be the first New Zealand ambassador to Peking: the toughest, ablest, most urbane and long-serving Western diplomat in the Far East.

My barefoot Canberra spies have already brought tidings that the first Aboriginal Kissinger will be either Dr Bruce Grant, the last of the Great Academic Reporters from the Far East, or Dr Ross Terrill, who has written excellent objective copy out of China. Hotel Canberra bar-betting, I understand, favours Dr Grant since he is on the spot and Dr Terrill is at Harvard. However, the consolation prize, I am assured, will be a United Nations posting.

All this is essentially drunken, unworthy gossip, but I have cunningly transmitted the betting odds to Comrade Chow here, hoping that inside information may lubricate my long-bogged attempts to re-enter China. (If Comrade Joseph Alsop comes, can spring be far behind?)

I still speculate over Peking speculation. Canberra and Wellington are again following a US lead. We Anzacs are once more heroically regrouping after a Far Eastern Dardanelles. Neither Singapore nor Kuala Lumpur is perturbed about the pending withdrawal of the mighty Anzac forces from its midst. SEATO's death rattle is loud in the land. Poor Taiwan? Does anyone care?

There will soon be Australian and New Zealand embassies in Peking. I am reliably informed that the Aussies had quietly drawn up their foreign office desk representation two weeks before the people's democratic vote.

And, of course, the good old Anzacs are following the lead of their good old enemies, the Japanese. This is a nice point that will enliven Peking speculation. Although, come to think of it, the Japanese Navy in World War I convoyed the Anzacs to Gallipoli.

Anyway all roads lead, these days, to Peking. Even Rome is humbly reversing its former once-proud and inviolate role, according to Vatican candle-signals.

As an expatriate foreign-devil, I would now like to recommend a comradely socialist, anti-imperialist, non-racial move by Premier Zhou Enlai, when the new men bow and protest too much. Let him try to persuade Australia and New Zealand to unite in an Anzac national and constitutional confederation. Each proud, independent, white Commonwealth state has now chosen to tread the socialist path. Why do their governments allow the Tas-

The principal failing occurred in the sailing,
And the Chairman, perplexed and distressed.
Said he hoped that at least, when the wind
blew due East,
That the ship would *not* travel due West!

With apologies to Lewis Carroll's
'The Bellman's Speech'

man Sea to separate them into two nations? Their natives happily and instinctively adjust, with a few reservations, on most personal, cultural, sporting and racial issues. The New Zealanders may lack the musical Australian accent and their ancestors weren't convicts, but their racehorses beat the Australians' in the Melbourne Cup, and their sheep grow better quality wool than the Aussie merinos.

Australians and the New Zealanders have a grudging mutual respect. Many Aussies reckon that the NZ Division was the best unit in Montgomery's 8th Army (including the two Aussie divisions). It was commanded by a general with the improbable Kiwi name of Freyberg, but it also had the best G-2 in the Middle East: an Irish-NZ Rhodes scholar, Paddy Costello who,

abominably, was never promoted above the rank of captain. He could learn any foreign language in a few months, and later opened the NZ embassy in Moscow.

To Peking, the continuing constitutional separation between New Zealand and Australia could look like a cunning denial of common and obvious parenthood.

In World War I, ANZAC meant "Australian–New Zealand Army Corps." Gallipoli was of course an Anzac disaster, though it could have been a decisive victory if Churchill had prevailed over the halfwit Kitchener. As a senile Anzac, I fear personally that ancient World War I memories of the military alliance shared between Australia and New Zealand may now lack contemporary appeal to the new non-Gallipoli generation in both countries. But the idea still attracts me.

29

1973 January

It was a chance — and for me, unprecedented — encounter in a cheap Tokyo *sukiyaki* restaurant, slap across the road from the old and now regrettably unlicensed Yoshiwara quarter. An amiable, slightly drunken, middle-aged worker with a younger attractive wife, seated on the *tatami* next to us, heard my distinguished guide and mentor, Dr Robert Guillain (*Le Monde* evangelist and author, and an old comrade in the Tokyo and Shanghai of 1940), speaking Japanese. He and Dr Guillain exchanged courtesies and, intrigued by the discovery that we had both been *gaijin* newspapermen harassed by the *kempeitai* in those evil Tojo days, our neighbour — let us call him Suzuki — civilly invited us to his home around the corner. His wife was clearly surprised, even embarrassed. But we went together into the dark rain and had an enjoyable and rewarding hour in their humble three-"room" worker's apartment.

The Suzukis lived on the ground floor: a common sliding door, opening on to the lane, also led to an upstairs apartment and we stumbled over the shoes of the unseen and presumably sleeping neighbours. Suzuki-san's wife had now rallied and relaxed, and we had a glimpse of the wardrobe-sized kitchen on the right as we passed with one stride the closed bedroom and squeezed into their immaculate "living-room" — about the size of my modest Hongkong bathroom. A colour TV set, an oil heater, a pigmy table and built-in cupboards barely left room for me to sprawl grossly and the Suzukis and Dr G. to kneel gracefully.

I learned more about the current mood of change, expectancy and speculation in Tokyo from that *sukiyaki* encounter than from Gaimusho and other briefings. Suzuki-san, it seems, is a printer by trade and he hand-printed his card for us with a small rubber stamp. He had served for one year in the home army in 1945, and is now a figure of mysterious Japanese-style union authority in the Tokyo ward. I got the impression of an old-fashioned Hongkong triad set-up, with correct but convenient and useful *kaifongs*.

Suzuki-san was contemptuously anti-communist, but he believed the Party's vote-seeking aspirations could help him and his neighbouring workers. They were prepared to use the Party but — let there be no doubt — the Party would never use them. If the Party went too far, the rightists — now organised in local minority groups — would take care of them. Of course, he was not a rightist, but he would cooperate with the rightists in any showdown with the Party.

The local communists were shrewd operators and cunning infiltrators. They were opposed to affiliation with the Peking or Moscow parties. Internally, they contrived to learn in advance of approved reforms in local government, road building, pollution, resettlement projects and so on, and immediately began to campaign fearlessly for these improvements before promulgation, so that they could then claim credit for accomplishment. "Japanese communist custom," Suzuki remarked

Nakasone in 1973: the man to watch.

with an indulgent smile.

He and his friends wanted no Japanese army expansion. But the Japanese would now have to defend themselves. They did not wish to rely indefinitely on US protection. And could they really trust the Americans? The Japanese people opposed restoration of Japanese army influence. He was as emphatic on this point as on his anti-communist stand.

The Japanese would be happier to be friendly with China than with Russia. He and his wife hoped to visit China one day.

He believed — instructively — that the man to watch in Japanese politics was still Yasuhiro Nakasone, the tough, nuclear-minded former Self-Defence chief, who is now marking time as Minister of International Trade and Industry.

But Prime Minister Kakuei Tanaka, Suzuki stressed, remained formidable and was digging in for four years. Japanese generally had been impressed by his short, sharp reply in the Diet to a socialist member who asked whether Tanaka did, in fact, keep a mistress — a question deplored even by the communists. "Yes," Tanaka had answered, "I do have a mistress. And I will not forget that *you* asked me the question."

● **Tanaka resigned as prime minister in 1974 and was arrested in connection with the Lockheed scandal in 1976. Nakasone, "the man to watch," became prime minister in December 1982.**

February

On my recent happy return visit to Taiwan, devoted to newspaper research, pious evangelism and gastronomic inquiry, I picked up some of that wayward, irrelevant information that always fascinates foreign-devils, no matter how long their expatriate residence along the China coast. This perverse marginalia, I discover guiltily, is more memorable than serious basic news about gross national product, political developments, land reform and synthetic fertiliser exports.

For example, I learned from my distinguished mentor, Dr Lawrence Chang, that Chinese sing-song girls have become a major export item as homesickness spreads among elderly wealthy Overseas Chinese in Hongkong, Thailand and Singapore. Once subsisting on a lower caste level than the hostesses in girlie bars, sing-song girls are now in lucrative demand for live performances in Chinese cabarets and restaurants abroad, reviving the old songs and lyrics that have become sad, blurred memories to venerable exiles. There are also, of course, pickings on the side — if that is the Confucian phrase I want — and a sing-song circuit can be more rewarding than a Chinese film role.

Perhaps Peking might have more success with proselytism by training and sending Party-line sing-song girls abroad instead of Chinese opera troupes, gymnasts and those now-boring pingpong players.

At home — in Taipei as well as fabled Peitao — the night life flourishes unobtrusively and with civilised tolerance. The humblest professional "light ladies" are organised, with triad protection, as "families," in three separate street districts in Taipei. Those who await thrifty native customers, knitting or playing mahjong as the Suzie Wongs once did in the cubicles of Hongkong's old Luk Kwok Hotel, are known as the *Lyu Teng Hu*, or Green Lamp Family. In progression from this base are the Tea-House Girls, then the Wine-House Girls, the Cabaret Girls and the Call Girls. Many are "foster daughters," adopted by rural families who had originally needed extra help on the farm but who now share the earnings of their adopted progeny in their new and more profitable service.

One Taipei "family" may number 10 to 20 girls, each of whom may average a modest US$75 a month from non-tourist custom. The earnings are naturally higher in Peitao, where the triads control up to 2,000 girls and where the free-spending tourists, especially Japanese, congregate. The hot-spring atmosphere still reflects Japanese cultural customs which did not vanish when Formosa was "liberated" from the old Japanese Empire.

The Chinese food in Taipei is unsurpassed in quality and variety, and is reasonably priced. In Taiwan the ancient Chinese practice of dedicated kitchen apprenticeship continues, paralleling the French system of patient training in cuisine. Allegedly, this honourable tradition has been denounced as imperialist, capitalist, decadent and class-conscious on the mainland, where Chinese master chefs, outside the Imperial City's VIP showplaces, may, alas, become a vanishing race.

Folklore and inscrutable table gossip enliven Chinese dining-out in Taipei. I am still haunted by a revelation of Chinese ceremonial hospitality and elaborate welcome for an honoured visitor on some remote historical occasion. The date and place are obscured by the fumes of *shaoshing* but the detail is unforgettable. According to legendary record, the celebrated host respectfully offered his guest a part-token but putative harem line-up of seven companions and attendants: his own wife; the leading provincial courtesan; an absent neighbour's errant concubine; the maid; the cook; the widow of a hunchback (whom he, the host, had strangled); and — rare collector's piece — the wife of a eunuch's adopted son.

The company at our table nodded warm approval as the roll-call was recapitulated to me but were surprised at my gaping incredulity and gibbering queries. "The host was merely being polite," my informant explained patiently. "Just Chinese respect and hospitality."

March

It was bound to happen; and my spies assure me that it has happened, six months or so ago, but discreetly hushed: the first hijacking of a Japanese tourist party in Hongkong.

The disciplined party — around a dozen strong — wove its way like a docile Nipponese crocodile into the crowded lobby of a well-known hotel at noon. The guide at the head of the procession beeped gently on his whistle, waved his flag, ordered the party to stand at ease, and then, excusing himself obliquely, disappeared into the Gents' Pavilion. Rashly, he laid his whistle and flag on the reception counter. A mischievous, alcohol-exhilarated foreign devil — we shall call him Jerry — emerged from the bar, appraised the scene, quietly appropriated whistle and flag, called "*Hai!*" with assurance, beeped and fluttered, and then strode out of the lobby into the street.

Naturally, the obedient visitors followed their counterfeit Pied Piper, who led them magisterially by a five-minute detour into the Star Ferry subway, where he motioned them, with an authoritative bleep, to another at-ease halt, told them to stay where they were, waved the flag and returned with quiet dignity to the hotel lobby. Here the distraught guide was frantically seeking his lost flock. Jerry unobtrusively replaced whistle and flag on the desk and resumed his seat over another juniper-strong martini at the bar.

The guide has since been suitably rebuked, and I am informed that an Imperial Rescript has now inserted a stern clause into the regulations for group tours, insisting that whistles and flags must be treasured like the guide's honour (or like his commission wallet) and never left on reception desks.

This is an appropriate text for a sermon on Japanese guided tours, which are now, collectively, a permanent and formidable procession of Asian life and living, if individually and locally transient. Their semi-military organisation, with whistles, flags and roll-calls, may be wide open to *gaijin* sneers and mockery. But they suit the Japanese temperament, and the Japanese tourist money suits any foreign community which receives them — and so often loots them (without hijacking). As organised world tourism expands, the Japanese pattern, alas, may well become the example.

The most impressive organised parades of Japanese-style organised tours tramp, of course, through Tokyo every Sunday and public holiday, especially outside the Imperial Palace, where the whistles and flags are mandatory to rally the ranks of rival marching columns pouring in from rural areas, and to sort them finally into waiting queues for mass photographs outside the Double Entrance. Self-discipline is instinctive and compulsive for the Japanese. Even their riots are orderly. They call their revolutions "restorations." All homage to the Sun-Goddess: they are not communists . . .

I recently took part in a guided tour of old stamping, drinking and preaching grounds in lovely Hakone. We dozen undisciplined tourists were all elderly *gaijin*. Our tour was meticulously planned, but

33

without whistles and flags; and we did tend to break off into wandering groups. The Japanese planners of our happy safari had craftily anticipated irrational non-Japanese behaviour by providing reasonable and flexible interludes in our timetable.

Their precaution had an instructive racial sequel. I wandered into my favourite old bar in the gracious Fujiya Hotel, after eight years' absence, to guard against the bracing blasts from Fuji-san. The ancient barkeep, with the frightening memory of his trade, croaked: "Ha, Hoojis-san, you will have double-gibson?" To save his face, I did indulge, and lingered, chatting, thereby missing the cultural tour of the art gallery and open-air museum, where my temperate fellow-tourists spent the hour, returning for coffee, to surprise me, sampling Japanese plonk after the gibsons. No one was openly hostile, but the party closed Western ranks against me in disapproval; I felt closer to the Japanese tour-announcer, who winked without discipline.

April

A huge Buddha-like statue of Chairman Mao, dominating the entrance hall, has driven the ghosts of the taipan money-changers out of the old Shanghai Club, once No. 3 on The Bund, but now 101, and a drab stopover hostelry for transient rustics. It is called the Dong Feng ("East Wind"). My old 1940 memories had ached when I re-inspected the hallowed premises in 1956, to discover that the celebrated Long Bar (110 ft) had been divided into three sections, over which ice-cream and peanuts were available for non-member children and women.

(Kids and women in the Long Bar! Sir Victor Sassoon would have leapt from the roof.)

But on this latest re-inspection, desecration had been deepened. The three sections of the Bar have been reassembled as a dump for "empties" and crates of soft drinks. Sacrilege has fattened on its own excesses. The sacrosanct smoking-room, opposite the Long Bar, where honourable, Scotch-sodden members dozed after a heavy tiffin, draped with copies of *The Times*, is now a communal overnight dormitory, with rolled mattresses and dangling patched underwear and dirty towels.

(On second thoughts, Sir Victor would have thrown himself under a rickshaw.)

Two army sentries have replaced the old bronze lions outside the palatial Hongkong and Shanghai Bank (now the Municipal Revolutionary Committee HQ). They showed no sign of post–Lin Biao tension: when I passed, one was scratching his groin with an unashamed abandon that would have provoked a bared *kukri* from a Gurkha sentry outside Government House.

The old Cathay is of course now the Hoping (Peace) Hotel and has — logically if capitalistically — taken control of the comfortable Palace Hotel, on the other corner of Nanjing Road.

The old racecourse — already a park and people's square when I returned in 1956 — is now the roof of the largest and deepest air-raid shelter in Shanghai, following underground the winding course of Nanjing Road, below the new Party store which replaced Wing On.

I hope I have at last cleared up the mystery of the "Dogs-and-Chinese-not-admitted" sign outside the park on the Bund. It was, in fact, a paragraph in a great list of municipal proscriptions — in Chinese, never in English — which was exhibited outside the park from 1868 until 1925. Following the May 30 demonstrations in that year, the British quietly removed it. Urbane representatives of the Foreign Affairs Ministry showed me a photograph of the original sign and indulgently blamed "wealthy Chinese" rather than "British imperialists" for its ban.

There is no evidence, however, that the notorious blunt version in English — so widely publicised but so implausible (who could read it?) — was ever displayed.

Broadway Mansion — now Shanghai Mansion (fair enough, but surely "Mansion" is a decadent term?) — has the most efficient elevator service in China; from its lofty roof, one can salute furtively the ancient British Consulate (sacked by the Red Guards), which is now a handsome restaurant for the Seamen's Club, with Friendship stores in the compound.

The old "King Kong" Hotel and the carnal French Club (across the road) were not accessible: "under repair," which, I surmise, means that modern hotel expansion or underground raid-shelter construction is afoot.

Not even veteran Party cadres could recall the sinister names of Delmonte's or Farren's — those infamous, delightful gambling casinos, now schools for dramatic and theatrical training . . . "Do you remember 'Demon' Hyde, the tough San Francisco boss of Delmonte's?" No one does.

Dirty linen, appropriately, hangs in public from the verandahs of those ancient millionaire residences which have survived along former Avenue Joffre in old Frenchtown — now converted into workers' tenements. Evil "Blood Alley," back of the Bund, is depressingly respectable, with only dens of Party virtue and haunts of self-criticism — and never, never, a sidelong feminine glance.

Those side-glances, alas, have been submerged by the most appalling mass confrontation of open-mouthed, cold-eyed gaping which this ancient foreign-devil has encountered anywhere, anytime, in Asia. Even in parochial Australia, a randy panda, suddenly engaged in intercourse in the street with a kangaroo, would not attract the incredulous attention and traffic jams which any commonplace foreigner ignites or explodes in 1973 Shanghai.

The Shanghai Chinese of 1956 had at least preserved some 1940 sophistication. The plague of the "cultural revolution" and the arrival of hordes of rustics from the outer regions — balancing the counter-migration of student "volunteers" from Shanghai — has made Shanghai more provincial than Peking. A nervous man, I abandoned my stately morning parades along the Bund; I always felt that I had come out without my trousers. No hostility — but also not a friendly smile. Just the Mass Gape — the psychic equivalent of a mass rape.

Today, Shanghai, bloated with more than 10 million inhabitants, is obviously a far better city for "the broad masses" than it was in its exciting, colourful and degenerate past. The Party there still has control over the Army. Peking's "collective leadership" still glances nervously over its right shoulder at the revolutionary committee sitting in the old Hongkong and Shanghai Bank. Shanghai has known only the worst of both possible worlds. Who can really doubt that communism, with its pious tyrannies, will pass, as imperialism, with its brazen tyrannies, has already passed, and that the Chinese people — terrifyingly patient — will at last reshape Shanghai into a Chinese city of their own choice, with Chinese charm, sophistication, dignity, progress, individual happiness and personal aspirations?

May

Is a poor man's Leaning Tower of Pisa worth more than a rich king's Treasure Tomb? That is the delicate, non-political, non-ideological problem awaiting a top-level Party decision in Peking. The ancient, seven-tiered Tiger Pagoda in Suzhou has tilted 15 degrees to the north and occasionally, in a high wind, showers loose bricks on to unwary strollers in the gardens below. The local comrades have managed to anchor the tower with an ingenious lining of steel-and-rock supports at a cost of 150,000 yuan. (An excellent achievement: shouldn't they send details to the distraught experts at Pisa?)

Now there is renewed hope in Suzhou that further excavations below a dark underground sea will finally uncover the long-lost tomb of the King of Wu, whose imperial politburo slaughtered all the workers who dug the tomb so that it would never be located. But this subterranean and submarine probing must extend under Tiger Hill and so will threaten the acupunctured stability of pagoda.

Hence the hard choice, which — the Suzhou comrades told our visiting evangelical group — has been referred to Persons of Responsibility. The discovery of the Wu Tomb would add another lustrous monument to the historic treasures of the 2,500-year-old city, so admirably preserved by the local inhabitants, who successfully restrained the cultural ravages of the rampaging Red Guards.

We foreign devils gratefully sipped local jasmine tea in the shadow of the Tiger Pagoda, which I had last seen in 1957, and laid odds in anticipation of ultimate approval by Peking of a resumed search for the buried tomb, which, we agreed, would somehow be accomplished with Chinese ingenuity and without sabotage to the reprieved leaning pagoda. Perhaps our optimism was partly attributable to the heady effects of the Suzhou spring water, which contains minerals strong enough to allow a coin to float on the surface of a filled glass.

Does the sustaining quality of this elixir help to explain the traditional beauty of the women of Suzhou and Hangzhou, and the serenity and charm of the hills and lakes, the gardens and canals, the pavilions and the trees? Here is unchanged and unchanging China.

In Suzhou's Embroidery Research Institute, we learned that *each* primary colour has 20 different shades, that a dozen colours are needed to embroider the eyes alone of another heroic reconstruction of the Canadian Dr Norman Bethune, that it can take one and a half months to embroider one flower, that Women's Lib has at last indulgently allowed males to graduate in embroidery . . .

The young, handsome, intense Party cadre who guided us through the incomparable *Cho-cheng-yuan* ("Humble Administrator's Garden") is one of China's leading, if anonymous, experts on dwarf trees. I had foolishly thought that dwarf trees — bonsai — were invented by the Japanese, but they were in fact discovered accidentally by an amiable drunken Chinese poet, Wang Wen, 1,200 years ago. He threw a handful of orchid seeds into a neglected thundermug, where they suddenly blossomed in miniature.

Our cadre explained apologetically in perfect English that the magnificent 11-acre garden, with its symbolic interwoven lakes, streams, pavilions, rocks and flowers, originally belonged to a former corrupt Censor and Imperial Envoy of the Forbidden City, who was supposed to suppress and punish pre-Maoist bribery. But, as a Liu Shaoqi–type arch-swindler, he had shared that bribery and had used the payoff to build the master-piece.

The inspired designer was Wen Chenming, a celebrated painter who, all agree today, could have improved the landscape miracle only by studying Chairman Mao's thoughts.

The son of the corrupt "Humble Administrator," it seems, was as decadent as, if less intelligent than, his father. He was an inveterate and reckless gambler and, in what must have been the most disastrous run of luck in Chinese gambling, lost his father's garden in one night's play. "Gambling is forbidden today in the People's Republic," our guide recalled.

God bless our guide, and may he achieve his shy ambition of growing (rather, stunting) the first Chinese 6-inch bamboo in a pot. He knew every curve and every legend of the gardens. He escorted us lovingly and proudly from the dwarf-tree conservatory to the central lake, which in the summer reflects lotus blossoms to the north, and in the spring camellias to the south. He showed us how a cunningly disguised mirror across the lake rediscovered and surprised us, eternally retracing our enchanted pilgrimage. He explained how some walls were shaped like dragons and some like clouds. He pointed out that there were 300 different patterns of "flowering windows" in one winding covered corridor.

Finally, as a curtain-call, he led us to the Pavilion of Breezes on a Moonlit Night to read to us the engraved couplets signed by Wen Chen-ming on the two red pillars:

The noise of the cicadas
Makes the forests more peaceful;
The twittering of the birds
Lends more tranquillity to the hills.

I genuflected. The garden was "perfection."

The cadre, alas, marred the memorable day: "No; there is not enough room in the garden for a mass Party rally."

Never mind. Eunuchs come and Parties go, but Suzhou and China remain forever — even if I have to wait another 16 years before I am able to return.

July

Whatever parochial or protective curbs Prime Minister Gough Whitlam may impose on Japanese investment in Australia, there is one corner of an Aussie field that is forever Nippon. It is a curiously green hillside in the brown, often drought-ridden landscape of Cowra, in central New South Wales.

Here are rows of simple brass plaques on 234 graves of Japanese prisoners of war who committed mass *hara-kiri* in a suicidal breakout 29 years ago. The 5 August 1944 anniversary may not be recalled by new-generation Australians, but it will certainly and correctly be honoured at the new army establishments in Japan: "Self-Defence" now; not, of course, "Imperial."

The slaughter — more than 100 other Japanese were wounded — set an all-time, hot-blood record for fair-dinkum Aussie (if we forget the systematic, cold-blooded massacre of hundreds of Aborigines in Tasmania in the 19th century). But I don't think it was ever property reported. Those of us Aussies, who were then involved in "the last civilised war" against the foreign-devil Nazis, heard little or nothing of the affair; and I have not yet read a detailed inside report.

But, clearly, it was unique, traditional and unchanging *Japanese* behaviourism, which it would be dangerous for non-Japanese to forget today. More than 1,000 prisoners were crowded into 20 huts, built originally for only 500 urbane Italian prisoners. Exercise *Hara-kiri* — or *seppuku*, if you want to be precious and pedantic — was opened by a midnight bugle blast, and the screaming prisoners, armed with knives, baseball bats, hooks and improvised weapons, hurled themselves against, across and over the three barbed-wire fences. The vanguard offered themselves as an agonised bridge for the second wave. The third and last wave set fire to the huts.

Four of the dozen Australian guards were killed, firing and defending the Vickers machinegun posts. One Australian — with the appropriate name of Hardy — rushed to an unmanned but fully-armed Vickers gun and coolly flung its trigger-case into the dark, foiling the selected group of prisoners who had hoped to operate it. (They trampled and tore him to death.)

Only one Vickers gun was seized, but was clumsily jammed by the excited Japanese, who had planned to sweep it against the other gunposts. The leader of this unit cut his throat in apologetic acceptance of responsibility.

Some of the prisoners who managed to escape and roam the farm areas at dawn hanged themselves before they were rounded up. At least two threw themselves, shouting "*Banzai!*," under a passing train on the Cowra railway.

The then Labor prime minister, John Curtin, a brave conchie in World War I, issued a brief statement, commending the "highly satisfactory action" of the army guards, but refraining from comment on the action of the Japanese prisoners.

Why recall this now? Well, why not? Where did Crown Prince Akihito and his lovely commoner wife, Michiko, insist on going when they visited Australia this year? To Cowra, mate, where they bowed in homage to the 234 *hara-kiri* dead, and planted a tree to commemorate their first Grand-Shrines-of-Ise appearance in White Australia. Even the Japanese commies would understand and applaud.

And why does that Nippon corner of a parched, alien Australian field remain forever green? Because Tokyo, cobber, paid and pays for the installation and upkeep of the irrigation system for the graves.

Happier footnote: In December, Broome, ancient sea-pearling port in northwest Australia, will again celebrate the oldest annual multiracial corroboree for *Shinju-Matsuri*, in remembrance of 300 original Japanese-Australians who were drowned while pearl-diving there in the 1890s.

August

Dick Noone, one of the original and greatest of Southeast Asian jungle fighters and counter-insurgency experts, has died in Bangkok of lung cancer. He was a brilliant anthropologist from Cambridge, fought with the Australians against the Japanese in 1941, served with Field Marshal Sir Gerald Templer and Robert Thompson in the Malayan jungle "Emergency" of the fifties, and had been a master security adviser with Seato's counter-subversion and counter-insurgency forces for the past six years. His toughness was matched by his modesty. He was 55 when he died.

Noone knew more than anyone else (no pun intended) about the unsolved mystery of the disappearance of legendary Jim Thompson, expatriate New York socialite, OSS jungle commando and millionaire founder of the first Thai international silk company. Thompson, who would be 67 if he were still alive, vanished into the thin, sweet-scented air of the Cameron Highlands on a post-prandial saunter, or encounter, one sunny Easter Sunday six years ago.

The circumstances of Thompson's hurried departure from Bangkok for Malaysia suggested hopes of delayed personal contact with mysterious Thai agents, who had fled to Laos in the aftermath of the abortive 1949 coup by the brave Free Thai leader Pridi Banomyong (now in exile in Paris). It was always insisted that Thompson, a strange and restless man of many interests, had retained no post-OSS ties, but CIA authorities in Bangkok made an unprecedented request for the services of Noone — allegedly undertaken and officially financed by Thompson's silk company — to probe the mystery on the spot.

Dick Noone went into the jungle where Thompson had taken his fateful stroll and talked with tribal chiefs whom Noone knew personally and whom he had interrogated 15 years previously to solve the more human and less complex mystery of the disappearance of his brother Pat, who had married into the aboriginal tribes. (Pat had been murdered by a native who coveted his pretty and devoted wife; the killer slew him with poisoned darts and a *parang*; you can read the story in *Rape of the Dream People*.)

Dick Noone made a long secret report to the CIA — I mean, the US Embassy in Bangkok, or was it Thompson's silk factory? Discreet always, he gave only one public statement: "I am fully convinced that Thompson was not lost in the jungle."

But we foreign-devil pressmen, who were honoured by his company, help and trust, agreed that Noone's taciturn asides and marginal observations or silences meant that Thompson had vanished by decision, not by force. A message or a personal contact on that last stroll could have attracted him to another secret rendezvous with old friends. He was then 61 and, I repeat, restless.

Noone's later work with Seato took him regularly to the curious *melange* underworld of Siamese, Lao and Vietnamese in the north-eastern territory (Issan), where many of Thompson's old double-agent contacts still roam.

Dick Noone never lost interest in the Thompson mystery. He returned for another hidden Holmesian, non-jungle inquiry into a Singapore lead: a Madam Florence Wong, who was certainly no Irene Adler because she couldn't fit her bottom into an economy-class seat on a jet plane, but who hinted that she knew that a disguised Thompson had arranged a clandestine journey to Hongkong on a Norwegian ship. Dick preserved his secrets.

Last time we lunched together at the old Oriental Hotel's Normandy restaurant in Bangkok, 18 months ago, I presumed tediously to reopen the affair.

"At least prepare material for a posthumous book on the Thompson search like your Pat-search book," I urged, little suspecting, alas, this month's obituary.

"Totally different subject, Richard," he insisted. "Some secrets are more secret than others. Must keep my name out of that one. Sometimes" — with a James Bond twinkle — "I realise that my father carelessly dropped a hyphen from our family name: it should be No-One." A fitting epitaph.

December

My friend and former colleague in young and happy days on the Victorian Railways, Dr Mick Feehan (now an active figure in the Chinese-Australian Friendship Society) brings me word of the recent death of a former railway union contemporary of ours, a man of enterprise and imagination. He was an assistant stationmaster in Victoria in the 1920s — never mind his name now — who committed the most bizarre offence in the history of the railway service (anywhere, I would think). An earnest messenger lad in the despatch office of railway head office in 1921, I read with awe the file of his trial before the Discipline Board and the dreadful penalty imposed by the Railway Commissioners. The judgment, I still recall, ran:

"It having been proved to our satisfac-

tion that you were guilty of grossly obscene and disgusting behaviour at Korong Vale in that you did:

"Cause a piece of cow manure to be coated with icing sugar, decorated with strawberries, and disposed of at a church bazaar, as a goodwill offering from the Victorian Railways, the deception being not discovered until the camouflaged cake had been sliced and served at a tea party;

"Therefore we have decided to:

"Fine you £5 *[which would have bought 400 genuine teacakes in those distant days]*;

"Reduce you to the position of Operating Porter; and

"Transfer you to Serviceton *[the Victorian Railways Siberia on the South Australian border]*."

The dossier of the file revealed that the lively offender was not only an able railway worker but was also — not surpris-

ingly — interested in the culinary arts and had indeed experimented, of all things, in Chinese cooking. I am convinced that, had he survived, he would have been a logical selection for the union board of control of the projected Chinese package tours.

This opinion would have been shared by the late and great Sir Harold Clapp, formidable Chairman of Railways Commissioners, who signed the punishment for the manure-cake crime. Greatly daring, I once asked Sir Harold, when I had become one of his public relations officers 12 years later, what eventually happened to the demoted assistant stationmaster. (We were travelling in the Chairman's carriage on one of his regular tours and had just bumped through Korong Vale.)

"Yes, a curious case," Sir Harold remarked pensively. "We had to punish him of course. But we recognised his imagination and innate abilities. I can tell you now confidentially that we did not keep him long in exile. He is now serving in a higher post and the offence will not be held against him."

At that moment, the railway dining-car steward arrived with our austere lunch. Sir Harold, a noted gourmet, surveyed the tray with compressed lips. "Sometimes," he added, "I think we should have put him in charge of our railway refreshment services."

A pity, I repeat after half a century, that he did not survive to help plan these foreign-devil tours of China.

● **The Australian trade-union movement had just announced a plan to run package tours to China for union members.**

1974 February

When I was last in Laos, a pious notice welcoming visitors was prominently displayed above the immigration counter at Vientiane airport:

> *"Hatred can never be ended with hatred anywhere. Hatred can be ended only by kindness and love. This is The Eternal Law."*
>
> — The Lord Buddha.
> — Kindly authorised by courtesy of Prof. Setha of India. *(Who he?)*

One wonders whether this admirable non-Marxist and non-imperialist law can help sustain the third and latest effort to establish a coalition government in "The land of a million elephants and the white umbrella." I wouldn't bet on it myself. On past and present form, the odds are heavily against any enduring political compromise between the two half-brothers: Prince Souvanna Phouma, 73, the prime minister, and "Red Prince" Souphanouvong, 63, alleged leader of the Hanoi-backed Pathet Lao forces.

I recall, with a sentimental oath, the forced but hopeful champagne toasts at the last coalition-reconciliation bid in Vientiane on 12 June 1962. It was tripartite then: Souvanna Phouma and the Red Prince posed for photographers and TV in a joint triangular handclasp with Prince Boun Oum (who privately ridiculed the notion that the pact would last, and bowed out within a week). Philosophic observers like myself were depressed by the portent that Souvanna Phouma, as the Centre Prince, gave his left hand to Boun Oum, the Right Prince, and his right hand to Souphanouvong, the Left Prince.

The new coalition project establishes a combined police force, and an agreed equal presence of both Royal and Pathet Lao troops in Vientiane, the administrative capital, and Luang Prabang, the royal capital. His Majesty King Savang Vathana needs no supernatural advice to remind him that the North Vietnamese military forces are firmly entrenched between his palace and Vientiane to the south, and that the Chinese army has built two military highways through Phong Saly and Sam Neua to the north, making those Lao provinces a Chinese buffer-state. (Lao keep out.)

The tragedy is that if the Chinese and North Vietnamese got out of Laos (as the Americans have now done), the two princes — both ranked as Serene Highness — could probably reach brotherly accord on a neutral Lao settlement, pacifying the million elephants and furling the white umbrella.

I have always doubted the sincerity of the Red Prince's communist dedication. He is essentially Laoist rather than Maoist, a swarthy, handsome man with horn-rimmed spectacles, carefully trimmed moustache and side-whiskers, an engineering diploma, an incongruous huntin'-and-shootin'-and-fishin' sartorial sense, an actor's vanity and a caustic wit. But he has a statuesque North Vietnamese communist wife who, I suspect, is the real Red negress in the Lao woodpile.

Prince Souvanna Phouma is obviously

fond of his bastard half-brother. He was educated in Hanoi and France and, according to his detractors, speaks French better than his native Laotian tongue. He is a patient, amiable compromiser, who prefers to negotiate rather than fight. He was one of the Laotian representatives who signed the convention with France in 1949, which endorsed the ingenious French invention of Laos as "a state."

It will be a miracle, the Lord Buddha Himself would be the first to acknowledge, if the joint police forces and the associated Pathet Lao–North Vietnam–Royal Army forces work together in trust and amity. In 1959, there were modest plans for the partial integration of the Pathet Lao with the Royal Army. After two years, the Pathet Lao battalions, under orders from Hanoi, bolted back to the jungle with Royal Laotian arms (supplied by the United States).

The Eternal Law for Laos, alas, has nothing to do with hatred or kindness. It simply is: "You can't trust the neighbours."

March

Down with Confucius, Lin Biao — and Sherlock Holmes.

The Baritsu Chapter of The Baker Street Irregulars (of which I have the honour of being Chief Banto) learns privily that Sherlock Holmes, Dr Watson and their publisher-agent, the late Sir Arthur Conan Doyle, will soon be placed on Peking's anti-Confucian list, along with Beethoven,

Mozart, Schubert and Michelangelo Antonioni.

There should be no real surprise at this politburo decision, though we Baritsu cosmopolites hotly resent the cultural denunciation of The Master of Baker Street. His immortal works have not had wide circulation in the People's Republic since "liberation." (I did buy a second-hand copy of *The Hound Of The Baskervilles* in the old market in former Morrison Street in 1957.) But with, one had hoped, still deepening contact between The Middle Peopledom and the barbarian West, the non-racist, non-political Baritsu Chapter had wishfully begun to plan new translations of some of the adventures for distribution to the broad masses in China.

The politburo's case against Holmes (and, by implication, his reactionary influence on his publisher Doyle) is that he is a decadent Confucian figure seeking, with Dr Watson as his disciple, to subvert the masses and restore rich landlords, capitalist hansom-cabs and London fogs to China. It is asserted that he was a kowtower to Queen Victoria (though he refused a knighthood in 1902 at the age of 48); that he was a male chauvinist (though, to him, Irene Adler was "always The Woman"); that he had a weakness for German music and played Beethoven on his violin; and that he used a needle for cocaine-drugging rather than for acupuncture.

On the current politburo argument that the hands may belong to Lin Biao but the voice is Confucius', Peking also asserts that Holmes' evil reactionary influence is mirrored in the Confucianist revisionism of Arthur Conan Doyle. Doyle, of course, was a lapsed, Jesuit-educated Catholic, who became an evangelic leader of Spiritualism, which is, by Party reckoning, the foreign-devil version of Confucian cosmology.

"Confucius absurdly argued," a local Party member told me angrily, "that impersonal cosmic energy and principle produce Yin and Yang, and these by their interaction produce heaven and earth and all living beings. That is the same anti-Party, pro-Soviet nonsense which the spiritualism of Conan Doyle and Sherlock Holmes disseminates."

The Party critic also made the point that Holmes' first adventure was entitled *A Study In Scarlet*, which, he alleged, was "a cheap sneer at the *Red Flag*." "And," he added, "Holmes declared cynically in that class-conscious manifesto: 'What you do in this world is a matter of no consequence. The question is: What can you make people believe that you have done?' This is rank pro-Confucian, pro-Khruschev, anti-Maoist heresy."

That, briefly, is the politburo's legalistic case for linking Sherlock Holmes with Confucius, Lin Biao, Beethoven, Mozart, Schubert and Michelangelo Antonioni. It is, of course, gross misrepresentation, and the Baritsu Chapter will make an honest, if futile, attempt to present a defence of The Master in consultation with The Sherlock Holmes Society in London and The Baker Street Irregulars in New York.

Holmes himself anticipated one of Chairman Mao's Thoughts *(The Sign of Four)*: "It is of the first importance not to allow your judgment to be biased by personal qualities." He also demonstrated that he was one of the first China-watchers when he warned Watson in 1914 *(His Last Bow)*: "There's an east wind coming, such a wind as never blew on England yet. It will be cold and bitter, Watson, and a good many of us may wither before its blast. But it's God's own wind nonetheless." Premier Zhou Enlai could construe that forecast as evidence that Holmes (God forbid) was a Party agent.

April

So dear Relman (Pat) Morin, we belatedly learn here, has kept his deadline — at 65, alone alas, in his New York apartment. Pat won two Pulitzer prizes for his Associated Press reporting: one, in 1951, for coverage of the Korean War; the other, in 1958, for coverage of the integration rioting at Little Rock.

I first met him in Tokyo in 1940, when he was AP bureau chief. He and I occasionally drank together with Richard Sorge of the Nazi Embassy in the old Imperial lounge, little knowing (as they say) that Sorge was the No. 1 Soviet spy in Japan. Pat helped me also in Shanghai at that time, when we sought news sources in the Park Hotel, the French Club, Blood Alley and Delmonte's cultural casino.

He stuck around in Japan when I quit Shanghai, running hard, in December 1940, convinced that the Japanese would be in the war in February instead of December 1941. The Japanese tried to cajole and then to force Pat to make propaganda broadcasts, after interning him for "espionage." He told them what to do; they kept him in jail.

I met him again in Cairo and Africa during the Rommel war — the last of the gentlemen's wars — and then in Korea, the first of the commy wars.

Pat was one of the best newspaper friends anyone could have. In salute, I would like to recall here his first by-lined story from Shanghai — the report of 10 murders in the old concession-city in 1930. I don't doubt that he would prefer this story to be recorded rather than one of his Pulitzer offerings — besides, it's the kind of story we're becoming acquainted with in Hongkong today. Pat wrote:

'Pat' Morin

❝Everyone remembers his first byline. I was lucky. A lesson came with mine. I had never handled a straight news story before. Up and down the length of the China coast, there was no other reporter so raw and green. On that day, the only real reporter on the Shanghai *Evening Post* failed to show up. He had been conscientiously investigating the night life of Shanghai and phoned, groaning, to claim that the gout was killing him again.

The managing editor, Al Meyer, had no choice but to assign me to the story. "Take a cab and skip out to this address in Frenchtown," he said. "It looks as though someone has wiped out a whole Chinese family."

The French police-captain would have made an admirable reporter; he told me the whole story in flawless English. Shortly before daybreak, a rickshaw boy, passing the house, heard screams inside. Suddenly a child, a boy of six or seven, ran into the street crying for help. The rickshaw boy found a policeman, who entered and went through room after room of headless bodies.

"It was someone who knew the house very well," the captain told me. "He must have gone to the kitchen first and taken the cleaver. No lights were turned on. Everyone was asleep. He moved quietly and killed the owner of the house and his wife, the owner's mother and father, three older children, the cook and two houseboys. It wasn't a *tong* killing; they kill for business, and naturally much more neatly. This fellow was in a murderous fury."

The master, it seemed, had fired an assistant cook several days before. The cook claimed wages were due, but the employer refused to pay him. "There was quite a row," said the captain. "The other servants beat him up. I think he may be the one."

"But why did he spare that little boy?"
"Ah, that also fits the theory. We know the child was his favourite. He often played with the little boy and gave him sweets. Picture him" — the captain mimed —

45

"standing over the sleeping child last night with the cleaver raised. Suppose at the last minute he recognised the boy. A bizarre picture, is it not? Worthy of your Edgar Allen Poe. Now, if you wish to see the bedroom — but be careful, the floors are slippery with blood."

When I came into the office, Al Meyer looked at me curiously. "You're a little green," he said. "How was it, pretty juicy?" I outlined the bare facts. "Now, let me give you a piece of advice," he went on, as I was rolling the paper into the typewriter, only half-listening. Mentally, I was trying to find a lead, something that would encompass the facts and the visual horror in one shattering, Grand Canyon lead. Like most cubs, I continually looked then for the big word, the erudite word, the off-beat word.

As though from a distance, I heard the boss saying "— don't write this story at all." I came to with a shock: "What do you mean?" "Don't write it," he repeated. "Let it tell itself. Tell it as you told it to me, in plain words, the plainer the better. For instance, you said a cop slipped in the blood and fell. What did he say when he fell?" "He said '*merde*'!" "Good. Use the quote. Use details that add to the visual picture. Take the customers inside that house and let them see it and smell it. But play it low. The story tells itself."

I tried not to look when they read the copy. How much were they cutting? How much re-writing? To escape the torture, I went out to Jimmy's Kitchen and drank coffee. Finally, the paper came up. There it was, under the main banner — and with a by-line. I read and re-read it. At some point — the fourth re-reading perhaps — I noticed that my name had been mis-spelled. It didn't matter . . . ❚

(Thanks, Pat. Be seeing you, mate.)

May

My senile hand has been happily guided to some yellowing parchments which provide more detailed and frightening background to last month's decision by Tokyo's Supreme Court to end the 26-year brawl over ownership of the sacred slopes of Mount Fuji.

The court, it will be recalled, awarded possession to the formidable Shinto Sengen Shrine. But less ghostly and more temporal consequences were involved — though not yet properly publicised — because the Sengen sect, which now rules the Fuji roost, is entrenched in the prefecture of Shizuoka (on which geographical entity I pen comment with due trepidation since I understand this noble prefecture is the birthplace of the noble wife of the editor of this noble publication). The court's judgment overruled the now forgotten, or non-published, counter-claim by Yamanashi prefecture.

Mt Fuji (12,461 ft) straddles the boundary separating the lush vineyards of Yamanashi, to the north, and the green tea plantations of Shizuoka, to the south.

The Sengen Shintoists were always supported by Shizuoka prefecture. The shrine on Fuji is administered from Fujiyama City in Shizuoka. The original and decisive document-claim was a 300-year-old scroll, vesting control of Fuji in the Sengen Shrine, under the seal of the great warrior shogun, Iyeyasu Tokugawa.

Sordid motives were promptly and angrily attributed to the claim by the Yamanashi people, who realised that legal ownership would carry the right to levy currency offerings and perhaps to peddle refreshments to the tens of thousands of visitors who scale the mountain each summer. The Yamanashi counter-claim, I now discover, sincerely admitted selfish interest in financial gain and based its case on the two interesting legal arguments that:

● Most of the winds which blow on Fuji also pass over Yamanashi;

● The snow lingers longer on the northern, Yamanashi, slope than on the southern, Shizuoka, slope.

Shizuoka, obviously in State-and-church consultation with the Sengen Shinto abbot, rallied with the two rejoinder claims that:

● The sun shines more strongly on the southern slopes of Fuji, clearly identifying Shizuoka more spiritually with the Sun goddess;

● Earthquakes are more frequent on the southern than the northern slopes (reconfirmed, alas, earlier this month).

Shizuoka and the Sengen abbot then established an Honourable Federation for Sincerely Opposing Private Ownership of Fujiyama.

Yamanashi, shaken but resolute, hit back with militant delegations of sturdy villagers, clad in ceremonial white hara-kiri costumes, who established their *makoto* (sincerity) by twice trying to storm the Diet, while carrying a large cardboard replica of Fuji and shouting: "Give us back our mountain," "Shinto robbers," and "Democracy first." Following through, a Yamanashi mystic threatened to commit hara-kiri on the summit of Fuji if it was surrendered to Shizuoka.

Shizuoka and Sengen at once responded with what must be regarded as a masterstroke of *makoto* by accepting the principle of hara-kiri but eclipsing the Yamanashi challenge by pledging: first, to stage a mass hara-kiri ceremony involving 20 volunteers (named); secondly, to consummate the ceremony with a spectacular group leap into the Fuji crater itself by the volunteers, roped together.

That threat, it was believed when I wrote my despatch then for foreign-devil readers, influenced the 1953 recommendation by the Government's harassed advisory committee, now sealed by the Supreme Court, that Fuji should become the property of Sengen and Shizuoka.

It could only happen in Japan. The hara-kiri hasn't started yet.

July

"Mr Chairman, ladies and gentlemen, and fellow hard-boiled eggs . . ."

Senile, drunken, absentee life-members of honourable clubs are often invited from afar, with a shrug of sentimental indulgence by the contemporary committee, to attend and address an anniversary meeting. So I was back in the old Tokyo

Foreign Correspondents' Club (still No. 1 Shimbun Alley) for a happy, crowded "Hongkong Night" last week.

Thirty-year-old ghosts from the past lurched in, singing the old "Sioux City Sue" club anthem; some evil, ancient contemporaries were wheeled in, hiccoughing. I am gratified to report that my blurred memories were suddenly nudged by an inspired wisecrack by the late Prince Tokugawa, who had given me an urbane interview for my first Tokyo front-page story for Aussie readers in July 1940.

Invoking his memory, I addressed for the first time a gathering of Asians and foreign-devils as "hard-boiled eggs." I commend this as a civilised, feudal Japanese introduction to similar addresses by any speaker at non-apartheid, peaceful-coexistence gatherings anywhere in Asia.

Prince Tokugawa, who would have been Emperor of Japan if there had been no Meiji Restoration, recalled to me that, during his term of office as Consul-General for Japan in Australia in the late 1930s (Canberra and Tokyo, incredibly, did not exchange ambassadors until the eve of Pearl Harbour), he had made a pioneering and hazardous private flight to Broome.

(Broome, the ancient sea-pearling port in northwest Australia, celebrates an annual corroboree every December: *Shinju-Matsuri*, in remembrance of the 300 Japanese who were drowned pearl-diving there in the 1890s. Native Australian aborigines then pay tribute to those first non-white Australian migrants in amiable unity with the local hybrid conglomeration of Japanese, Malays, Chinese, Indonesians, Filipinos and post-convict Aussies.)

Prince Tokugawa's flight from Perth to Broome took three days and, because he had been discreetly warned of gastronomic austerities at his two night stops, he prudently carried a large stock of hard-boiled eggs for basic emergency nourishment. He told me, with a chuckle, that he mentioned this nutritive stratagam when he replied to the welcoming speech by the Mayor of Broome.

"It occurred to me," he told his cheering luncheon audience, "as I flew up, nestling among my hard-boiled eggs, that there was a moral for East and West, Asians and Europeans, yellow and white, in my choice of this safe and rewarding diet. If there is too much white or too much yellow in a hard-boiled egg, it is unsatisfactory and even indigestible. But if there are correct and cooperative proportions of yellow and white, with the white not smothering the yellow, and the yellow not flooding the white, the hard-boiled egg is surely the most wholesome, durable and satisfying diet you can have."

The reaction of my compulsive audience at No. 1 Shimbun Alley last week was identical to that of Prince Tokugawa's audience in Broome four decades ago. Long live hard-boiled eggs! . . .

Japanese bar (not menu) postscript: I had not been back in Tokyo's American Club for eight years. No one knew I was arriving with friends. I could not recognise the new structure behind the Russky Embassy. The handsome and still youthful *maitre* approached me: "Welcome back, Mr Hughes. You will of course have double Gibson?"

"Thank you," I replied, shaking hands

and adding clumsily: "But not too much yellow — I mean, vermouth."

August

It now looks as though "The Third China" may at last have to haul down its proud flag in northern Thailand and eastern Burma. But where will the expatriates go? Their leaders are two durable Chinese Nationalist generals who have, in effect, ruled "The Golden Triangle" since 1950, commanding the former 3rd and 5th Kuomintang armies (now the Chinese Irregular Forces — 5,000 men), controlling and taxing opium-smugglers and trade caravans, educating and training their descendants and cooperating actively with Taiwan's Intelligence Bureau of National Defence (IBMND) in "Region 1920" (as The Third China is known in Taipei).

The two veteran generals — tough carbon copies of the old pre-"liberation" warlords — are Chao Fa ("Prince") Lao Li, based on Tham Ngob, and Tuan Hsi-wen, based on Mae Salong.

My old friend Dr Theh Chonghadiky has given the best report on The Third China in recent issues of the *Bangkok Post*. "They levy taxes on the inhabitants of their fiefdom — be they Thai, Burmese or refugees," he summarised. "They also impose taxes on merchants and traders who travel through their areas and they have raised and maintained armies which ensure the continued existence of their domains."

It is an astonishing story; but, to repeat, it now looks like drawing to a close after two crowded decades. The previous Thai governments accepted The Third China; so did Rangoon, which for six years subsidised and armed ethnic border groups, cooperating with the Chinese Irregular Forces and fighting Burmese communists.

Now, Rangoon has disowned the freelance border groups, and Bangkok has ordered Taiwan to disband the units of IBMND. The pious aim of the involuntary non-Chinese protectors of The Third China is to absorb the expatriates and their second generation into peaceful restricted areas, to persuade them to lay down their arms and join the ranks of other Overseas Chinese. It is claimed that the IBMND has already closed its "branch units" in Burma.

Thailand's Deputy Foreign Minister Chatichai Choonhavan, who personally directed the withdrawal of 7,000 KMT troops from northern Thailand in 1950, hopes that under the new campaign most of the remaining soldiers will go to Taiwan.

Bangkok has also ordered the closure of schools operated by the Chinese Irregular Forces in northern Thailand, unless they make Thai the principal language and teach Chinese only as a foreign language up to primary standard.

(In The Third China, students at the two main schools in Tham Ngob and Mae Salong are given standard Chinese secondary education and on graduation can attend university in Taiwan. Some of the 600 students come from Chinese families resident in Bangkok.)

No one can yet pretend to know what the ultimate reaction of "Prince" Li and Gen. Tuan will be. But the IBMND is discreetly curtailing, or concealing, its operations in Thailand as well as Burma, which suggests that Taiwan will not encourage The Third China to resist combined Thai and Burmese pressure.

In the 1960s, we barefoot newspaper evangelists in Luang Prabang and Sam Neua frequently encountered, or knew the operations of, IBMND agents in northern Laos. They were well organised with top contacts, enjoyed their liquor and made regular forays for intelligence and sabotage across the border into Yunnan. Their base was Ban Nam Kueung.

Since the withdrawal of the Americans — though not, naturally, of the North Vietnamese — their presence has evaporated. But, like the North Vietnamese, the Chinese Army, which built the two roads from Yunnan into northern Laos, still occupies the two northern provinces — never, of course, as a Third China, but only as a "liberated" buffer-state.

● **The Kuomintang forces are still operating to this day in the remote north of Thailand.**

September

I hesitate to write about this incident, which somehow seems inappropriate for public print. But sympathetic Chinese friends, after earnest discussion, have urged me to ventilate it — if that's the word I want — because it is an ear-witness report which stresses difficulties and complexities of human Sino-*gweilo* (foreigner)

communications and relations. One broods over possible reactions to a similar incident during a top-level Sino-Australian diplomatic conference.

I was taking my daily early-morning walk in Hongkong's Mid-Levels. Dawn was coming up like thunder out of the South China Sea across the bay at 6:30 as I rounded the corner of a seemingly deserted street beside respectable apartments. Here, the ground-floor servants' dunny windows front the street. One was lit, and someone inside broke wind with the most deafening roar I have heard since the Alamein barrage. The initial thunder was followed by a percussion of small-arms fire and then another nuclear blast which sent me reeling into the gutter and blew a covey of terrified birds from trees across the road.

I could not restrain myself and, noting the apparent absence of any other audience, clapped my hands loudly and shouted: "Bravo! Encore!" Alas, I discovered, to my dismay, that an ancient, frail, aristocratic Chinese lady, who paces to and fro each morning, had paused for a rest in the hidden entrance to the block, next to the dunny. I always give her a correctly respectful bow when we pass and she rewards me with a sweet and gentle smile. Now I hung my head as she transfixed me with compressed lips and contemptuous eyes. I don't think she blamed me personally for the explosions, but she had seen and heard me cheering and clapping. There was nothing I could do. I lumbered past, clutching my throat.

She continues to avert her delicate, imperial profile when we now pass, disdaining all my penitent attempts to restore recognition.

I urgently sought the advice of male Chinese friends at the Foreign Correspondents' Club and other cultural centres. Two sympathetic Japanese friends have also taken the problem under sincere advisement. At least they don't jeer like fellow foreign-devils. They agree that Chaucer, Shakespeare and Mark Twain have recorded similar incidents in classic masterpieces, reflecting no personal embarrassment among mixed-company participants. But they seize on a plausible point: No Asians were involved in those scenarios — only foreign-devils. The argument, they suggest, cuts — or blows — either way.

Simply, they argue that, had I been a Chinese male, the Chinese lady would have ignored my behaviour; that, had I been accompanied by a Chinese male, she would merely have lowered her eyes (whether or not he was sharing my applause); that, had she been a Chinese male, he would either have agreeably accepted my demonstration, or, if race-conscious, passed with quiet superiority. (It is, of course, assumed that the unseen *fung-pei* master was Chinese — probably from the north or, perhaps, Sichuan.)

The Japanese reaction would irritate Women's Lib. They say that, in either Japanese or multi-racial company, such a masculine demonstration would provoke amiable discussion and reminiscences, and even stimulate spirited competition. But for Japanese ladies — never. (There is, indeed, a folklore story of a Yedo *samurai* whose No. 1 *geisha* performed accidentally at a banquet; her inadvertence was gallantly ignored at the time, but the infuriated *samurai*, who had lost more face than she had lost wind, then sold her into the Yoshiwara; she thanked him for not having ordered her to commit *hara-kiri*.)

Meanwhile, I am now making a shamed detour to leeward on my Mid-Levels patrols. Can happy, peaceful accord be restored? Or will the East Wind continue to rise?

October

The first world ginseng symposium, convened in Seoul last week, was attended by 98 scientists and businessmen from Japan, the United States, Britain, Germany, Taiwan, Thailand, Singapore, Switzerland, the Netherlands, Belgium, Sweden and Turkey.

According to the Director-General of the Office of Monopoly, which controls the export and guarantees the quality of red ginseng, the symposium as designed "to improve the image of ginseng" — i.e. to establish medical endorsement for some legendary elixir claims, to adopt a conservative and scientific posture, and to down-pedal — but never dismiss — the dirty jokes about old men and young wives.

The visiting, pampered troupe of 30 invited journalists — only one from Hongkong — agreed that the symposium was restrained but persuasive. Most of them left laden — some furtively — with samples of ginseng products, ranging from roots (still the operative word) to liquor, and including tea, powder, cosmetics, soup, cigarettes, jam and confectionery.

This superficial report will make no attempt to present an analysis of the learned treatises read by the 14 specialists — four from Korea, four from Japan, three from Germany, and one each from Yugoslavia, Denmark and the United States.

In brief, the notion that the ginseng root, which looks like the foetus of a nymphomaniac witch, was a panacea or even "a wonder drug" was rejected, but documented evidence was presented to confirm that the unique root does help to promote energy (yes, and virility), prolong life, remedy anaemia, rheumatism, "women's diseases," diabetes and liver complaints, and to inhibit the growth of cancer cells.

There are strange contradictions. Small doses of ginseng allegedly increase weight, but large doses reduce weight. Ginseng is now the basis of a wide range of wines, mixed liqueurs, and cocktails of authority, but it is also supposed to relieve hangovers sustained from more conventional alcohol. Human trust and belief doubtless play a decisive role in the real or imaginary effects. (And why not?)

A shy but sly personal inquiry about the recent angry pronouncement by New York Attorney-General Lefkowitz that "ginseng tablets are absolutely worthless as a sexual stimulant, aphrodisiac or cure for impotency," evoked indulgent comment by two amused European scientists:

"The term aphrodisiac is in poor taste. Tablets, anyway, are not the most rewarding version of ginseng. But good health and virility are undoubtedly encouraged —

more impressively by red ginseng [six years old] than by white [four years]. It is a tonic which certainly aids digestion and reduces blood pressure. Most Korean boxers and swimmers drink ginseng tea."

The visiting journalists soon shifted from normal foreign-devil drinks to ginseng varieties when they discovered that a straight double vodka or scotch cost Won 2,300 (nearly US$5), while a double ginseng "wine" — which looks and tastes like an agreeable medicinal whisky with a pleasant lingering after-effect — costs only Won 700.

Doubtless French cognac-sellers would be distressed by the lifelike counterfeit "Napoleon," five-star labelled bottle from which ginseng "brandy" is poured. Scotch distillers would be similarly disturbed by the precise appearance and white label on the bottles of ginseng "whisky."

East meets West in ginseng cocktails: ginseng "old-fashioneds," ginseng "Manhattans," ginseng "gimlets" and ginseng "brandy slings."

Export trade is booming. South Korean ginseng shipments were worth more than US$14 million in 1972, US$23 million last year and should rise to nearly US$31 million this year.

The Korean Office of Monopoly announced at the symposium that it would build "a large-scale, up-to-date, integrated red ginseng plant" near Puyo at a cost of nearly US$15 million and capable of producing 1.2 million tons a year.

China is now becoming a keen competitor, but in Korean judgment, the communist product is inferior, largely because the root is cultivated with artificial fertiliser — abominable. An enterprising cadre unit in Honan was recently applauded by the Peking *People's Daily* for producing ginseng from natural fertiliser, but they mixed birds' dung with fallen leaves and so spoiled the vintage flavour. Besides, the Chinese product, it seems, is not properly matured.

The new Chinese product of brandy ginseng toothpaste is dismissed with a Korean shrug. The rival Japanese product is marred by over-modernised methods of mass production and relies on white rather than red ginseng.

One of the specific aims of the world symposium was to secure a lifting of the current ban in England and United States on the "longer life and vivid vigour and vitality" advertisement claims for ginseng. These advertisements are permitted throughout Europe, and the increasing world demand — especially in the United States — is expected to break down prudish censorship elsewhere.

There will be a second world ginseng symposium in Zurich early next year and most visiting pressmen who attended the Seoul inaugural hope that they will be again invited. As in Korea, the clear Swiss Alpine air encourages a proper appreciation of ginseng-tasting.

November

My favourite ruined temple, I note with a reverent genuflexion, is back in the news. Preah Vihear, the crumbling, thousand-year-old Hindu "centre of the world," is perched precariously on the disputed Thai-Cambodian frontier — pavilions of sandstone monuments, with explicit and amorous carvings and mouldering pillars thrown down over the centuries by impetuous and itchy-backsided elephants. The historic complex tilts giddily into northern Cambodian space over an inbuilt precipice and is more easily accessible — even in peacetime — from Thailand than Cambodia.

According to legendary gossip, a debonair young French cartographer, on the spot in 1904 and distracted by imported champagne and beautiful native girls, ran an erratic blue-pencil across the old map which then delineated the border between Siam and Cambodia and literally flicked the Preah Vihear temple across the precipice into Cambodia.

The dispute over territorial ownership persisted until Prince Norodom Sihanouk, as resident Cambodian ruler, appealed to the foreign-devil–dominated World Court, which ruled in 1962 — a nine-to-three vote — that Preah Vihear belonged to Cambodia and confirmed the dubious 1904 redemarcation.

Some of us barefoot pressmen recall an impromptu news conference, just after the international judgment was handed down, with Marshal Sarit Thanarat, the tough and choleric then prime minister, in northeastern Thailand. (Curiously, in retrospect, we were reporting the welcome arrival of a fighter squadron on the borders of Laos to help defend Thailand against North Vietnam commies.) Sarit roared at us: "We shall shoot down the dogs as soon as they attack!" We all thought he meant the real and mounting communist threat across the Mekong. But he meant the prospect of Cambodian forces re-occupying Preah Vihear.

In the wash-up, however, both the Thais and Cambodians behaved very reasonably. The Thais reserved the right to appeal against the divided World Court ruling (they never did), and they dropped their early threat to boycott the Southeast Asian Treaty Organisation. Sihanouk — always, I insist, a man of charm, wit and sophistication — invited all Thais and tourists from Thailand to visit Preah Vihear without asking for visas and graciously waived the World Court's supplementary ruling that statuary and carvings removed by the Thais must be restored.

Now we learn that a beleaguered Phnom Penh military force continues to occupy Preah Vihear against the heavy build-up of Khmer Rouge rebels and communist invaders (I mean, "liberators") in the Cambodian plains below the temple. But the isolated force survives only because of the presence of Thai paramilitary units on the heights behind the temple ruins. Whatever the Western mapdrawers may say, Preah Vihear belongs culturally to Cambodia, but geographically to Thailand.

Before the Cambodian tragedy, Bangkok and Phnom Penh had reached an amicable, Southeast Asian compromise. That non-ideological partnership abides.

The vulnerable Phnom Penh troops fly the blue and white flag of the 1954 Hague Convention above Preah Vihear — invoking the international ban on involvement of cultural monuments in military action. But their continuing presence and the safety of the temple depend on the Thai flag flying behind them. (An interesting coincidence, because the Thai troops had temporarily seized the temple ruins in 1954.)

It is difficult to doubt that in Peking, Sihanouk, the improbable royal front-man for communism, is now privately saluting the Thais for their cultural intervention. Madame Indira Gandhi should be interested also: Indian missionaries blessed the Hindu temple centuries before Comrades Buddha and Marx arrived.

December

I deliberately postponed comment on Taiwan's decision the other week to substitute the gas-chamber for the gallows because I thought there might be a correction of the report. It seems now to be fair dinkum. My caution was understandable. To my grievous embarrassment, I had been personally involved in a false alarm over Japan's suspected switch from hanging to the hot squat during the early days of the Occupation. There was, in fact, a scurrilous file on me in Gen. Douglas MacArthur's archives. An old Aussie friend in New York, Harry Lee (book reviewer for *Time*; now, alas, RIP), had sent me as a Christmas card, in execrable taste, a postcard with a dramatic close-up in colour of the death-chair in Sing Sing. Typewritten on the other side, clear for all to read, was his deadpan message:

The Lee Exporting Co., New York.
December 1947.
Richard Hughes, Esq.,
Posing as a Foreign Correspondent,
Press Club, Shimbun Alley, Tokyo.

Dear Sir: In response to your welcome inquiry, we have pleasure in submitting sample illustration of the type of goods which you wish to import to help democratise Japan. This is a sturdy but elegant model, easy on power, maintenance and the eye, if hard on the seat, and has given satisfaction to all users. Testimonials available. Pray advise numbers required as quantity will of course govern price (f.o.b. San Francisco–Yokohama).
With personal respects and greetings for Christmas and the New Year to both yourself and General MacArthur in your noble labours.
(signed) HARRY LEE, President and Managing Director.

This had been intercepted and read by a sincere Tokyo postal official, who then called to see me with another sincere Japanese "adviser" on trade, liaison matters and import and export licences, in the Occupation set-up. Simply, they had taken the message seriously and wanted to see if they could cash in with me on arranging the orders at a fixed price.

"It is, as you know, sometimes unusual for a newspaper correspondent, Mr Hooje, to hold also import licence under Occupation law," the postal man pointed out. (It was, as both well knew, downright illegal.) "We did not know that Supreme Commander was intending to change our barbarous Japanese form of hanging for democratic electrocution method. It seemed to us *(voice lowered)* that it would be useful to you and Mr Lee if we could have private information of the number of electric chairs which General MacArthur thinks might be necessary and we could then, ahem, help you to fix fair and reasonable price — ha, ha."

It was a frustrating interview — however amusing in retrospect. I could hear Harry Lee's mocking laughter in New York. My visitors, of course, flatly refused to believe my frantic attempts to explain that the message was only a joke. They clearly suspected that I was only being discreet, or else evilly manoeuvring for a better bargaining approach. After a maddening argument, they politely left, but promised to send a more authoritative agent, who turned up a couple of days later. He was an influential industrialist of honourable lineage who obviously had undercover Japanese and, alas, Occupation contacts. He rejected my explanation with more open derision than the earlier visitors, but finally decided that I had either withdrawn from the deal or appointed a front man with an authorised licence.

I suppose I should have tried to find out what graft was being offered and how they were manipulating exchange grants, but I could never take the matter seriously. (Some time later, an Occupation official, with a grin, asked me how electric chairs were selling.)

Anyway, there seems to be no doubt that the Chinese Nationalists are now officially dumping the gallows. I guess they preferred the gas-chamber to the electric-chair because of the energy crisis. They are still hanging them — in theory — in traditional Japan.

55

1975 January

It is encouraging to note that Peking's new English-language trade magazine is seeking to promote world sales of deer antlers. The antlers' "albumin, hormones, calcium phosphate and gelatinous cartilege," the sales campaign claims, "have therapeutic value in combating loss of memory, pain in the joints and malnutrition, and restoring virility [of course]." It is also randily recalled — in a mood of happy disharmony with Party puritanism — that antlers are "believed to have aphrodisiac qualities." (China is, and will remain, Chinese first and communist second.)

Significantly, these attributes are lifted, word-for-word, from an authoritative survey of ancient and honourable Chinese animal drugs, *Chinese Materia Medica*, compiled by Dr Bernard Read in 1931, and first published by *Peking Natural History Bulletin*. (Copies of the historic book are still on limited sale in Peking; I got mine from a diplomat who visited the Forbidden City a few months ago.)

Today, China's deer antlers are being prepared for export as "bottled liquid extract," or as "two- or three-branch horns" (a better term than "antlers"), graded in three qualities.

If I were PR cadre for any of the communes preparing deer horns, I would refer more closely to *Chinese Materia Medica* and widen the variety of products in different categories, with a selective eye and descriptive tongue for barbarian weaknesses.

For instance, it seems that the best horns come from sika deer *(lu)* and elk or moose *(mi)*. The sika deer (abundant in all China's mountain forests) sheds its celebrated "velvet horns" *(jung)* in late summer: "They are licentious, one male serving many females; they like to eat turtles and good grass; they sleep together in a ring, head to tail, to sustain posterior circulation." (Old Hands will remember that this is the dormitory habit of Peking swallows.)

The antler harvest: varied attributes.

The elk (hailing from south China and the Huai River region) sheds its horns in the winter solstice and is therefore logically classified as *"yin"* to blend with the sika *"yang."* The horns of the elk are longer than those of the sika.

The elk has one notable advantage over the sika: "It has two openings below the eyes called 'night eyes.' If seen accidentally by a pregnant woman, her child will be born with four eyes." This surely would be an admirable sales-plug for eye-improvement from powdered elk horn — now neglected.

The sika horn offers more varied attributes, most of which still escape the attention of current Peking trade development propaganda: "Good also for stomach upset after alcohol, for decayed teeth, vertigo and nymphomania." (A British Medical Association specialist could very well brood over that last claim: What does "good" or "bad" mean when nymphomania is under treatment, remembering shrewdly that the basic influence of deer horn is "improved virility.")

Sika and elk horns also produce a "deer glue" *(pai chiao)*, which could be effectively promoted in foreign-devil — rather foreign-angel — beauty shops. Powdered burnt horn is boiled over a mulberry wood fire for seven days, with stirred water and vinegar. "It is paler than asses' glue and, when applied to the face, its cosmetic effect is like jade and the complexion is most lovable."

To repeat, here is a dramatic challenge to PR promotion on the world horn market. Already the Chinese are vigorously pushing their world sales of ginseng — though the Koreans, North and South, dismiss it scornfully as a No. 2 virility rival. China, alas, cannot offer rhinoceros horn, which many of my elderly, drooping friends applaud. And "drunken shrimps" cannot be canned. But *king ning-hualon* — "gold and silver flowers" — should soon join deer horns and ginseng.

February

Belatedly, I have just heard, with deep sorrow, of the death of one of the greatest Japanese I had the honour of knowing: Mitsugoro Bando VIII, the gifted 69-year-old Kabuki actor. When I first met him in the Kansai Theatre in 1946 — introduced by the late Torao (Tiger) Saito, Japan's No. 1 war correspondent and photographer — his stage name was Minosuka Bando VI. We discovered that we had both been born in the same Year of the Horse (1906), and I always gratefully and selfishly imposed my foreign-devil presence on him whenever I visited Kyoto.

He was a generous host and a great gourmet — ironically, that was the cause of his death — and some of my most memorable Japanese meals were enjoyed at his table. In 1973 he was officially designated by the Japanese Government as an "Intangible Cultural Asset," so he was the only "living national treasure" I shall ever know.

The circumstances of his death were properly theatrical and uniquely Japanese, and I do not doubt that when he died his mobile philosophic features reflected a classical Kabuki smile. He had dined with four friends at the celebrated Masa Restaurant in Kyoto — where he had frequently honoured me — on the delicious but sometimes deadly dish to which he introduced me: *fugu*, or Japanese globefish or blowfish. The menu included *fugu sashimi* (sliced raw) and *chiri nabe* (casserole), and Bando insisted on eating the liver of the *fugu*, which many Japanese diners avoid. That's what killed him.

Globefish poisoning is caused by tetrotoxin, usually found in *fugu* liver or ovaries, which can be far deadlier than potassium cyanide and causes violent paralysis. Since 1958, when a total of 289 diners suffered from globefish poisoning in Japan and 167 died, only licensed cooks have been authorised to prepare *fugu* dishes. Even so, about 80 people suffer from globefish poisoning in Japan each year, and 22 died in 1972 and 27 in 1973.

(Police are now questioning the heartbroken cook at the Masa Restaurant who served the *fugu* at the Bando party.)

My one-time boss and old friend, Ian Fleming, thoroughly enjoyed his only *fugu* dinner with "Tiger" Saito and me at a first-class inn in Fukuoka, when he was absorbing local colour and detail for his penultimate James Bond adventure, *You Only Live Twice*. (Both "Tiger" and I are shamefully lampooned as "secret agents" in this book.)

"Tiger" well knew the hazards of *fugu* dishes, but made a careful reconnaissance of the kitchen and returned with an "all-clear" signal. I can still see Fleming confirming detachedly with a hot match-end the claim that the insidious and delicious authority of the blowfish does temporarily deaden the lips of the eater. "It makes me feel like a leper," he remarked. He then brooded aloud over the possibility — and some excellent *sake* — of introducing a fatal *fugu* poisoning into the plot of *You Only Live Twice*, but had decided next morning that "no one in the barbarian West would ever believe that such poisoning was possible."

In retrospect, it is an encouraging fact that dear Ian — eventually to die all too soon — at least established, with "Tiger" and me, that some people can still live twice after *fugu* liver.

Certainly Mitsugoro Bando VIII knew the risk that he was taking when he relished that last supper last month. Appropriately perhaps, he was then playing his last role as an elderly tea master in the Kabuki drama, "*Ogin-Sama*." And he would have applauded the shrugged comment of one of his mourning friends who was asked whether he would continue eating *fugu*: "Of course, one can get killed far less pleasantly by stepping in front of a taxi."

March

With a sad *sake* hiccough, I learn from Tokyo's *Shukan Sankei* that, following the current clampdown by Japanese firms on "entertainment" expenses, the most popular hostesses in the Ginza cultural area are being peddled from bar to bar on sharply competitive bids by rival proprietors. Seductive hostesses naturally command loyal personal retinues of the dwindling spenders, who follow them to new nightclubs — just as Hongkong gourmets follow a favourite Chinese chef when he moves to a new kitchen.

According to this report (translated for me by my old cobber, Dr Bob Horiguchi), some of these transactions involve a bid of more than ¥1 million (US$3,247), and the magnetic hostess, under contract, must accept compulsory transfer.

It seems that retrenching *zaibatsu*, as previously reported, are not only cutting back on expenses, but are delaying payment of "entertainment" bills from the old honourable limit of 90 days to 120 days or more, and are even then hiding behind promissory notes. Therefore, the personal fidelity of durable drinkers to any one hostess becomes a rewarding investment.

Old *gaijin* hands, remembering the romantic Ginza days of the 1940s and 1950s, will share my nostalgic regret at this sordid commercialism. For example, I recall, with moist eyes, the delicate cold war between "Beautiful Crystal" and "Dawn of Love" for pre-eminence in Tokyo's sophisticated nightclub life in the late 1950s. "Beautiful Crystal," an elegant one-time dancer, presided over the celebrated L'Espoir ("Hope"), a golden-walled cabaret with a tiny bar, which was a gay rendezvous for Tokyo's smart, intellectual set. Then "Dawn of Love," a voluptuous *geisha*, arrived from Kyoto to set up her rival establishment Osome ("Modesty"). She struck sharply and successfully at the heart of "Beautiful Crystal's" prestigious custom with a modernistic, lantern-hung, L-shaped sanctuary, modelled on the Gion entertainment area in Kyoto. The two ladies operated their cold war with suave and subtle Japanese feminine methods.

Whenever an especially distinguished man of letters or art visited L'Espoir, "Beautiful Crystal" would herself escort him later through the narrow winding lanes to Osome to introduce him modestly to "Dawn of Love," who naturally admitted herself prostrated by the honour, though aware that observant drinkers in her cabaret were witnessing a notable psychological victory for "Beautiful Crystal," far transcending the sordid value of the few drinks which the patron enjoyed in the rival establishment.

At the first available opportunity, of course, "Dawn of Love" would launch a similar counter-attack on "Beautiful Crystal" with equal self-deprecation, charm and craft.

A best-selling novel, *Black Butterfly*, was based on the nightclub cold war by an eminent author, Matsutaro Kawafajuchi. This in turn became a house-packing movie, *Night Butterfly*, in which two leading actresses played the roles of "Beautiful Crystal" and "Dawn of Love." In the climax, "Dawn of Love" won the cold war, but "Beautiful Crystal" won the man they both wanted; "Dawn of Love" pursued the two lovers in a night car chase, and all three were killed in a *kamikaze* collision.

I never discovered who actually and ultimately prevailed. But I got instructive replies when I asked them both separately, in late 1958, what they thought of their fate as portrayed in the book and film.

"These stories are absurd," said "Beautiful Crystal," shyly. "She is my sincere friend. As for the film, perhaps an insignificant and helpless woman needs the support of an honourable business as much as the devotion of a dedicated lover."

" 'Beautiful Crystal' is my sincere friend," said "Dawn of Love," shyly. "The film? We dull and flighty women naturally cannot depend on the enduring loyalty of men; we must humbly seek to protect our foolish old age by our own modest efforts."

April

There should, please, be a minute or two of silent prayer and homage for the two dedicated martyrs to Southeast Asia's unofficial and non-ideological, but resolute and admirable, refusal to pay blackmail to terrorist guerillas. They are the two foreign-angel missionary nurses who were treating lepers in the Yala province of Thailand and who were kidnapped nearly a year ago by a Muslim bandit bastard called Poh Su: Miss Margaret Morgan, 39 (from Wales), and Miss Minka Hanskamp, 40 (a Dutch-born naturalised New Zealander).

Their abduction was followed by demands for a ransom of US$500,000 and "political independence" for four southern provinces of Thailand. After tortured consideration, the Singapore-based Overseas Missionary Fellowship, for whom they selflessly laboured, made the heroic decision to reject any deal. (The letter which the foreign-angels were compelled to sign ended, movingly, with the invocation: "May God guide you in your choice." I think He did.)

Now their corpses have been discovered (RIP) in the same province where they had been treating and comforting native lepers.

The vital and encouraging point to stress is that these heroines paid the price for what appears to be an unofficial agreement by government authorities in Southeast Asia that no ransoms will be paid for terrorist kidnappings in their part of the world. On all the evidence, Burma, Singapore, Malaysia, Thailand, the Philippines and Laos — with the tacit endorsement of Soviet, Chinese and US ambassadors — are in complete agreement that any blackmailed surrender in these abominable circumstances would only encourage a Latin American–type extension of kidnapping and terrorism. Here, indeed, is an example for the world.

We should recall the happier climax to Burma's refusal to yield to blackmail demands for the release of two Soviet doctors who were similarly kidnapped, two years ago, in an allegedly "secure" area, 200 miles north of Rangoon. Their abductors demanded a US$2 million ransom and the release of their Chinese-born leader, Chang Chi-fu, who had commanded a private army in the opium-rich Golden Triangle and who is still — 100 cheers! — serving a life sentence in a Rangoon prison.

The Burmese Government flatly refused even to consider negotiations and just tightened security over Chang. The ransom demands were then vainly repeated by the frustrated kidnappers to Burmese diplomats in Thailand and Laos, implying that the Soviet victims were being shifted and re-shifted across the common Golden Triangle borders.

The strong stand of the Burmese Government was warmly if privately commended by foreign diplomats in the area, including, instructively and uniquely, both the Soviet and Chinese embassies. There was wise and apolitical agreement that any weak concession to the Sino-Burmese kidnappers would automatically promote further kidnappings and more arrogant blackmail.

A welcome and unpublicised byproduct of that kidnapping was the unofficial co-operation by US CIA and anti-narcotics agents with the Burmese military and Thai security authorities in the jungle search of the two Soviet doctors. Ultimately, both hostages were sullenly released. At least, their Burmese kidnappers were not as vicious as the abominable Poh Su.

Communist representatives in Hongkong privately commended the Singaporean and Burmese reaction to the kidnapping of the Soviet doctors and the Overseas Missionary Fellowship reaction to the kidnapping of the two dear nurses. The angry outburst of a local party official at Kaitak, when revolutionary students from the Philippines hijacked a plane from Manila to Canton in 1973, is apposite: "China will never become another Cuba!" Those students are still engaged in "voluntary reproductive work" on a commune reformatory outside Peking. (Perhaps President Ferdinand Marcos will talk with them on his projected goodwill visit.)

May

More than 33 years have elapsed since I was expelled, weeping and blaspheming, from the press galleries of both the Senate and the House of Representatives in Canberra because of a trivial and boring newspaper column which I had written criticising an irresponsible and parochial Senate vote against John Curtin's Labor war-time government.

I admit — nay, insist — that I was delighted to re-seat myself humbly in the galleries this week with no hostile reception; old memories stirred happily, but no wounds ached. The Canberra press remains, as always, one of the friendliest in the world, and the younger generation urbanely conceals its apprehension of detailed reminiscences about the Boer War when a senile expatriate colleague is wheeled in.

Prime Minister Gough Whitlam, alas, was not in the House during my brief re-emergence — indeed, only two Government and three Opposition members were yawningly present — but I was impressed by the courtly replies of Foreign Minister Willesee to long-winded questions.

Another gratifying reflection was the impression that at long last we Aussies have outgrown the warranted jibe of Singapore's Prime Minister Lee Kuan Yew in an interview six years ago with British journalist James Cameron. Lee, ironically and correctly, then deplored "the strange reluctance of Australia to accept promotion above the rank of deputy sheriff in Southeast Asia."

That reluctance, it seems to me, has now passed. Any expatriate Australian — whatever his political persuasion — will applaud the Whitlam instinct — whatever his non-political goad — to show the Aussie flag in foreign states, riding astride a kangaroo, with a boomerang in his hand (right or left).

It was, for me, at once *(a)* gratifying to learn that Whitlam will leave this week to shout "Cooee!" in Latin America and expound his version of Australian independence (right or wrong), but *(b)* bewildering to discover that he is being denounced by both his own party's lefty faction and the new leader of his rightist opposition, Malcolm Fraser, for his "poor-man's Kissinger" visit to another part of the world when so many problems are mounting on the home front.

The trouble with the Aussies — as frustrated Asian neighbours have known for so long — was that they did not like to "mix" with the others. The reason, I reckoned, was shyness, stupidity and parochialism, rather than reputed "White Australian" aloofness.

Current portents — those old "well-informed sources" tell me in Canberra — indicate, happily, closer Australian relations with Indonesia, Singapore and Japan, in particular, for the best of all possible reasons: mutual advantage.

Anzus, alas, seems to have gone down the drain. Who can trust the Yanks these days?

Anzac, alasser, is broken. Identity cards must now be carried by Aussies and NZedders visiting each other's country. I guess only old men now recall that ancient honourable Gallipoli alliance. (It was once seriously suggested by some idealists that Australia and New Zealand should unite constitutionally in the same parliament under the name of Anzac — Australia New Zealand Allied Commonwealth.)

Give Whitlam current credit (my old and new Canberra colleagues assured me): Australia will not retreat again behind the boomerang curtain; "White" Australia has gone with the East Wind; and Australia now aspires to the rank of a full-sheriff-plus.

But does it have two guns? Or even one? That is another story — on which Australian defence authorities have strong opinions.

June

The scene is China, in the Year of the Ox, 1949, precisely 26 years ago. A revolutionary leader called Mao Zedong has entered Peking; his military commander, Lin Biao, with Soviet aid, has seized Shanghai and is sweeping south; and the Americans are trying, in embarrassed defeat, to divest themselves of continuing support for the overthrown Chiang Kaishek (then commuting between Canton and Formosa).

I try to resurrect the mood and confusion of those mid-1949 days with contemporary extracts from on-the-spot news reports and comment by distinguished by-liners (old cobbers, and some of them now dead, alas), available from yellowing files on my praying-stool. Earnest readers are invited to make their own deductions and comparisons between June-July 1949 and June-July 1975 *(or today — Ed.).* "The historian is a prophet looking backward" — Comrade Schlegel.

■   ■   ■

"A promise to Shanghai residents that the nationalists would recapture the city from the communists within four months was made by Generalissimo Chiang Kaishek in a broadcast last night from Formosa. He said that he would commit suicide if he was unable to fulfil the promise. He apologised to the people of Shanghai for losing the city to the communists, explaining that his planned 'fight to the last man' miscarried because the troops in the rear were 'bought off by others'." — *United Press (Shanghai)*

*   *   *

"Communist leader Mao Zedong broadcast from Peking a message to Chinese workers, telling them that they must 'cooperate with the capitalists so that maximum production can be attained' . . . He warned that the Party's present labour policy called not for unrestricted license but rather for control and cooperation with capital." — *Associated Press (Nanking)*

*   *   *

"The Chinese communists, in what appeared to be the opening of a war of nerves against Hongkong, today blasted British 'oppression of the Chinese people.' The propaganda broadcast was fired as British Defence Minister Alexander arrived in the colony, and the nearest Chinese communist troops were reported in Kian, only 300 miles to the north." — *United Press (Hongkong)*

"Whatever controversies there are on other aspects of American foreign policy in Asia, there should be agreement on the value to the US of encouraging the intense desire of Asians to govern themselves . . . Communism may provide worse exploitation of Asians than they ever suffered in colonial times, and that possibility should be stressed on every appropriate occasion." — *New York Herald Tribune*

*   *   *

"Only the Chinese communists can now provide what the Western nations desperately want: a China independent of the Kremlin. But only the Western nations can provide what the Chinese communists desperately want: the wherewithal from machine tools and capitalist technical skills to industrialise their country . . . The aim [for the West] must emphatically not be to interfere with Mao Zedong's organisation of China. The sole aim must be to promote the Western contacts and the spirit of Chinese national independence." — *Stewart Alsop (Hongkong)*

*   *   *

"General Claire Chennault said that 'a third and more horrible war is inevitable if the US permits communism to conquer China.' The former chief of the Flying Tigers added: 'We will make 1,000 million enemies. Communism will conquer Asia and encroach on the islands of the Pacific. The Americans who died to sweep the Japanese from those islands will have died in vain. Indochina, Indonesia, Burma, Thailand and Cambodia will fall. Japan, the Ryukyus and the Philippines will be threatened'." — *United Press (Washington)*

July

I sincerely hope that I did not provoke the North Korean guards' assault on the Americans at the truce village of Panmunjom. I had been deliberately provocative on my invited visit last week for the 25th invasion anniversary when the arrogant communist soldiers, as usual, photographed me, close-up, as a senile reporter who had covered the Korean War. I glared at them through my old 8th Army (North Africa) fake monocle — the first time, according to our tough but urbane, 6-ft 3-in US captain escort, their insolent commy Rogues' Gallery would have a photograph of a monocled visitor (without cord, of course).

"It will confuse the hell out of them," he said, with an amused oath. "They may think you are from Sandhurst — posturing as a pressman — or perhaps from Prussia. Over the years of confrontation here, we have had our Battle of the Flags, Battle of the Doves and Battle of the Buildings. Perhaps they will regard this as a challenge for more Upmanship, and will now train and turn out an officer or visitor wearing two monocles. Their flags are bigger and higher than ours. They made their official matching building one metre higher and one metre longer than our Friendship Villa."

However, the commies lost the Battle of the Doves. They had developed a pious habit of releasing a covey of doves after each truce meeting, and indicating significantly that all the doves always preferred to settle on the roof of their original northern building — instructively sensing that that was the centre of true peace. The cunning plot was detected, however, when the new UN-US pagoda villa was built opposite. The basic colour in the decorative paint on the villa resembled that on the rival communist roof, which the doves had been eye-washed to select as their perch, and so they began to settle on the more attractive southern building. They don't appear now . . .

Anyway, it is a curious coincidence that the dozen North Korean Army guards and reporters chose to beat up the two Americans so soon after our anniversary visit. None of them, it seems, sported a retaliatory party-line monocle; though — come to think of it — the North Korean Army breeches and knee-boots — modelled on the Soviet revisionist, instead of the Peking peace-loving, uniform — could appropriately justify a monocle.

In fact, the moon-face of President Kim Il Sung, "the poor man's Chairman Mao," would look more dignified with an eye-glass — but he, of course, being basically an insecure man, would have to have it taped.

When our group gazed across the Bridge of No Return and past the dusty and empty buildings of the artificial North Korean "propaganda village," we could discern on a distant hillside, above some lingering Kaesong gingseng crops, a huge cult statue of President Kim. He is in profile and is not surveying the South. But the hills and land on the northern side of the demilitarised zone are honeycombed with hundreds of bunkers, army outposts, and ack-ack and artillery strongpoints, and at least 17 tunnels have been burrowed under the 38th Parallel. (Kim's new title in the South is "the light at the end of the tunnel.")

The tunnels are under observation, and two have now been physically "intercepted" by the South Korean garrison forces. Our visiting group was taken by helicopter to the original tunnel. Booby-traps and mines along the tractor-rails have been systematically destroyed — with casualties — and a steel wall will be erected underground, correctly and precisely, at the official line of demarcation in the DMZ. Formidable people, the Koreans — North and South, Park Chung Hee and Kim.

Of course, Kim (grooming his 35-year-old son as heir) wants to push south — with or without monocle. But the unspectacled view, on the spot, is that both Peking and Moscow prefer to keep Korea divided.

September

That unique Japanese institution, *sokai-ya*, is still on the march, reinforced — appropriately enough, in this International Women's Year — by the first infiltration of enterprising Japanese womanhood.

I am indebted to my Tokyo mentor, Dr Bob Horiguchi, for recent scholarly research, updating my own blurred recollections of this subtle blackmail operation, which has defied all attempts at suppression by the Japanese police, but which, strangely, has never prompted even attempts at duplication in other Asian states.

Sokai-ya must not be blasphemously confused with *Sokka-Gakkai*, the enigmatic, neo-Buddhist political body, which last month signed an amusing 10-year pact of peaceful co-existence with the Japanese Communist Party (world peace, freedom of religion, anti-nuclear war, anti-fascism, pro-Rotary, etc.).

Members of *sokai-ya* buy a few shares in Japanese companies, which are tradiatically anxious to conduct formal shareholders' meetings with speed, goodwill, deep bows and unanimous votes. The *sokai-ya* — no one is quite sure how many there are, as groups often nominate a single representative — customarily represent themselves as editors or publishers of financial bulletins and newsletters, economic "analyses" and stock-exchange guides.

They are, bluntly, paid off by the companies to refrain from causing commotion, moving minority votes of censure or demanding sub-committee inquiries at shareholders' meetings which they are technically entitled to attend. They demand a substantial fee for this restraint. The companies, alas, pay this blackmail and, with Japanese sincerity, do not cooperate with the baffled police.

This compliance does not mean that the company directors are guilty of administrative malpractice. They simply feel that unruly shareholders' meetings or minority challenges on the floor to the board's recommendations involve a loss of face for the company and offer encouragement to rival companies (similarly nurturing the *sokai-ya* parasites).

The first detailed report I have seen of alleged earnings by a typical *sokai-ya* has been translated by Dr Horiguchi from a recent report in the Tokyo weekly *Shukan Shincho*. One of the first of the seven women to join the *sokai-ya* is Ms Asako Taira, described as: "Fiftyish. Pretty, wise and courageous. The brightest gem among the female *sokai-ya*." Her *New Japan Economic News* costs ¥8,000 for a six-month subscription. Six hundred client companies are now dutifully subscribing. It is also alleged that she receives payments from various firms, ranging from ¥20-30,000 to "support" her fearless *News*. Four leading Japanese security houses, it is said, make these payments five to six times a year, and beer companies every two months. Naturally, revenue soars with the opening of the season for general shareholders' meetings.

(I was myself once approached by a smiling *sokai-ya* in late 1947, when I was temporarily out of a press job because of a cultural breach with my then Sydney boss — RIP — and was presumptuously pretending to "manage" the Foreign Correspondents' Club [FCC] in Tokyo's Shimbun Alley. The *sokai-ya* made it clear, through a suborned student interpreter, that regular payments — to be determined — by the FCC for the publication of an Occupation-approved newsletter would be an insurance against looming disaffection among my loyal FCC Japanese staff. Hastily, I briefed fellow-member Larry Tighe — a Golden Gloves champion — in the bar, and introduced him to the *sokai-ya*, whom Larry civilly invited to step outside. Larry returned five minutes later, rubbing his knuckles: "Left eye black; nose scarlet; okay, Dick?" It was. The FCC staff thanked us.)

One still wonders why the *sokai-ya* trick has not been tried elsewhere in Asia: Jakarta, pre-Marcos Manila, Bangkok, Rangoon? Was this essentially Japanese *sokai-ya* mood spiritually responsible for Tokyo's shameful surrender to the Japanese terrorists at Kuala Lumpur?

● **Leftwing militants of the Japanese Red Army had recently seized a multi-storey building and a number of hostages in Kuala Lumpur. In exchange for the release of their hostages Japan agreed to release seven convicted Red Army members.**

October

This deplorable incident is now four months old and has caused me grievous embarrassment, though arousing hilarity among evil *gweilo* mates. It could happen elsewhere in Asia to any language-inhibited foreign-devil — though especially in Hongkong. And last week, it was partly and alarmingly revived. It has nothing to do with politics, but it could become a blackmail racket and might sabotage my job as a columnist for the REVIEW.

The setting was one of the two unmanned elevators in the old Gloucester Building. The time was after 7 p.m. — otherwise, I would, as usual, have waited for one of the three manned elevators in the charge of one of my old friends who have acted as lift-men since the old Gloucester Hotel days.

I had respectfully delivered a front-page exclusive (ha, ha) for *The Times* at Reuters on the 7th floor and, in the empty elevator, efficiently pressed the button for the 4th floor to enjoy my daily ration of one martini at the ancient and honourable Cosmo Club. The elevator halted at the 6th floor and a modest, elegant, sad-eyed Chinese girl entered, burst into tears and, turning her back on me, began to sob out her heart into a handkerchief. With Holmesian perception, I recalled that there are several doctors' clinics on the 6th floor and made sympathetic and helpful mumbles in Melbourne English, which she gently silenced with apologetic waves of her free hand. I brooded over what bad news her doctor must have given her. "There is no justice," I murmured.

But then the elevator halted at the 5th floor and two obese, arrogant, well-dressed, Rotarian-type Chinese entered. They did not know each other. But their joint reaction was spontaneous and understandable: a terrified Chinese girl weeping in one corner; a randy, gross foreign-devil crouched at the closing doors. They exchanged fiery glances, glaring at me; one tried to speak to her and was similarly waved away; the other pointed a denunciatory finger at me and exploded in threatening Cantonese. I mumbled again, and then, when the elevator stopped at the 4th floor, dived out, while both Chinese shouted warnings at me as the doors closed. Clearly, they sensed that I was escaping.

Shaken, I related the incident to Chinese and *gweilo* friends at the Cosmo Club bar. The *gweilos*, I repeat, roared with laughter and obscenely challenged my details. The Chinese exchanged hasty and concerned comment: "Go down immediately and report the facts to the two security guards on the ground floor; we will accompany you; you can be sure the two witnesses from the 5th floor will have reported it — even if the girl hurried away."

Alas, I was a coward. (What would you have done?) I took refuge in martinis (increasing my daily ration to three over half-an-hour), crept down the stairs instead of taking either of the two elevators, noted gratefully that the two security guards had quit their table and were studying some traffic hold-up in Des Voeux Road, and nicked undetected into Pedder Street.

Okay. And may God bless and help that distraught, harmless and helpless girl.

But this week, I again encountered the more aggressive and fuller-bellied of the two Chinese "witnesses," with another companion, in the same unmanned elevator at the 5th floor. He pointed accusingly at me — I had an instinct to drive my old left into his Arbuckle stomach — and began to recount his version of the incident, as I again — once more in apparent guilt — dived out at the Cosmo Club floor.

What the devil should I do now? Some *gweilo* friends clearly ridicule my explanation. Chinese friends — with coughs of forced sympathy — regret that I failed to report the incident. Should I paste this column in the two unmanned elevators in the Gloucester Building? Or thrust copies furtively under the door of every office on the 5th floor? A legal friend advises me to use the stairs always instead of the unmanned elevators.

Could this not become another Hongkong racket?

November

This month marks the 34th anniversary of the mysterious murder of T. R. ("Demon") Hyde, proprietor of Delmonte's, the celebrated pre-war Shanghai gambling casino and dance-hall. I have never met anyone who knew the full facts or outcome of the shooting of "Demon" Hyde, nor have I been able to research any reliable written record of the mystery.

It was a double mystery, because no one seems to know why Hyde returned to Shanghai in 1941, after he deliberately and wisely elected to leave late in 1940 for the US, aboard the Japanese luxury liner, Chichibu Maru, with most of his art treasures and a lovely Chinese mistress.

I got to know him when he presided over Delmonte's during my own 1940 evangelical residence. And we travelled together on the Chichibu from Shanghai to Kobe, where I dis-embarked to return to Australia (no aircraft in those days), while he continued his retreat to the US.

He was an amiable and humorous but formidable companion, with a weakness for grog, golf, gambling and women. Like me, he had decided in late 1940 that the Japanese, bloating Shanghai as civilians and "liberating" north China militarily, would be in the world war on the side of Hitler and Mussolini in 1941. (Many of the "old hands" in Shanghai disagreed.) His art treasures were safely loaded in the hold, but he kept "open house," night and day at sea, with a beautiful, generously equipped, carved Chinese bar in his suite.

I recall that he confused the hell out of the Japanese migration official when presenting his and his mistress' passports for transit-stamping. Beside the query "Mar-

Shanghai today: eternal magnetism.

ried?" he had written "Yes and No." "What does this mean?" asked the gaping migration officer. " 'Yes,' I am married," Hyde replied soberly, "but 'No,' I am not working at it now" — jerking his thumb at the blushing Chinese mistress, standing between him and me.

We had a sentimental farewell. "We shall meet again, Richard, but I don't reckon it will ever be in Shanghai," he said, "Chiang Kai-shek or the Japs will take over. If I am ever back in Japan, it will be in the company of invading US troops."

I never heard from him again. I never had his American address. And I have never heard a satisfactory explanation of his strange decision to return to Shanghai. The reason could have been the eternal magnetism of Old Shanghai for all Old China Hands. Or perhaps he needed more funds. Or maybe he had changed his mind about the Japanese challenge. Or a combination of all those reasons. (So many foreign-devils who leave the Far East become bored after a spell and want to return.)

Anyway, whatever the reason, he was shot dead on his return — either at his palatial home or in his casino. Some reports say that his wife — who had remained in Shanghai — shot him. But the details, I repeat, remain unconfirmed and indeed unknown.

Had he not been shot, he would have been imprisoned in Shanghai by the Japanese after Pearl Harbour. But, of course, he would never have been able, after "liberation," to re-open Delmonte's — that decadent symbol of foreign-devil creation of the City of the Mudflats.

I tried to re-discover the old casino when I was allowed to return to Shanghai in 1973. But my amiable newspaper guide had never heard of it. Or of "Demon" Hyde. (I was told vaguely on visits in 1956 and 1957 that Delmonte's had become a Party school for dramatic training.)

Perhaps it was better that I did not physically revive Delmonte memories, after my shocked reaction to the changes in the old Shanghai Club, with the decapitation of the Long Bar and the conversion of the members' smoking-lounge into a third-class dormitory for rural travellers, who hang their soiled underwear from the windows overlooking the Bund.

Anyway, R. I. P., "Demon."

December

Hongkong's deputy CID director, Mike Davies, recently coined an excellent unofficial definition of the rival local leaders of the new splintered groups of triads: "baboons." Officially, my triad wire-tappers tell me, they are known as "area bosses." There are supposed to be about 200 of them, with now only 20-odd lodge-masters (shan chu). In effect, the former "Mr Bigs," since the new Triad Society Bureau swung into action, are being replaced by youthful "Master Bigs." So, paradoxically, the rise in violent crime in Hongkong can be partly attributed to the success of the new Bureau, which has struck at the traditional "Mr Bigs" and their set-up, and broken the old triads into juvenile factions.

The big bosses of the triads in the past were the lodge-master, his deputy, the master of incense *(hsiang-chu)* and the vanguard *(hsien-feng)*. The non-commissioned officers were the red staff (sergeant-major), the white fan (orderly room sergeant) and straw sandals (messenger). The ordinary member (or private) was called a forty-nine.

Today, as the Triad Society Bureau infiltrates and strikes, the red staffs and white fans — "Master Bigs" or "baboons" — are proliferating. The forty-nines are seldom properly and formally initiated by the master of incense, often jeer or present a cleaver at a rival upstart lodge-master, and probably don't know the elementary identification gestures and code phrases.

In older, more reverent days, formal initiation ceremonies into, say, the honourable "14-K," or the ancient Shanghai "Greens," lasted throughout the night. Before smouldering joss-sticks on a Buddhist-style altar, the candidates swore no fewer than 36 life-and-death oaths, and drank from deep bowls of wine, cinnabar, rooster's blood and a drop or two from their own fingers. They also bowed to the Ten Precious Articles, which included a red lamp (distinguishing the true from the false), a white paper fan (which strikes down all traitors) and a sword of peach-wood (which can decapitate enemies when merely flourished in the air). And finally they cast their joss-sticks to the floor with the solemn request that their own lives be similarly extinguished if they were untrue to their pledges or unfaithful to their brothers.

Now, triad initiation in Hongkong — if any — has been debased to a perfunctory exchange of finger-pricking in a hillside squatter's hut or a slum cockloft. And rival extortion, racketeering, blackmail and violence, like mass rape of young girls as an introduction to prostitution, have spread under the sundered triad groups of the "Master Bigs."

The most active and dangerous triad members probably number around 80,000. Their "stand-over" persecution would be crippled if their victims would only call their bluff and name them to the police. There is evidence that this self-defence or counter-action is now spreading.

In official opinion, there are at least six major triads in Hongkong, but the transient splinter factions, under the rival "area bosses," though nominally dedicated to one of the triads, are also at one another's throats. The six ruling triads are the "14-K" *(Sap Sei Ho)*, the *Wo*, the *Luen*, the *Tung*, the *Hoklo* and the *Chuen*.

It is a far cry from the concentrated authoritarianism of the old, all-powerful "Greens" in Shanghai of the 1930s and 1940s, whose two "Mr Bigs" — Tu Yuet-seng and Wang Tsin-yung — maintained an iron discipline which the Hongkong triads, in their strongest "Mr Big" period, have never pretended to wield. Tu and Wang managed to lead Jekyll-and-Hyde lives, combining banking, commercial and municipal interests with their organised terror and murder . . . I saw Wang once at the French Club in Shanghai in 1940. He was a hulking yellow nightmare of man and was known as "Smallpox" or Million-Dollar Wang — a real "Mr Big," more like a gorilla than a baboon.

1976 January

(Chairman Mao and Premier Zhou Enlai are discovered, relaxed, in a private hospital room overlooking a lake in the Forbidden City. Mao is sipping mao-tai, Zhou jasmine tea.)

Premier Zhou *(bowing)*: Again, Chairman, my warm thanks for the honour of your visit. You are too kind.

Chairman Mao: An honour to call on you, Comrade Premier, on the eve of our New Year — the Year of the Dragon, you will recall.

Zhou *(smiling)*: I have not forgotten our — I mean, my — decadent upbringing, Chairman, and the superstitious traditions of our lunar zodiac . . . I was born, you may remember, in 1899 — a Wild Boar, or Pig, as the unkind say; and I have no reason *(leaning back in reflection)* to remember Dragon years with satisfaction.

Mao *(sipping)*: Nor I. I am, of course, a Snake, born in 1893 — or, as I prefer to say, a Serpent. The Dragon years were not propitious for me either: when I was 11 in 1904, my first Dragon year, I was feuding with my father and objecting — I must, alas, admit — to digging rice-fields and collecting manure. Then, in the next cycle, I was running ignorantly with the 1916 young lions of the Changsha Students' Association. Let us forget 1928 *(Zhou coughs and gropes for his jasmine tea)* when Comrade Li Lisan denounced me as "a perfidious spokesman for deviationist peasant mentality" at our 6th National Congress in Moscow. In 1940, I published two of my most unworthy books: *Study Style, Language Style and Party Style*, and *On New Democracy*. And in 1952, I was fooled by the Russkies and caught holding the chamber-pot for the cost of the Korean War. Then 1964 — but enough . . .

Zhou *(refilling Mao's mao-tai cup)*: I agree, Chairman. And may I repeat, as we recall those old days, that I also have no reason to encourage memories of the Dragon. *(Another cough.)* You have not forgotten my own "confession of errors" in penitent sequel to the Li Lisan scandal of the 1928 Dragon year.

Mao *(raising his mao-tai cup in salute)*: We understand each other, Comrade. We have survived. China has survived. Our Asian Dragon, after all, has the claws of an eagle, the horns of a deer, the head of a horse, the eyes of a devil, the ears of a cow and the paws of a tiger. A significant combination and far superior to the Russky and European dragons, which are winged serpents *(spreads his arms mockingly)* with a crocodile's tail.

Zhou *(even more relaxed)*: My dear Chairman, how well you summarise and adapt. Dragons may come and go but the Serpent thrusts on forever. Your own next Serpent year will be 1977. My Wild Boar year will not recur until 1983.

Mao *(a sharp glance)*: Another point, Comrade Premier. This Dragon year coincides with the birth year of our resuscitated Vice-Premier, Deng Xiaoping. He was born in 1904 and, as a Dragon, has had a singularly fortuitous run of success in those years: 1928, organiser of the 7th and 8th Army commands, after his return from the kitchens of Paris; 1940, political commissar of the 129th Division, conducting our first successful anti-encirclement operation in Tai-hang; 1952, Vice-Premier; 1964, Acting Premier during your tours of Africa and Southeast Asia.

Zhou: Your memory is infallible, Chairman. As for me (*glances at the medical chart at the foot of his bed*), there certainly will be no more world tours. As for Deng, he has triumphed over his indignities during the non-Dragon years of "the Cultural Revolution." Let us hope that the coming Dragon year will confirm his resurrection and strengthen his Party command of the gun.

Mao (*clapping for more mao-tai*): He, like you and me, Comrade, will not be here to welcome the next Dragon year (1988). But, while the serpents and the wild boars, like the dragons, eventually pass, China is immortal. Another New Year toast. And hell to the Russkies. (*A tucket. Curtain.*)

● **By a macabre coincidence this column appeared on the day Zhou died, 8 January 1976. Meanwhile, Deng Xiaoping, 80 in 1984 and by then the undisputed leader of China, expressed the wish to live until 1997.**

May I suggest a deep non-ideological bow of reverent sympathy to Ms Deng Yingchao, the brave, devoted and modest widow of Premier Zhou Enlai, who affectionately dubbed her "Shou Zhou" or "little Zhou."

She is now in her 72nd year and has been a member of the Party Central Committee and leader of the Chinese Women's Federation since 1949. Unlike Ms Jiang Qing, she has never sought public attention or political influence. She ran the Zhou household, usually did the cooking and took special care of her hard-driven husband. She virtually introduced "women's lib" to China — but with true feminine charm and traditional Chinese dignity and none of the loutish excesses of the shrill Western bitches who seek to drag women down to the level of mere men.

When I was back in China in March-April 1974, she was still held in the same high esteem and respect by foreign-devil diplomats which she had rightly enjoyed when I was permitted to engage in evangelic labours there in 1956 and 1957.

She was born in Nanning in 1904 (Year of the Dragon, as also was Deng Xiaoping). Her father died bankrupt when she was a child and her mother, who first worked in a Tianjin orphanage, was personally responsible for her early education. She was a victim of tuberculosis — which could have been fatal — when she was at school, and became involved in political affairs when the Japanese served their abominable 21 Demands on China in 1919.

This was when she first met Zhou, the handsome, dynamic editor of the students' paper in Tianjin, pursued by the girls, and also a noted amateur actor — excelling (instructively) in female roles. She helped him to found what was called the "Awakening Society." Zhou was jailed for six months for his rebel student activities. He went to France when he was 21, corresponded regularly with her and — again, instructively — proposed marriage to her by mail.

They were married when he returned to China in 1925. It was one of the first of the Chinese Party's "no-ceremony" marriages — only a formal meeting with friends before whom the joint "eight mutual pledges" were made: "to love, to respect, to help, to encourage and to console each other, to have consideration for each other, to have confidence and mutual understanding."

After 1927, they were among the members of the young Communist Party who were hunted by Chiang Kai-shek's Nationalists. Yingchao then had their first and only baby in Canton, but it died and they fled to Shanghai, where they hid for five years. (I have never been able to trace whether this baby was a son or a daughter, but I would say, according to the Malt-Hughesian Theory, that it was a girl.)

Yingchao was still suffering badly from TB but survived the Long March in 1934, when she had to be carried on a stretcher. Strangely, that ordeal rallied her from her illness; she gives most of the credit to the fresh air and sunshine. The point is naturally not laboured today, but she also received skilful treatment at a sanatorium in Moscow in 1939. (A couple of years later, let it be recalled, Mao's third wife was shunted off to Moscow for "medical treatment" so that Mao could divorce her and, despite the strong disapproval of the politburo, marry the intriguing former B-movie starlet from Shanghai, Jiang, whose husband was shunted back to Shanghai. No one seems to know what happened to her predecessor; the Russkies, strangely, have

never used her fate — and their then comradely cooperation — for anti-Mao propaganda purposes.)

According to Peking gossip, Ms Zhou seldom meets Ms Mao. She remains a close friend of the lonely and almost forgotten Soong sister, Chingling, widow of Dr Sun Yat-sen and sister-in-law of the late President Chiang Kai-shek, now in her 80s. And she has also bridged the generation-gap with Ms Wang Hai-jung, the relative of Chairman Mao, who is a vice–foreign minister — and a "liberated" woman to watch ... Again, a sympathetic bow to now lonely Madam Zhou.

● **Deng Yingchao was in 1984 an influential member of the Chinese National People's Congress.**

February

Another old mate, Tom Harrisson, has been killed in one of those damnable road accidents in Thailand, after having miraculously survived war against the Japanese in Borneo, where he was the first soldier to be parachuted behind the enemy lines to organise head-hunters in preparation for Gen. Douglas MacArthur's landings. Anthropologist, ornithologist, explorer, author and TV director, he was only 64 — six years my junior — when the tourist bus in which he and his wife were travelling was transfixed last week on a Thai highway by an overloaded truck.

He was a world authority on Borneo; he helped to save orang-outangs from extinction; he amiably assisted all ignorant pressmen like myself who visited Borneo when he was based in Sarawak; he sustained an ever-youthful and alert eye of appreciation for the ladies. He organised my first and only night's stay in a Borneo longhouse when I was pretending — as a terrified hanger-on with the Gurkhas — to cover the 1964 border "confrontation" against randy "Bung" Sukarno.

Like all really brave men, he was modest and unassuming and deserved more than the DSO which he was awarded for his parachute landing — "on my backside," as he ruefully recalled — in the Kelabiti mountain village of Bario in 1944.

When we intrusive and irritating press visitors descended on him in the 1960s, he was curator of the celebrated Sarawak Museum — where, I trust, a memorial will be erected in his honour. (He wouldn't want that to happen, but if justice is done to him, the monument should show him embracing an orang-outang, with a pot of strong Borneo *borak* rice-wine in his free hand.)

No foreign-devil ever knew the Borneo jungle tribes like Tom Harrisson did. His book, *World Within* (Cresset Press, 1959), is still the definitive, scientific and human close-up of the original Borneo head-hunters. He advised me on protocol when I spent a night in the Bario longhouse — a rambling 250 feet-long, plank-and-thatched hut, housing about 100 pleasant, hard-working, hard-drinking tribespeople, who could become head-hunters when they wished, but were then happily settled together.

The "upper class," as I recall, lived in the central, semi-divided section of the longhouse and the farther you retreated to either flank, the lower was your status. But everyone seemed to mix happily and the *borak* flowed freely from huge jars, with good-humoured communal belching and singing and the occasional sounding of brass gongs. I averted my eyes, with heightened colour, from lumped silhouettes of intimate connubial bliss along the matted floors, or out on the verandah. (The single men are supposed to sleep alone on the front verandah, but the Borneo sleeping-mat can wrap two as easily as one.)

There were more embarrassing moments for me when — as warned by Tom — I discovered, after being aroused by the gibbons' call of "Wa! Wa! Wa!" at dawn, that there were no private or separate toilet facilities in the longhouse and you were expected to squat over accepted gaps in the planked flooring, 30 ft above the jungle undergrowth and the trampling buffaloes, scraping their back-sides against the foundation poles.

The little children scampered around freely among the different family groups and it was apparent, even to a foreign-devil being tolerated in the "upper-class" family section, that no one was supposed to indicate publicly that he or his family were superior to the neighbours. Indeed (as Harrisson says in *World Within*), that arrogance is one of the Five Deadly Sins of the Borneo hillmen. The other four are incest, neglect of orphans, ridicule of animals and failure to offer hospitality. Pretty civilised — with or without blowpipes, head-hunters' knives and two-feet-stretched ear-lobes . . .

Thank you, Tom. RIP. And you should be buried, with your dear wife, in Bario instead of Bangkok.

March

The ludicrous but instructive expansion of the Kim Il Sung family-cult idolisation campaign proceeds apace in tightly-sealed North Korea. The "poor man's Chairman Mao," 64 this year, has reappeared briefly after a strange and uncharacteristic disappearance from public view for more than a month, which had deepened speculation over persistent reports that he is suffering from incurable malignant neck cancer.

Many of my barefoot spies in Peking and Seoul believe that when Kim Il Sung sought medical advice in Rumania in 1974, he was told that he could expect to "continue in public office" for only two more years. This story certainly helps to explain his family-cult buffoonery and the controversial promotion of his 37-year-old son, Kim Jong Il, as his successor. (The Chinese comrades handle these matters far more deviously and skilfully.)

Kim junior's portrait now hangs beside all those of his father in public places. The numerous huge bronze statues of Daddy

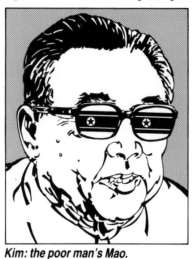

Kim: the poor man's Mao.

have all been gilded and the Kim family tombs, significantly, have been declared "sanctuaries."

No matter how crowded the subway trains are at peak hours, a leading carriage in one consecrated train always runs empty because it enshrines the seat hallowed by the ample buttocks of Daddy Kim when he made his first formal trip at the opening of the subway. There is known opposition by some senior members of the ruling Korean Workers' Party to Kim junior's promotion.

Taped speeches by Kim junior are now imposed on all captive Party audiences, following the reading of the infallible "Thoughts" of Daddy Kim. Honorifics which were once reserved exclusively for the old man — "beloved and respected" and "respected leader" — are now extended to Kim junior, whose birthday, like his father's, has become a "great national holiday." Yet before the old man went to Eastern Europe and had that medical examination in 1974, Kim junior was only a "guidance member" of the Workers' Party.

Even Grandad is being resurrected. Kim Il Sung claims that his father, Kim Hyong Jik, organised a "Korean National Council" as a revolutionary body "which waged anti-Japanese patriotic struggle" in the early 1900s. But historic records in Korea and Japan do not mention this alleged heroic-body or Grandad Kim.

Evidence of factional opposition to Kim Il Sung — under-played abroad — is also clearer and stronger in the Pyongyang Party press than the current "anti-capitalist-roader" line in the Peking press and on Peking walls. The State Council's mouthpiece, the *Rodong Shinmun*, ran a recent editorial demanding that "merciless struggle be staged because today many Party members and workers receive Party policies as words only, neglecting their faithful implementation . . . they show an irresponsible and insincere attitude in which they shun one task when another is imposed, or give up implementation of Party policies halfway at the sightest difficulty . . . they harbour various unhealthy thoughts such as shrewdness, formalism and self-protection."

Accordingly, this was an appropriate time for Sir Robert Thompson, Britain's counter-insurgency expert, to make an unpublicised 20-day visit to Seoul, when he not only paid tribute to South Korea's US-backed "short, violent war" defence policy and preparations, but also warned that Kim Il Sung was "the most unpredictable" leader in the communist world. In an address at South Korea's National War College, he applauded the defence strategy, which is based on an immediate counter-invasion of North Korea on the western front-line. And neither Russia nor China wanted another armed conflict in Korea, he stressed.

But could the unpredictable Kim, a poor man's Samson, scratching his cancerous neck, pull down the Korean pillars?

April

The sad personal news continues to trickle out of Saigon. Old barefoot reporters like myself will drink a silent toast to our long-time friend from the 1960 days of murdered President Diem: Tran Chanh Thanh, who, I have just learned, committed suicide with honour and dignity after the 30 April surrender. Thanh, a brilliant and heroic young Vietnamese, was the masterly official interpreter at press conferences with President Diem, to whom he was deeply devoted — whatever his hidden reservations about nepotism.

At the first presidential conference into which I gapingly inserted myself in Saigon in 1958, a respected mate in the front row, who had perhaps spent too much time over wine at the Continental, secured permission with outflung arm to ask a question. Then, in the sudden silence, he rolled his eyes, buried his face in his hands, and gulped, "I have forgotten what I was going to ask." Without hesitation, Dr Thanh turned to the bewildered president and coolly invented a question, the president's reply to which gave us all a hot news-lead.

Thanh reeled after the "Big" Minh coup of 1963 and the murder of Diem and his crafty brother, Ngo. We had lunch at the Caravelle and the tears poured unashamedly down his cheeks — to the angry perplexity of the waiters, who suspected that I was threatening him — as he expressed his own personal desolation and anxiety for the future.

"Why don't you get out and join your wife in Switzerland?" I asked (knowing

'Big' Minh

that he had been offered a professorial post in Geneva). "I am a Vietnamese," he told me, rallying with surprise at my question. "Of course, I remain here." Remain, he did. He edited a Saigon paper, was director of information and won a Magsaysay prize.

Incidentally, he indirectly saved the lives of myself and a couple of transients in Saigon in the mid-60s when, on the roof of the Caravelle, we were discussing, after the sudden Saigon twilight, our destination for an austere dinner. I suggested the floating restaurant on the river near the Majestic. "But I know you ate there last night, Richard, with Stan Karnow [*Time*] and Til Durdin [*New York Times*]," said Tran Chanh. "Let us stay here" — summoning more medicinal encouragement.

One hour later, there were two shattering explosions on the river-front and we raced downstairs to pick up a couple of those ancient, Parisian taxis and to discover that the floating restaurant had been blasted apart by two Vietcong bombs and that the bodies were being stretcher-carried across, literally, a river of blood. (The second bomb had been set, with comradely-IRA efficiency, to catch survivors of the first as they scrambled over the gangway.) I recognised the legless body of the charming waitress who had served Stan, Til and me the night before . . .

My informant of Tran Chanh Thanh's fate is Lieut-Gen. *(retired)* Tran Van Don, who had prolonged and dedicated military, political and legislative service in Saigon from Emperor Bao Dai's days and was Deputy Prime Minister and Defence Minister on the eve of surrender.

At dinner in Hongkong, with a small cultural if senile group, he told us that two Hanoi "liberators" and "unifiers" knocked on the front door of Thanh's home in Saigon on the night of 30 April, after "Big" Minh had signed off at 8 a.m. They were respectfully told that he would not be home until "later." "We shall be back in the morning," they promised. In his bedroom, Tran Chanh Thanh quietly took some pills, bowed and died peacefully.

He had remained. RIP. A great and honest Vietnamese hero.

May

The sacred turf was uprooted and the historical emblems were moved up The Peak last year. But now the holy and empty pavilion (*not* the Imperial Pavilion in the Forbidden City) has been demolished and Hongkong's 125-year-old cultural link with the Opium War days has vanished. It is not surprising that some dignified veteran members of THE Hongkong Club, across the road, were seen to be weeping as they passed the vanishing landmark last month.

It was, of course, a smart and heroic decision to shift the old Hongkong Cricket Club to another site, even if there had been no vital underground railway project on the drawing-board, appropriating that old and friendly green oasis in Hongkong's soaring cement desert. Its passing follows the similarly wise decision to keep Queen Victoria's nobly ridiculous statue out of Statue Square, and precedes, the necessary demolition of the 60-year-old Supreme Court and the venerable Post Office. Only the Hongkong Club, charmingly turn-of-the-century (1898) in its architectural whimsy, will remain.

There was controversy — my old friend, Dr Arnold Graham, the Wisden of the Far East and founder of the China Old Hands' Association, reminds me — over the founding of the Hongkong Cricket Club in 1851 (three years before the birth of Sherlock Holmes, but only 63 years after the first game at Lords).

The former part-time military parade ground was originally designated "a place for public recreation." But a Mr W. T. Bridges, newly-arrived articulate lawyer, good bowler and No. 3 batsman, who boasted that his "principal luggage on landing was a cricket bat and wickets," insisted — fair enough — that a British colony without a cricket-ground was like a church without a cross, and that "public recreation" should logically give priority to the grand old game. He won. Good on him.

It is forgotten that the Shanghai cricket ground — now a people's park above the deepest anti-nuclear shelter in the old City of the Mudflats — was founded about the same time as THE Hongkong Club and that the first match between the foreign devils of the two interloping cities took place in Hongkong in 1866. (The home-side won by an innings and 264 runs.) There was then cricket, too, in Hangkow and matches in Kobe and Yokohama. Altogether, Hongkong and Shanghai, in those decadent, unliberated days, played Test matches over a period of 43 years.

Anyway, a salute now to the transferred Hongkong Cricket Club. It never accepted apartheid, though the Chinese, alas, have shown little interest in cricket. (I reckon Mao would have been a first-class opening bat and Zhou Enlai a deceptive slow bowler.) A rough run-down of club membership today (around 1,000) discloses a wider range of different races than in any other club in Hongkong. And anyone could enter the ground free, at any time, to watch a match from the benches. Even baseball — "the poor man's cricket" — has been tolerated on the sacred turf.

To close on a happy note. One "rule" of the old club, strictly unofficial though never political or racial, offered a prize of a case of champagne to any batsman who broke a window in the building towering across the road and impeding his sight of the ball from the western end after the tea interval. That building happens to be the Bank of China. (Similarly, a case of champagne is available for any batsman who breaks the clock above the members' stand at Lords.) No one ever won the "unofficial, unadmitted" Hongkong prize.

I once asked a sophisticated Party-member of the People's Bank, who sometimes drank with me in the old pavilion bar, whether he knew of the prize. "Of course," he said, with a Zhou Enlai smile. "But we knew it was never intended to be imperialist or belligerent. Had we been the Hongkong and Shanghai Bank, the prize might have been more attractive."

● **Only the Supreme Court building now remains, and that is no longer used for court hearings. The Hongkong Club was demolished to make way for a multi-storey block, though the new block still houses the club.**

June

"We are very sad to hear of the sudden passing of Richard Hughes last Thursday (April 29). We expected to see him this week in San Francisco. Just two weeks ago, we received an invitation to have lunch with him at the San Francisco Press Club.

"Hughes, an Australian, had been covering the Far East as correspondent for The Times, The Sunday Times, The Economist, *Australian newspapers and columnist for the* Far Eastern Economic Review . . . *He was 76."*
— East-West,
*Chinese-American Journal,
San Francisco, May 5.*

So, like Lazarus, Mark Twain and Morrison of Peking (also working for *The Times*, if not the *Far Eastern Economic Review*), I have had the strange satisfaction of reading my obituary.

I am writing a letter of profound gratification to the *East-West*'s gracious editor (Mr Gordon Lew). His documented obit, seriously, was moving and flattering — including references to my Sherlock Holmes and Baritsu Chapter associations — and I am sending photocopies to friends whose Christmas and birthday cards (70, not 76) I had not acknowledged, reproaching them for not sending flowers for my coffin.

Editor Gordon Lew, like many other friends in the US, had of course mistaken humble me, the R. H. Pretender, for THE Richard Hughes, whose sudden death — six years my senior — was briefly and vaguely announced on world radio as I undertook my topless-performance lecture tour of the United States last month, confusing the hell out of my sponsors, the Hongkong Tourist Association and an airline.

Alas, I never met THE Richard Hughes. Over the years he and I exchanged incestuous porno-Welsh encyclicals after he wrote a mock-serious letter — 20 years ago — to editor Denis Hamilton, warning that he would not take personal responsibility for — and might launch legal action against — Far East stories in *The Sunday Times* bylined in his name. In our communications, I always pleaded hypocritical Welsh modesty. He always denounced Welsh poverty: "Why couldn't Dad afford a middle initial for his bastard son?"

THE Richard Hughes was a genius, but a lazy writer. I admired his *In Hazard* even more than *A High Wind in Jamaica*, and of course he never completed his trilogy, *The Human Predicament*, writing only the first two sections, *The Fox in the Attic* (1961) and *The Wooden Shepherdess* (1973). A great man. I hoped he would visit Hongkong, when I swore that I would wear a false beard. (RIP) . . .

His death prompted me to re-study the recently published *Correspondence of G. E. Morrison (Vol. 1, 1895-1912)*, covering part of the 23 years when Morrison, who read his fake obituary in Peking, had worked "for England and China" for *The Times*. Another Australian, he also never condescended to learn Chinese. (No "Chinese" Gordon him.)

Morrison of Peking forecast Japanese dominance in the Far East. (What would he predict now, one wonders.) He was seldom objective but always non-ideologically pro-Chinese in his reportage: "Their remarkable capacity for hard work — capable of anything." In those days, I learn with envy, you didn't cable news from China, but *The Times* ran regular 8,000-word sea-mailers . . .

November

Estimates of the number of Korean expatriates compelled to continue living in Soviet-"liberated" Sakhalin range from 40,000 to 60,000. Many are now the descendants of the Koreans who were shipped as work-slaves from Japan and Japanese-occupied Korea during the Pacific War for prison labour on the island, but plenty of sturdy originals still survive.

They are back in the news again, to the embarrassment, it seems, of both Japan and the Soviet Union. Of course, they want to get out — either to Japan or Korea. (One should add *South* Korea; none, absolutely

none, has applied to go back to the *north*.) But neither the Russians nor the Japanese are making swift or effective responses. In theory, the Russians have said they would consider negotiating the return of some; and, in theory, the Japanese have said that they would consider assisting repatriation of some. In fact, the harsh, generation-long imprisonment in exile persists for all.

There are technical difficulties. Most of the original Korean victims married Japanese wives. Some, not surprisingly, agreed to accept formal Soviet or North Korean nationality (after the Korean War) to lighten the ordeal of their work and harsh life on the island. But South Korea will accept all who wish to return.

Last week, a faint light of hope flickered between Tokyo and Seoul, when the South Korean Government announced that the Japanese Government had transmitted to Moscow and Seoul the names and family backgrounds of a first batch of approximately 300 Koreans who had formally applied for Japanese transit visas. South Korea has immediately identified half of the applicants as Koreans, but the Soviet reaction is still awaited. North Korea, of course, refrains from all comment.

China, Soviet Russia and the European communist bloc now permit the regular exchange of letters between Korean expatriates living in their areas and South Koreans. North Korea alone — abominably, if fearfully — forbids this contact between separated families and friends.

There is an ever-flowing flood of letters to South Korea, in particular from the 1.5 million Koreans who are now living in China and who are trying frantically to locate their relatives at lost and vanished addresses. (Seoul postal authorities, with volunteer public cooperation, have organised a characteristically Korean system by which the undelivered mail is retained and listed in all post offices for checks by eagerly waiting recipients.)

Kim Il Sung has flatly rejected President Park Chung Hee's proposals for regular brief visits between separated families in North and South Korea. He knows, too well, the universal reactions of those Koreans who have the misfortune to live in his bankrupt animal-kingdom when they compare, on the spot, living conditions in the South.

His Pyongyang, spy-ruled set-up for resident Koreans in Japan with northern ties, *Chochongnyon*, has already been split. Many of the 10,000 Korean members of the Pyongyang expatriate commune who defied their comrade-masters and visited South Korea by invitation have now formed a breakaway group known as *Chominnyon*.

Japanese security has remained strangely tolerant of the excesses of *Chochongnyon*, whose agents have been guilty of at least three kidnappings *en famille* in Tokyo to seek to deter Koreans from visiting relatives and friends in South Korea.

The Japanese must know the extent of North Korean spy operations in their country, originally directed by the Fourth Bureau of the Interior Ministry (shades of Moscow's Fourth Bureau of the Red Army!), but now revamped as North Korea's Social Security Ministry. Maybe, if the Japanese at last pressure the Russkies to release some of the existing Korean prisoners in Sakhalin, they will then deport some of the existing Korean spies in Japan.

December

Two off-beat stories were smuggled to my bathroom praying-stool this week — both dealing with drugs (though not really illicit).

The first drug I had never heard of: Gerovital, an "eternal youth" product, which was compounded in Rumania in 1947 by a woman, Dr A. Aslan. Its base is GH-3, which includes procaine, potassium and hypersulphuric acid. It is dispensed in expensive clinics in Europe (three in Rumania, still operated by Dr Aslan) and Mexico over two- to four-week periods, and must then be sustained by regular pill-taking and annual booster injections.

Rumanian clinic treatment costs US$1,800 (meals and drinks additional) and in Mexico up to US$5,000. Britons seeking longevity have to pay up to US$3,000 for local non-residential surgery injections.

I am indebted to my old friend, Dr Bob Horiguchi of Tokyo, for this background information. He has translated a report about Gerovital from the Japanese weekly, *Shukan Yomiuri*, which asserts that Japanese *zaibatsu* interests will soon open a Japan Life Medical Centre in Manila to dispense Gerovital, which is still banned in Japan. The medical staff will be American doctors: interestingly, GH-3 is also banned in the US.

Dr Yasuo Matsuki, a leading Tokyo gerontologist, who respects the governmental ban but is interested professionally in the drug because it has maintained its reputation in Europe for so many years, has agreed to examine all Japanese "patients" before they leave for the Life Medical Centre in Manila and after they return.

(Gerovital publicity claims that original GH-3 addicts included Khrushchev, Konrad Adenaeur, Aristotle Onassis, Field Marshal Montgomery and — wait for it — Mao Zedong! What about Kim Il Sung, I wonder?) . . .

The other drug story — if beer, as puritans claim, is also a drug of sorts — concerns the recent massive and unique transformation at the Hongkong United Dockyards of a French-built passenger-rail-car ferry, which will now operate across Cook Strait between the north and south islands of New Zealand.

My informant, another old friend, Dr Derek Round, Far Eastern mission father for the New Zealand Press Association, points out that the main purpose of the reconstruction of the ferry's decks was to enable beer-tankers to drive aboard the boat and to pump their beer straight into the three 150-gallon tanks in the main bar, which is one of the crowded attractions of the busy ferry trips. This direct delivery of New Zealand beer will reduce the current "turn-around" time by eliminating the need for reception and replacement of kegs at Wellington (North Island) and Picton (South Island).

The shrewd New Zealanders have anticipated an inevitable by-product of the inflated beer demands on the ferry, Aratika, which can accommodate 800 passengers — all putative beer-swillers — as well as 70 motor-cars.

"We have also installed a new Electrolux vacuum sewerage system for the Aratika's 28 lavatories," the master, Captain Lawrie Collins, announced proudly if primly. "We will now carry enough fresh water for 6,000 flushes — at 1½ litres a flush — in case of emergency."

Appropriately, the Aratika Sino-Maori innovation coincided with an analysis by Dr Richard Batt, professor of biochemistry at Massey University, of the drinking habits of the New Zealand crews of 70 boats in a yacht race between Whangarei and Noumea.

"They took on board 3,000 bottles of spirits for the cold night watch and 20,000 cans of beer," he told an impressed convention in Christchurch. "Calculations based on body metabolism meant that their livers were operating at a maximum capacity for 23.3 hours a day. I hear that the ocean floor between Whangarei and Noumea is littered with beer-cans. One wonders how they ever found Noumea."

This report and ferry reconstruction should stir some resentful reaction from dinkum Aussies, who always insist that they drink, understand and appreciate beer better than the New Zealanders. According to my latest confessional information, the alcoholic content of Aussie beer ranges from 3.5% to 4.5% by weight, compared with the New Zealand average of 5.64%. (The average strength of Pommy beer is only 2.8%, but their noble strong brews hit a high of 11%.)

1977 January

Foreign correspondents throughout the East — or even if now exiled elsewhere — will raise glasses in sad salute to Maurice Cavallerie's celebrated Constellation Hotel in Vientiane, which has now been "communised" by the new Lao regime.

The Constellation was the last lingering "private" hotel in Vientiane, a homely, happy inn, with 54 simple but comfortable airconditioned rooms (US$3-7, single; US$5.50-10, double), a spacious bar-lounge opening on the street, first-class kitchen, and a suave, tough, sophisticated owner-manager (whose life history I would have liked to research and write).

Over 20 years, I never stopped at any other hotel in Vientiane. It was, of course, the unofficial Foreign Correspondents' Club in Laos. The venerable row of individual mail boxes was preserved inviolate on the wall opposite the bar. You always met old mates there when a news story broke anywhere in "The land of a million elephants and the white umbrella." To us all, the Constellation was the human heart of that one-time soft, lazy, dusty, curly amalgam of villages called Vientiane.

Dr Oden Meeker first noted the curls: "Everything in Laos seems peaceful and nicely curly: the roof-tops and the lottery tickets, the long serpent balustrades that lead up to the pagodas, the water buffaloes' horns and the carts that the beasts pull, the heavy flat-irons with the curlicue, cast-iron roosters sitting on them, and the Lao language itself. On a typewriter keyboard, the symbols @ and ? are the most Lao-looking things I can find."

Appropriately, it was in the bar of the Constellation that Dr Bob Miller, now UPI despot in Honolulu and the Pacific, told me a memorable story that still crystallises what must now, alas, be the vanishing Lao scene, as the bleak, "liberating," Soviet-Marxist wind blows the once free and happy Lao curls away. The story is Bob's — so, of course, it is reliable. Nationality, names and the year have been discarded to protect the guilty.

A new foreign-devil embassy had been established in Vientiane. Counsellor J., a bachelor, had arrived to act as majordomo until his ambassador was appointed. A tall, handsome, randy, fair-haired fellow, he soon found the curly Lao girl he proposed to install as his embassy "housekeeper." Housekeeping was of secondary importance; he wanted to learn the language the right way. He found her, with quick intuition, after guidance from the Constellation, at Vientiane's No. 1 bordello, then down on the river past the old slaughter-house and its black muster of buzzards in the tall trees.

She was a typical, supple Lao beauty with soft eyes, hot lips, black hair curled in a gold chain behind her left ear, slim waist wrapped in the gold-embroidered, midi-length cotton sarong (felicitously called *sin*).

He effected a satisfactory, three-way financial arrangement to buy her from the fat madam, pay her a fixed generous income, and endow her with a handsome gratuity when he departed. It was virtuously agreed that she should cease, of course, to be on call, and J. departed, happily and foolishly, to Bangkok to complete some unfinished personal business.

He returned in two days to discover, to his shocked rage, that during his absence his deputy, Secretary B., a tall, handsome, randy, black-haired fellow, who had arrived in Vientiane as he left, had enjoyed the putative housekeeper's favours on his first and only social call at the bordello.

"She thought it was *you!*" the madam protested to the disgusted J., as he cancelled the house-keeping agreement and tramped away, disillusioned, past the slaughter-house and under the hooded gaze of the attentive buzzards.

The innocent girl shrugged off the shock of her abortive release from the bordello with true Lao philosophy. "All those fat, red-faced foreign-devils with the big noses look the same to me," she explained . . .

A macabre, if suitable, curtain-fall for the Constellation Hotel, as well as, apparently, for the lost curls of happy Laos.

February

Interestingly, most of the visiting delegates to last week's Hongkong convention of the Pacific Area Travel Association whom I know sought, privately and sometimes furtively, recommended local addresses — not of topless, massage or music parlours, but of Chinese fortune-tellers. Evidently, this is a cultural tourist attraction which Hongkong could develop rewardingly.

I couldn't help them directly. The only Chinese fortune-teller I ever consulted was a venerable, goat-bearded man who, curiously, was still allowed to operate on the zig-zag bridge near Shanghai's old "secret garden" during my sojourn there in 1957, and who confidently assured me that I would "return very soon" to Shanghai. As it happened, it took me 17 years to wangle my next visa . . .

But, in all fairness, I must report that I had two frightening consultations with the celebrated Blind Bonze of Luang Prabang, one-time royal capital of Laos, when — for no fee and on a reluctant religious rather than commercial basis — I was correctly told both the past and the future. He was venerated as the holiest man in Laos. Tales of his prophecies, warnings, miracles and healings were legendary among the faithful. (He died in 1967 at the estimated age of 87.)

On a brief first visit to Luang Prabang in 1959, I decided to see him at his *wat* (temple) and ask him some questions in bad taste for a frivolous news-feature. My driver-interpreter, a dedicated Buddhist from Bangkok, and I climbed a creaking ladder to his stilted hut and entered on hands and knees. The Blind Bonze, a wrinkled ancient, wrapped in a yellow blanket despite the heat, was squatting on the matted floor, praying and chewing betel nut. He turned his staring, blue-white, cataract-hooded eyeballs in our direction, pointed and cried out aloud.

My guide was clearly surprised and looked at me hesitantly. Then light dawned on him. "Mister Huggers," he asked, "is your wife dead?"

Taken aback in turn, I said: "Yes," He was vastly relieved: "Oh, it is all right then. I thought The Master made a mistake. He called out, 'That man has brought his wife with him.' Of course, he saw — I mean, sees — the spirit."

"Ask him some more," I said, shaken. The holy man raised his terrible, unseeing eyeballs to the thatched roof and, with unconcealed impatience, crackled out a few sentences in reply to my guide's apologetic questions.

"Holy man says your wife is always with you," the interpreter said, "but she came specially today because she wishes to tell you so. Holy man says she died maybe 10 years ago; he thinks perhaps in Japan but he has not been there and so does not recognise the landscape. She is small, dark-haired woman, laughing, very gay. That is all."

I forgot my shrewd newspaper questions. My wife did die in Japan (Tokyo) on April Fool's Day, 1950. The Blind Bonze's description was precise. The exact and evocative word "gay," surviving awkward and defective vocabulary and translation, seemed to haunt the hot shadows of the Asian hut . . .

I visited the Blind Bonze again about a year later. He looked frailer but was still chewing and mumbling his prayers and appeared to recognise me — or affected to do so. He was more brusque and even less interested in impressing me with clairvoyant insight. Staring at us sightlessly, he got across the message that he was no idle fortune-teller with the time or interest to ponder personal inquiries by stray visitors.

I bowed to the inevitable and we humbly withdrew. As we crawled out, he relented and called out (my interpreter was surprised): "Be sure to say goodbye to your friend!" I shrugged.

My old friend, Frank Corrigan, Irish-American Pacific and Korean war veteran turned United States information Service employee, drove me to the airstrip an hour later. I told Frank that I would be back in a month's time. He walked off briefly to talk to technicians unloading another aircraft. I was called aboard the DC-3 to take me back to Vientiane and Bangkok. I waved perfunctorily through a window. Frank didn't really see me as he hurried back, peering through the dust.

I did not say goodbye to him. I never saw him again. He was killed accidentally the next week, taking off in a small aircraft.

I revisited Luang Prabang several times but I never had the courage to call on the Blind Bonze again.

March

Whampoa, in the Pearl River, surrounded by the lingering ruins of the Opium War fortresses, was certainly the correct setting for Peking's belated welcome-back to Chinese territorial waters of a foreign-devil tourist cruiser last week. From there, the 300 visitors, without any personal search for heroin or opium, were whisked 12 miles in the care of the efficient China Travel Service to Canton for three days' sightseeing, merrymaking and over-eating.

Whampoa, of course, was the original

public anchorage for East India Company trade with China via Canton, and the disguised "honest" trade front for the contraband centre of opium-smuggling in the 18th and 19th centuries at Lintin ("Solitary Nail") island, 10 miles nearer Macau.

Some old ghosts must have stirred at Whampoa, and in the ancient "Hog Lane" approach to the 13 historic foreign "factories" on the Canton waterfront, when the new tourists arrived. The opium deliveries, in those old days of honourable "squeeze," were made by hulks and barges from Lintin, manned by wretched Chinese coolies, who were sometimes arrested and strangled by the "squeezers" to sustain the fiction that opium-smuggling was illegal. But the British and other foreign-devil crews on the ships, which respectfully waited at Whampoa for the legitimate reciprocal deliveries of Chinese tea, silk and rhubarb, were all allowed to visit the Canton waterfront in groups of 20 — like last week's holiday visitors.

The salty pioneers certainly then had a livelier reception than the sanctioned tourists did. Mine hosts at intimate bars in Hog Lane welcomed the eager Jack Tars with shouts in pidgin of "Hallo, Jack! Fine day, old boy!" and with an encouraging cocktail, Canton Gunpowder, which comprised alcohol, tobacco juice, sugar and arsenic. (It would have been a good news story if the China Travel Service had included Canton Gunpowder in the menus for their new tourists.)

Presumably, also, there was no encouragement — and, of course, no necessity — for last week's tourists to sneak back grog to their cruise ship, which the original Whampoa-anchored seamen were wont to do, as liquor, very properly, was forbidden for the crews of East India Company ships. So the original visitors had the habit of filling bladders and teapots with grog to carry back when they boarded their waiting lighters for return to Whampoa. The bladders could be lowered or forced down a sailor's trousers, and a carefully carried teapot testified of course to the bearer's temperance . . . old days, old deceptions.

Another difference in the restored Whampoa connection would have been the conspicuous absence of the customary public notices which the old court official known as the *Hai kwan pu* (rendered as "Hoppo" in pidgin) posted up on the waterfront to warn the locals of the then only partly-guided "tours."

"About this time the devil ships are arriving and it is feared that the lawless vagabonds will again tread their old habits," one typical warning read. "Let them not dare to employ young boys as servants to lead them to brothels nor to bring prostitutes into their factories . . ."

But then, the abiding Chinese realism and superiority intervened: "It is also the duty of our *hong* merchants continually to instruct the barbarians.

"Since our merchants are men of property and good families, it becomes them to have a tender [*sic*] regard for the new faces, not to cheat them, but to trade justly and so win their confidence."

So the Canton Gunpowder and the warning posters may have passed from the scene, but the traditional, unchanging, non-ideological Chinese desire for reward and profit seems to be extending happily now to the non-opium tourist trade. Later this year, after the restoration of entry into territorial waters, groups of foreign tourists for the first time will be allowed to travel from Canton to Peking.

But no "squeeze" now for anyone, comrades.

The 10th anniversary of the haunting disappearance of legendary Jim Thompson, Thai Silk King and former Office of Strategic Services–Central Intelligence Agency (OSS-CIA) operator falls on 26 March. Even I, one of his old friends and admirers, who had sullenly clung to the hope that he might have secretly survived a last-minute personal decision to vanish, now concede that he must be dead.

James Thompson, the wealthy expatriate New York socialite and OSS jungle commander against the Japanese, would have been 71 this month. (When we met in Bangkok, we always toasted our common birth year and month: March 1906, Year of the Horse.) A post-war Bangkok resident, he vanished into thin, sweet-scented air in the Malayan Cameron Highlands on a post-prandial holiday saunter on Easter Sunday, 1967, while his old-friend host was enjoying a siesta. No one knows how, where or why he so mysteriously departed. But I still insist — like others who know far more about the affair than I do — that he disappeared by his own choice and will, and not by force.

He did not become a millionaire through his development of the highly marketable beautiful Thai silk. He was a strange and restless man of many interests: architect,

interior decorator, painter, art collector and shrewd investor. Like so many *farangs* (foreigners), he became almost more Siamese than the Thais and preferred the old name Siam to Thailand.

But once a CIA man always a CIA man (unless you decide to become a traitor). Thompson had remained an unofficial political adviser to his old friend, United States ambassador Edward Stanton, after he became a business executive in Thailand. The CIA in Bangkok immediately, quietly and efficiently organised an air-and-land search for him after he vanished on that after-lunch stroll.

Richard Noone (RIP), one-time Southeast Asian Treaty Organisation officer and veteran of the Malayan Emergency, who knew the Cameron Highlands better than anyone, also visited the jungles where Thompson disappeared, saw tribal chiefs whom he knew and, agreeing with the CIA hunters, said positively: "I am fully convinced that Thompson was never lost or killed in the jungle."

Dick Noone — another old friend of mine — would never discuss, very correctly, the Vanished Thompson Affair. But he knew, of course, of the Tao Oum association. And this year — a decade later — it is essential to recall Jim's personal connection with Tao Oum, his former No. 1 assistant in the foundation of the still-flourishing Thai Silk Company.

Tao Oum was born in Laos and operated inside Thailand against the French. He was lucky to escape from Bangkok after the abortive February 1949 coup bid by the Free Thai leader Pridi (now in exile in France). He was one of the close inner circle who really knew Thompson; four others of that group, also involved in the coup, were arrested and shot. Thompson personally sheltered Tao Oum in the old Oriental Hotel and then helped him to return to Laos, where he resumed operations in twilight politics instead of sun-bright silks.

There can be little doubt that Thompson and Tao Oum maintained contact, which would surely have interested Thompson's old pre-silk associates, who rushed the helicopters to look for him in the Cameron Highlands and to direct the most exhaustive jungle search in Malayan history.

Accordingly, one plausible inside theory persists that Thompson, after an urgent message from Tao Oum, left at the last minute to meet him or an emissary in the Cameron Highlands. (Both knew that an old friend would always welcome Thompson at his "hill station" home there.) He certainly left in a hurry: there was embarrassment at Bangkok's airport when it was discovered that he did not have medical or immigration clearance to Penang.

Nobody has ever heard since about Tao Oum, though, if still alive, he would certainly be actively interested in events today on the Lao-Thai border.

A possible Sherlock Holmesian reflection at this point could be that, like so many men in their late 60s, Jim Thompson had become bored and restless and would have welcomed an adventurous challenge.

Anyway, a 71-gun salute to him, wherever he is.

May

As Richard Lovelace meant to say: "Stone graves do not a news column make, nor RIP memories a newspage." But as one of the 80 war correspondents from 17 countries who survived coverage of the Korean War and who were invited to South Korea last week to attend the unveiling of the unique monument to 18 colleagues who did not survive, I reckoned I could ignore Lovelace (who was, after all, a member of Ben Jonson's Cavalier "gang of three") and take a risk — even after a quarter of a century.

It was a moving and historic event. No other country anywhere has honoured the memory of foreign newsmen who were killed covering a war on its native soil. A characteristic Korean precedent.

The monument is a 30-foot, olive-green, granite-and-copper carving which resembles the letter "J" (for journalist) as a curved teletype sheet of copypaper on a pedestal shaped like a giant typewriter. The names of the 18 correspondents are inscribed below. The memorial cost more than Won 31 million (US$63,000), raised by the Journalists' Association of Korea. It is located at Tongli Park, close to the demilitarised zone and adjacent to the Munsan stop on the old Pusan-to-Paris railway, where some of the dead and living correspondents once lived and worked in parked railway cars.

Veteran correspondent Bob miller, now United Press International chief in Honolulu, pointed out — in dubious taste, as I warned him — that in the trees behind was a large communal nest of noisy magpies, whose screeching commentary of the wreath-laying ceremony, he argued, was appropriately symbolic of newsmen's style when seeking a front-page headline.

We visitors — many of whom had not seen one another since the war days — agreed that our unluckier mates would prefer that our assembly and tribute should not be unduly gloomy, but obviously all were brooding over why some people are luckier than others . . .

The engraved names of two close friends of mine, Ian Morrison of *The Times* and Christopher Buckley of *The Daily Telegraph*, haunted me. They were blown up together in a jeep which was being driven by another old friend, Col Unni Nayar, Indian army public relations officer, who drove Christopher and I around when we were with the Eighth Army in the Montgomery-Eisenhower-Rommel desert war.

I was in Tokyo on a three-week spell from front reporting when the three arrived there on their way to Korea in August 1950. I wanted selfishly to go back with them — war correspondents who know one another like to travel in a group — but my cabled request was amiably dismissed by my then boss, 007 Ian Fleming, foreign manager of *The Sunday Times* of London, who told me to wait out my three weeks.

So we had a *sayonara* lunch, *à quatre*, at Tokyo's Marunouchi Hotel — "See you later, mate! " — and they were then blown to pieces on a mined road in the jeep in which I also would certainly have been reclining. (Ian, the son of "Morrison of Peking," where he was born, was 37; Christopher was 45 — just married.)

Later, our party flew to the United Nations Memorial Cemetery in Pusan, where I located Christopher's grave among the 2,271 bodies still buried there. Ian was buried separately — I do not know why — in a church graveyard at Taeku, which, like all South Korea since the war, has been so expanded, rebuilt and modernised that we could not launch an exploration for it.

For me — ignorant always — it was instructive to learn that the United States exhumed and repatriated all identified bodies of its soldiers killed and originally buried in Korea. So did Belgium, the Philippines, Thailand, Greece, India, Columbia and Ethiopia. France and Norway also exhumed most of their dead. But Britain (884 graves still there), Turkey (462), Canada (378), Australia (281), The Netherlands (117), New Zealand (34) and South Africa (11) did not move any.

Happier footnote: The visiting war correspondents, learning from Korea, will now provide a fund for welfare development of a Korean hamlet, where 18 trees will be planted and which will be renamed The Village of Eighteen Trees. (RIP)

June

It may seem strange to be writing about Australian "blacktrackers" in Oriental jungles. But I reckon there could be useful work for them today and tomorrow in the

Philippines, Thailand and along the Malaysian-Thai border. They are undoubtedly the best trackers in the world.

Last week's report of the successful tracking, detection and killing of four communist terrorists of the communist New People's Army by a government force in the Philippines stirred reflections on the possibility of recruiting selected Australian blacktrackers as talented advisers and guides in the insurgency areas.

This proposal was being seriously considered, I remember, by heads of the Gurkha units which patrolled the Borneo border in search of infiltrators during the "Bung" Sukarno Confrontation. The Gurkhas themselves were of course first-class, but I recall nervous nights when they lost the tracks of raiding parties from the south in the thick undergrowth. Trained Aussie blacktrackers work as effectively in the night as in the day.

How many are available or working with the Australian police these days, I wonder? I knew the No. 1 blacktracker of the New South Wales police force and watched him, in awe, at work on a hunt for murder victims in the scrub near Dubbo and Narromine. But that was 40 years ago, when all rural police forces had their trained Aborigines.

He was Alec Riley — dead now, alas. Shy and quiet, he wore riding breeches, leggings, blue coat and a neat cravat. He could pick up a trail three weeks old, but he did not like reading small print. He had found more bodies than any other police searcher in Australia, but he admitted a personal superstitious fear of corpses. He would dive fully clothed into a dam to locate a body, but he objected to kneeling in the dirt. He trod lightly, never raising his head, giving the impression that he was looking with his ears, nose and tight-lipped mouth, as well as his eyes — which seldom blinked. He held his hands slightly in front of his hips, palms facing the ground, fingers extended and separated, like a fortune-teller using the earth for a crystal ball.

"Wherever a man goes, he leaves marks," he told me. "He can't help it. He kicks stones; he breaks twigs and sticks; he steps in soft earth or sand. The wilder the country, the easier it is to follow the trail. Every man walks his own different way. Every man's shoes and boots are different.

"Sometimes men walk backwards when they know they are being followed. But they get tired of that very soon. Very few do it for more than 50 yards. You try it yourself. You stumble and you can't see where you are going and you think you look stupid. Black people do it better than white. They're more patient.

"To know which way a motorcar was travelling, look at the marks on the stones and twigs which the wheels passed over and displaced. The wheels always throw them behind the car."

Alec's most difficult job was tracking the notorious Roy Governor, "last of the bushrangers." His success indicates what a challenge he would have been to lurking terrorists on the Thai-Malay border, with or without booby-traps.

For one month, a police party led by Alec trailed Governor, a cunning, armed native who knew every inch of the country in the wild bush north of Gilgandra. Governor wrapped sheepskins over his feet, doubled, circled, played every trick he knew to confuse his trackers. He would lead the party to a water-course, apparently enter the stream, leap into a tree on the bank, swing Tarzan-like to other trees, drop to the ground perhaps 50 yd from the point where his trail ended in the water, then steal boldly back in the direction from which his hunters were coming. Yet every night on that month's relentless search, Alec and the police camped right on his heels. They got him at last — after he had put a bullet through one of the constables.

Alec himself never drank but he could tell whether another man had by looking at his footprints: "He leans forward a little on his toes, slightly turns one, or sometimes both, of his feet in; drags his heels."

Ever since, I have tried to remember to walk with my weight self-consciously on firm heels.

August

It is appropriate that the 50th anniversary of the founding of the People's Liberation Army should coincide this month with the current drive for army modernisation in China. The PLA, let us recall, was founded in Hunan as the "First Division of the First Peasants' and Workers' Army" (later simplified as "the Red Army") and comprised only three regiments, which were recruited and united in the first open and definite breakaway from Chiang Kaishek's relatively modernised Kuomintang (KMT) forces.

Party leaders prefer now to forget the Red Army's stormy conception — ridiculed originally as "The Rifle Movement" by the Politburo, which expelled Mao Zedong from its inner circle and the Party Front Committee. Mao was able then to demonstrate the same survival qualities (including a miraculous, shoeless escape from an execution squad) as Deng Xiaoping does today.

His tiny "army" fought many, and lost several, battles with the KMT as it struggled through Hunan. "Discipline was poor, political training was at a low level, and there were many desertions and wavering elements among the men and officers," Mao himself related. "When the little band" (now the PLA) "finally climbed up to Chingkanshan in the winter of 1927, they numbered in all about one thousand."

Amusingly — how history repeats itself — the Mao line, half-a-century ago at the birth of the PLA, was denounced as "deviationist" by both the party's "rightist opportunists," who wanted continuing concessions to the KMT, and the "party putschists" (as Mao called them in 1936), "who were demanding a terrorist policy of raiding and the burning and killing of landlords."

The Red Army's first vital reinforcements — ironically, once more — were supplied by (again Mao's description) "two former bandit leaders, Wang Tso and Yuan Wentsai," who restored the Red Army's strength to three regiments. While Mao was there, they supported him as "faithful communists and carried out the orders of the party," but when, later, he was temporarily absent from Chingkanshan, they resumed "bandit operations" and were executed by Mao's peasants, "by then organised and able to defend themselves."

Lin Biao

Corresponding to today's five "modernisations," Mao's formation of the Red Army was one of the five basic undertakings which comprised his so-called "Autumn Crop Uprising": complete severance from the KMT; organisation of the peasant-worker revolutionary army; confiscation of the property of small and middle, as well as great, landlords; establishment of Communist Party power in Hunan; organisation of Soviets. (Of course, that last party word, which is sound Marxist-Leninist jargon for any communist government bodies, would be untactful in a Chinese party programme today because of its parochial semantic connotations.)

The ancient — and now largely forgotten — historic facts show that, though the Red Army was technically born in 1927, it was not officially legitimised and given Politburo sanction for puberty until the winter of 1928, following the Sixth Party Congress in, of all places, Moscow.

The great — and still enshrined — Zhu Deh had arrived in 1928 in Chingkanshan (which, appropriately again, also invoked and conformed to the "five" tradition, because it was named after five mountain wells — *ta, hsiao, shang, hsia* and *chang*). The great, if now reviled, Lin Biao had also then appeared on the army scene.

Lin Biao, in fact, was commended by Mao for his two personal "rules for discipline" accepted by the Red Army: "Soldiers must always pay for all articles obtained from the people; soldiers must always establish" dunnies [I mean, latrines] "at a safe distance from people's homes."

But, even until 1930, the infant Red Army, Mao faithfully records, was weakened by "partisanism" ("lack of discipline, exaggerated ideas of democracy"), "vagabondism" ("a love of movement, change and new experience") and "militarism" ("commanders maltreating or even beating the men and showing favouritism").

Mao himself would probably say that the Red Army achieved puberty in October 1935, when it settled in at Shensi — eight years old.

September

Interpol, it seems, has very correctly and discreetly prepared a documented dossier on the two recent North Korean Marxist-Leninist kidnapping ventures by Asia's Idi Amin, Comrade Kim Il Sung, and his heir-apparent, Kim Jong Il. Copies of the dossier will be available for the United Nations Secretary-General, the two governments territorially involved — Yugoslavia and Iraq — and indeed for any other interested authorities, which should surely mean any state that tolerates a North Korean presence.

The two incidents, let us briefly recall, involved art and sport — the piano and table-tennis. They were both planned and foiled in late July. The more publicity that is given to them the more hazardous encores will become. So let me pray patience for these recapitulated details, originally reported by newsagencies, confirmed by the local press and the escaped victims-to-be and now supplemented and expanded by Interpol's inquiries.

The major attempted abduction was organised by former North Korean ambassador to Albania and Bulgaria, Yim Chun Chu, now Chief Secretary of Kim Il Sung, and involved the special operation of a North Korean airliner. The target victims were distinguished Korean pianist, Paik Kun Woo, and his actress wife, who now live in Paris and who were invited to visit Zagreb in Yugoslavia to give recitals to local celebrities.

They scented trouble as soon as they arrived, and pianist Paik sighted the waiting North Korean Tu 154. He shrewdly played for time and the couple, with their five-month-old baby, found sanctuary in the United States consulate and returned safely to Paris.

Comrade Yim flew back empty-handed to Pyongyang — and no doubt a cold-handed reception by Kim Il Sung.

The Interpol report names Yim's agents in Paris as Lee Ung No, expatriate Korean painter (once involved in a Berlin-based North Korean espionage ring), and his nephew, Lee Hui Se, who publishes a tolerated communist magazine, *Unification of Motherland*.

The second North Korean kidnap target was Kim Chang Je, South Korean coach of Libya's national table-tennis team, in Baghdad during the Arab Youth Games in July. (He is certainly lucky that the abduction bid was not made in Libya.)

Also attending the Youth Games was a North Korean gymnastic coach, Lee Chol, who made cordial non-political approaches to Kim and transmitted a personal invitation to dinner from the counsellor at the North Korean Embassy in Baghdad. Kim — no half-wit, he — refused politely and, scenting further trouble, did not attend a farewell party (13 July) for players and officials. He locked himself in his hotel room and, sure enough, at 10 p.m., the communist coach and a couple of members of the North Korean diplomatic staff tried to force their way in. Kim summoned Iraqi police and the kidnappers sullenly withdrew.

The Beirut daily, *Al-Bairak*, carried a straight news report of the incident on 27 August, under the heading, "Diplomats Try To Kidnap A Sports Instructor" — duly included in Interpol's dossier.

How, one wonders, would the North Koreans have got a kidnapped Korean out of Baghdad? No waiting airliner there, as in Zagreb. But let us remember how Kim Philby, "the British spy who betrayed a generation," got that back-stabbed KGB defector-to-be, Soviet consul Konstatin Volkov, out of Istanbul and back to Moscow in 1945, "heavily bandaged and unconscious on a stretcher."

What real advantage — apart from revenge — would the North Koreans have secured by either the Zagreb or Baghdad kidnapping? The theorists say that the disappearances could have been represented as a voluntary preference to live in animal-kingdom North Korea. That curious argument certainly won't stand up in the future. No one knows yet if Interpol has offered an opinion.

And did the Iraqi Government, whose police saved table-tennis coach Kim, make a private protest to the North Korean Embassy? They made no public protest.

Previous North Korean diplomatic offences, belatedly discovered, included, of course, the smuggling of narcotics and local blackmarketing of embassy tax-exempted commodities, grog and cigarettes.

Let us hope that, when President Tito gives his first press conference on his return to Yugoslavia, he will be asked whether he demanded an explanation of the Zagreb incident after he had his public embraces with President Kim in Pyongyang. If he didn't, why not?

November

Random personal jottings from my praying-stool diary of a recent visit to Tokyo:

My return, after six years' absence, to one of my favourite Asian cities, in which I lived for 12 happy years before and after the war, re-twitched my senile anxieties about the overdue encore of the catastrophic 1926 earthquake. The skyscrapers are soaring from Shinjuku and Shibuya to downtown Marunouchi. From the 25th floor of the Yurakucho Denki Building, where the august and venerable Foreign Correspondents' Club is now located, one can toast the shape of Mt Fuji through the bar windows on rare unpolluted days.

But club members are aggrieved by the fact that another skyscraper will soon obscure that holy view. And I discovered that resident Old Hands share my doubts that capitalist builders have actually devised a unique and untested combination of flexible cement and pliable architecture which will enable the skyscrapers to flutter their backsides gracefully and remain safely erect when the next giant shake hits Tokyo. It is admitted that those trapped in the halted elevators "must remain patient, correct and sincere" as the huge new buildings to their hoped-for slow and serene rock-and-roll.

I would still prefer to be in the top fifth floor of the original Foreign Correspondents' Club in Shimbun Alley than in the Club's new 25th floor when that quake hits. (Come to think of it, some members might still prefer the alternative view from the curtained southern windows of the old Club to the new fleeting glimpses of Fuji-*san*: night and morning close-ups of the uncurtained windows of the ladies' shower-cubicles in the adjoining dormitory of the Soviet Occupation . . .)

The Japanese, I was glad to note, are drinking more grape wine — even if the local product is generally still too sweet. A variety — new to me — is *Suntory* (not to be confused with the traditional Japanese whisky). The Japanese wine comes chiefly from hill vineyards around Kofu, capital of Yamanashi prefecture (northwest of Tokyo).

The high price of Japanese wine — what isn't high-priced in Japan for visitors? — is partly attributable to taxation, which still makes it cheaper to grow grapes for fruit rather than for *gaijin* wine. Nevertheless, Japan is still giving a welcome lead to other Asian countries in the fermenting of light dry plonk. Just use the grapes and the quality of the Asian wine will improve . . .

The treatise which fascinated me most at "the First World Conference of Journalists" — my excuse and opportunity for re-visiting Tokyo — was a learned paper by genial and gentle Sheik Ali A. Hafiz, former mayor of Almadina, "the holy city of Saudi Arabia," and founding editor of its local daily.

"We in the Arabian peninsula [Jordan, Syria and Iraq in the north, the Arabian Gulf in the east, the Red Sea in the west, and the Indian Ocean in the south] practised the art of journalism thousands of years before the dawn of Islam," he claimed.

"The largest newspaper was established in the Arabian peninsula in the year 500 A.D., during the pre-Islamic age and was known as *Okaz*."

(That certainly puts my paper, *The Times*, in its place, I brooded gloomily.)

Okaz, it seems, covered "trade, leaders' speeches, literature and tradition, as well as news and symposia of poetry, sports and glorious deeds." Prophet Muhammad ("peace be on Him") used *Okaz* editorials "to spread the Islam faith to all corners of the world," and Omar ibn Al-Khattao, second Caliph of Islam, was a sports and wrestling reporter for *Okaz*.

Alas, I then belatedly discovered that *Okaz* was "verbal journalism" and reflected only "personal comments of news events and other information" proclaimed by visiting bedouin at the monthly and weekly fairs at Okaz (near Mecca), which prevailed until 1908, "when a few modest Saudi newspapers appeared."

Anyway, a newspaperman's toast to *Okaz*. No libel risks, union brawls or advertisement domination in those days.

December

An expatriate foreign-devil who tearfully has not been able to cast his compulsory democratic vote in an Australian election since pre–Pearl Harbour days, I was gratified to discover, during my recent one-week return to the old Sydney homestead, that electioneering standards and speeches remain toughly and vulgarly Aussie.

I still recall the violent language of P. M. Billy Hughes' (no relative) abortive proconscription campaign, resisting the disguised-IRA Archbishop Danny Mannix's "vote no" sabotage, which involved me and other Christian Brothers' boys in fist- and stone-throwing battles with similarly organised "vote yes" state schoolboy revisionists after the Gallipoli disaster.

So, while newly arrived foreign diplomats in Canberra might have been taken aback, I was racially relieved to read that Labor leader Gough Whitlam had called the press "bastards" and, in a Disraelian election aside, had claimed grazier-P. M. Malcolm Fraser's "rams on his sheep-farm are shitting themselves this weekend because they fear he might be back as their master." (Neither of my favourite Aussie political leaders — P. M. Ben Chifley, old railwayman like myself, and treasurer E. G. Theodore, another former railwayman who should have been our ablest P. M. — would have used that language themselves, but they would have understood, accepted and encouraged it.)

For me, the major surprise was to discover that so many of my well-informed sources in Sydney thought (or feared) that Labor, despite the Whitlam handicap, could beat Fraser in the premature election. I note that current opinion polls dispute this belief. It was generally agreed, however, that, if Labor does scrape back, No. 2 Bill Hayden, a competent former cop, will soon replace Whitlam.

Anyway, Fraser won't lose his command of the Senate until mid-1978 even if he is tripped from the House on 10 December. The Senate, with its parochial state representation, can override the voice and will of the Australian people in the House. That strange Aussie constitutional combination of Westminster and Washington systems, of course, brought Whitlam down in 1975 and flung his House majority to the wind.

I was myself a humiliated victim of Senate irresponsibility when I was expelled as a barefoot columnist from both the Senate and House press galleries for an article of mild reproof which I wrote in 1942, criticising the halfwit President Cunningham for giving a casting-vote against his own Labor Party's urgent bill, rushed through the House, to release supplies of urgently-needed beef for the newly-arrived US forces of Gen. MacArthur. (The details are too technical to report here and now, but P. M. Curtin had Cunningham dragged before him next day and the disputed bill was approved by the Senate when next presented.)

The senators, like the House MPs, would not have endorsed my expulsion, but Cunningham — who had been heavily liquored and fell on his knees when he crossed the floor to cast his original vote — had constitutional authority to kick me out personally and then talked his running-dog, Speaker Nairn, into ejecting me from the House gallery.

My then Sydney boss, Frank Packer, used strong language in rejecting the demand for apology and withdrawal. So, unbelievably, Cunningham and Nairn then extended the expulsion to all my Packer colleagues, who had not had the slightest connection with my gentle criticism.

For three months we had to cover debates and the Canberra scene, appropriately, from an undertaker's office near Parliament House. But justice at last prevailed and we were re-admitted, without apology or withdrawal, to applause from the floor of both the Senate and the House, while Cunningham and Nairn glared helpless from their chairs.

I then left to advise Eisenhower at the Casablanca landing and never saw Cunningham or Nairn again. But — a tip now to Whitlam and/or Fraser, whatever the election results and the expedient role of the Senate — whenever I return to Canberra, a group of us mature pressmen parade and thumb our noses collectively and publicly at the painting of Cunningham and the photograph of Nairn in Parliament House entrance hall.

1978 January

By happy coincidence, 47-year-old Malcolm Fraser opened his third year as Prime Minister of Australia in the same week as this senile expatriate, waving well-bloodied boomerangs, returned for a sentimental one-month survey of the old homeland. Fraser emerged from three weeks' seclusion and, at the time of writing, was expected to summon his first new Cabinet meeting.

Well-entrenched ambushes and deep elephant traps evidently threaten him on the long and arduous bush-track ahead. He will have to disperse and suppress a curious Australian opposition melange of rival factions — political and bureaucratic, trade unions and big bosses.

My barefoot advisers tell me that he is studying a basic programme for the diversification of Australian export markets in the Far East as the Japanese continue to cut back imports of Australian mining products. This bid for expansion must involve a corresponding reduction of Aussie protectionism, which has for so long sustained and encouraged inefficient local manufacturing methods, inflated wages and swollen unemployment.

Unemployment generally has risen from 66,900 in 1966 — when the Aussie labour force was 4.8 million — to 322,400 in 1977 (labour force then 6.1 million). Youth unemployment (between the ages of 15 and 20) was around 20,000 in the late 1960s but hit 88,000 in 1976, 118,000 in August last year and 171,000 in December.

Strikes are the correlated problem. In September, strikes cost nearly 123,000 workers A$9.9 million (US$11.25 million) in wages through loss of 272,000 working days.

This gloomy picture is deepened by the gathering flight home of disillusioned British migrants — including significantly many family

Fraser

groups. The number of Pommy arrivals in 1975 had fallen to 17,800, and 10,000 former happy residents returned to the Old Country in the same year. However, incestuous racial ghettos of Italians and Greeks and expanding in Sydney and Melbourne.

Asian migrants continue to arrive — including, naturally, a large proportion of Filipina maids-to-be, who are being exploited as widely in Australia as elsewhere. They are paid around A$5,000 a year, compared with an average A$15,000 for Australian domestic staff.

At least 15 foreign embassies in Canberra employ maids, cooks and other house workers from the Philippines. Currently there is an indignant uproar over the harsh conditions of work and even physical ill-treatment of Philippine staff by foreign diplomats, who were publicly denounced but not named last week by Foreign Minister Andrew Peacock.

A doctor at a Canberra hospital has

treated six domestic servants from embassies for "severe mental strain" and even physical beatings. Under international law, the government can do nothing to rectify the so-called "slave scandal" and the terrified victims refuse to testify. Australia's Special Branch has files on two incidents but can take no action.

On the brighter side of the boomerang, the local Chinese communities stand firm and happy and Chinese restaurants and cuisine become increasingly popular — in suburbs and country towns as well as vulnerable city Chinatowns. Asian students continue to gain admittance to Australian universities and last week 200 Aussie students flew to Japan, the United States and Germany under a Rotary International student exchange programme.

The Aussie vineyards still flourish. Despite drought this year there will be a bumper harvest, with a surplus of about 45,000 tons, chiefly in black grape varieties.

Today, the Aussies, who tend to keep their best wine for themselves, are preferring white to red wine. They drank nearly 823 million litres of wine last year. Like Hongkong's Chinese, they are plunging more deeply into the brandy bottle: sales were up nearly 1 million litres last year to a record 13 million litres.

There is scornful and universal white-Aussie denial that the brandy trend in any way reflects the Hongkong belief that the noble spirit has aphrodisiac, ginseng-style quality.

Yet, to a shocked expatriate like myself with puritanical instincts, the scores of frank "massage parlour" and explicit "man to woman invitation" advertisements in the personal columns of the city press — which would have Hongkong's vice squad on heat — must reflect a vital degeneration, or perhaps "uplift" would be a better term, on the sex front.

February

Chinese cuisine continues to gain popularity in Australia, where there is still no real honest Aussie variation on the theme of world cooking.

As a lively local pamphlet (issued weekly by Peter Isaacson Publications) points out: "Although many attempts have been made to try to prove the contrary, indigenous Australian cooking remains at the level of 'the bush damper' (mix flour and water, cook), 'witchetty grubs' (do not cook, do not kill, just eat) and 'cockatoo stew' (boil a cockatoo in water with an old boot; when cooked throw away the cockatoo and eat the boot)."

Old expatriate Chinese friends assure me that Chinese restaurants in the Chinatowns of Melbourne and Sydney are spreading and improving, that takeaway *dim sum* (Cantonese food speciality) shops are spreading in suburbs and country towns and that Aussies generally are becoming connoisseurs in Chinese taste.

Melbourne's Little Bourke Street Chinatown is now more elegant than its Sydney counterpart around Dixon Street, with coloured shrines and illuminated pagodas. But both areas report crowded cafes for lunch and dinner, and Chinese cooks, it seems, are infiltrating the kitchens of hotels and restaurants which concentrate on Western-style cooking.

Dim sum and Cantonese cuisine, not surprisingly, are favourites in Australia, but an old Melbourne mate, Jimmy Lee (shall we call him), who offered me some excellent smoked Sichuan duck, said that he was getting demands for a longer menu and a wider variety of Chinese dishes.

"You Aussies are travelling more often to Hongkong, Southeast Asia and now China," he explained. "I get demands for 'drunken shrimps' and even birds nest soup. Of course, most of you Aussies [a shrug] don't know the true flavour of natural birds nest soup.

"You can't even tell the difference between red nest and white-grey or even green nests and some of you — believe it or not — pour it on noodles." He lowered his voice. "Of course our soup is canned. Aussies don't grow any real sea swallows."

Australians generally are queuing up to buy tickets for new approved tours to Peking. Few of them are China-watchers and most of them couldn't care less about Canberra's abolition of any Taiwan presence in Australia. (But a record number of Kuomintang delegates will be indulgently permitted to attend the projected International Press Institute conference in Australia.)

Trapped in a couple of radio interviews, I learned that popular Australian interest in China generally and Hongkong in particular is based largely on working hours, strikes, police corruption, cheongsams and the attractions of Chinese women. There was envious reaction to the discovery that Hongkong's maximum income tax is only 15% and its average taxi fares less than one-fifth Aussie rates.

The old Hongkong corruption scandals still hang heavily and darkly in the polluted Australian urban air. But there is also confusion over how the current controversial "amnesty" could apply definitely in retrospect when exception can be made at any time by the ICAC or the police chief if any crime is discovered to be allegedly "heinous."

"Our cops would use that exception whenever they wanted to do so," one seasoned newspaper police roundsman pointed out. "We could brand 'two-up' as more heinous than gang rape if it suited. You Chows seem to be pretty cunning."

Envy is also aroused by the absence of serious strikes and the length of working hours in Hongkong. (Australian unions are currently seeking an unprecedented cutback from 40 to 37½ hours a week.)

Some Australian union secretaries and shop stewards are becoming increasingly unpopular, though the stature and influence of the formidable but discerning and adaptable top union boss, Bob Hawke, dominates the labour and indeed employer scene. Most Australians I met — whatever their political or class differences — admire him. "The man to watch," all seem to agree.

However, the crude question about Hongkong, "Whatever happened to Suzie Wong?" kept cropping up. Naturally and embarrassedly, I had no firm answer.

March

We foreign devils who have been permitted to visit and even to work humbly in "liberated" China know that mainland Chinese all like to drink, though they never seem to be able to indulge on the same scale and spending, and certainly not with the same variety of grog, as their unliberated compatriots in Hongkong in particular and Taiwan and overseas Chinatowns generally.

Latest amendments to the Constitution indulgently permit the comrades to "enjoy freedom of speech, assembly and association," but regrettably Chairman Hua Guofeng and Vice-Premier Deng Xiaoping have yielded no specific or veiled concessions on the booze front. A pity, I reckon, as a senile but reasonably light dry-wine taster myself.

Faction critics of the new party set-up could plausibly insist that a liberalised liquor policy for the masses would be in step — if sometimes lurching — with the "modernisation" programme. Because, curiously, the historical record of Chinese alcoholic prohibition or restriction is plain, sobering and basically Mandarin — going back, in fact, centuries to the fall of the Yin territories and the directive of the stern Duke of Chow, which reads like a Gang of Four manifesto.

"The virtue in drinking is not to get drunken," the duke insisted, decreeing, first, that the drinking of wine and spirits must be confined to "sacrifices and festivals," and, secondly, that any intemperate revisionists must be carried in irons to the homeland of Chow and executed.

In the BC era, the decision was made to heat Chinese wine before serving, permissively, "with meals or in company only," on the Chinese theory that a boozer drank more slowly when his grog was warm. This argument derived dramatic support from the legend that a teetotal Prince of Tsou lost a war in 250 BC because he mistook cold wine for mineral water and, indulging inordinately but understandably this pleasurable variant on insipidity, passed out at a critical stage in battle.

Here is the often forgotten contrast between Japanese and Chinese temperament and philosophy. The Japanese have always gone for the grog, ever since drunken Emperor Ojin, in the fourth century, established that desire, in *vino*, need not outrun performance, on the *tatami*. A tireless lecher, poet and carouser, he imported from China not only Japan's first authentic copy of the Confucian *Analects*, but also Peking's top if suppressed brewer, who was rechristened Susukori.

In one period of exhilaration, Emperor Ojin wrote a verse:

> *Susukori has intoxicated me with fine*
> *wine*
> *And now I am so drunken that I have lost*
> *my tongue*
> *And feel so happy.*

He then staggered outside, bowed to Mt Fuji and proceeded to strike and roll aside boulders on the highway with his imperial staff, inspiring the Japanese proverb: "Even hard stones make way for a drinker."

May I respectfully suggest to Premier

Fukuda that Japan, as Peking-Tokyo detente strengthens, could try to brainwash Chinese party contacts into adopting some Japanese drinking protocol at official banquets where plenty of *mao-tai* and *shao-shing* is usually, if temporarily, on call, but where variety, guidance and indulgence could be transmitted to rural cadres and other provincial visitors.

The Japanese of course call beer *biru* but they have the generic word, *yoshu*, for all Western alcohol — brandy, gin, whisky, wine. And the most discerning demand that beer or light, dry plonk should be poured, like *sake*, from opaque rather than glass containers on the perceptive theory that "half the pleasure of drinking is lost when you know how much [or how little] is left in the bottle."

Also, Peking bosses might be interested in the comradely *kenshu* climax to a formal *sake* dinner when the diners exchange beer mugs or *sake* cups to carry away as a mark of mateship.

More grog must surely lubricate both detente and "modernisation."

April

It was gratifying to note that the 25th anniversary of the first James Bond 007 adventure (*Casino Royale*) was recorded with proper respect by the London press earlier this month.

His creator, Ian Fleming, called to his reward 14 years ago, was my first Fleet Street boss in 1946. He was foreign manager of *The Sunday Times* for which I was based in Tokyo. I twice had the honour of accompanying him as a valet-comrade in his search for folklore and local spiritual colour through Bangkok, Hong-kong, Macau and Japan — *Thrilling Cities* (1960) and the solitary Asian Bond adventure, *You Only Live Twice* (1962).

He told me in Japan that he wanted to send James Bond on his last adventure into communist China. Fleming knew he had not long to live, but he

Fleming in Japan: Cavalier.

would not attempt such a setting unless he had been able personally to visit China. That attention to detail was characteristic.

His last — appropriately 13th — Bond story, *Man with the Golden Gun*, was written in early 1964 at his Jamaican home, when he was in semi-retirement. (He had also hoped to visit Panama so that 007 could have been involved in some cunning and crafty canal crisis that would have had special interest today.)

Ian was one of the best friends you could ever have — a tough, laughing cavalier, and always a newspaperman. He had been a Reuter correspondent in Moscow during Stalin's day, and had served with Naval

Intelligence during the Hitler war. He told his best stories against himself.

The 25th anniversary persuaded me to re-read *You Only Live Twice*, in which he has criminally lampooned me as Dikko Henderson, the evil sensual Australian secret service chief in post-war Japan. The story recalls his precise and correct attention to detail during our tour of Japan — evocative of the similar research methods of John le Carré, alias David Cornwell. (I am relieved to know that my Chinese wife does not understand — or pretends she does not understand — some of the Fleming implications. When I threatened him with a libel suit, he wrote in reply: "Go ahead, Dikko, and I will then write the truth about you.")

I have uncovered some of his unwritten asides:

"Women take happiness for granted; they never realise that it is something which must be earned."

"That man is a scoundrel" — a fellow passenger on the train from Kyoto to Tokyo — "he has not had his hair cut for more than a month."

"Young eccentrics will always be old England's salvation."

I once asked him why he drank bourbon instead of Scotch. "The muscles *expand* under bourbon, Dikko, but they *contract* under Scotch," he told me, spreading and bunching his long fingers.

That ingenious theory was also an excuse for his cigarette smoking. He was not supposed, I knew, to smoke heavily, but he was constantly screwing his Bondian cigarettes into a long holder. He protested, deadpan, that the non-Scotch-like influence which bourbon exercised on his cardiac muscles also tended to correct ill-effects from nicotine.

"In other words," I argued, "the more bourbon you drink and the more cigarettes you smoke, the better for your heart?"

"Come, come, Dikko," he replied. "A little common sense, please. You are not writing a story for *The Lancet*."

Fleming's cable address in London was "Vagabond." He was always a Happy Wanderer.

May

Gallantry and gullibility are the contrasted themes of this week's intrusion on REVIEW readers. But I reckon each is another tribute, for vastly differing reasons, to the persons involved.

I am indebted, as always, to my old mate Denis Warner, former Australian army commando, then war correspondent, now author and president of the Free Tasmania (non-terrorist) Movement, for the following unknown or forgotten incident in the heroic career of Gen. John Singlaub, who, regrettably if inevitably, has resigned from the US Army because of his voluble differences of opinion on strategy and policy with his C-in-C, Supreme Commander Jimmy Carter.

We senile war correspondents who heard Singlaub — and all other resident US military chiefs — logically denounce the projected pullout of the US garrison when we went to South Korea last year, admired him greatly. Warner now recalls the parachute landing of Singlaub — then a major, who had led guerilla forces in the French resistance and in China more than three decades ago — into Hainan Island on 26 August 1945.

The Japanese had officially surrendered two weeks before, but the local Japanese camp commandant at Hachau (on the southwest coast of Hainan) was still holding about 200 dying Australian and Dutch prisoners, who were the survivors of a 400-man group brought from Indonesia in 1942 and compelled to build the railway viaduct which the Chinese use today to carry iron ore from Five Finger Mountain. The *gaijin* prisoners were then living on rats, with a generous low-protein Japanese diet of two sweet potatoes a day.

Maj. Singlaub bluffed the Japanese commandant into believing that he was in constant communication with HQ and that a formidable US force was on its way to Hainan. (Actually, his radio equipment had been broken in his parachute descent.) After one day's resistance, the Japanese commandant surrendered. Singlaub rushed food and medical supplies, which had also been parachuted, to the prisoners, seized the Japanese radio and summoned three British destroyers to crush the last Japanese resistance in the Far East.

The Warner records also disclose that only 600 Chinese labourers survived of the 30,000 brought to Hainan to work in the iron-ore mines. He quotes an Aussie survivor, Capt. Philip Misken: "I doubt if anyone in our camp would have been alive in another four weeks if Major Singlaub hadn't arrived. The rats had eaten all our rice and we had eaten most of the rats. You can't live long on sweet potatoes."

One wonders what happened to the Japanese commandant, and whether the Chinese comrades, now modernising Hainan Island, have put up a monument to Maj. Singlaub as well as to the 29,000 Chinese workers who died there.

And now from gallantry to gullibility. Last month I reported the East-meeting-West appeal by Dr Ronald Burt De Waal, librarian at the Colorado State University and the world's leading bibliographer of Sherlock Holmes. He sought help for an American, John E. Moss, serving a 15-20 year prison sentence for having killed a man who allegedly raped and murdered one of his twin teenage daughters.

In my continuing and undeserved post since 1948 as Chief Banto of the Baritsu Chapter of the Baker Street Irregulars (founded in Tokyo, with then Prime Minister Shigeru Yoshida and Count Makino as two of the original 25 members), I took the liberty of publishing this appeal in the REVIEW — with responses from other Far Eastern Sherlockians.

It had been sent to 150 scion societies of the Baker Street Irregulars — in England, US, Canada, Sweden, Holland, Denmark, Australia, New Zealand, Japan and Hong-kong, proving that one touch of Sherlock Holmes still makes the whole world kin.

Now De Waal has written to report in dignified apology that he had been misled by Moss, who has admitted that "there was a relationship between the man I'm supposed to have killed and my daughter. He didn't kill her but he did try to rape her at one time."

De Waal, who is still helping the imprisoned Moss, while returning the cheques, wrote me ruefully: "There is at least one trait I have in common with Sir Arthur Conan Doyle: gullibility."

Also, I would add, generosity and humanitarianism. ("A good man and a good friend, Watson," I can hear Holmes remarking.)

June

It is always self-salutary for a senile reporter — especially a war correspondent — to re-read, gulping and groaning, the utter nonsense which he sometimes (shall we say?) wrote pompously in the past. On the eve of my latest return to Kinmen (Quemoy) last week, for the 20th anniversary of the frustrated 42-day bombardment of the island outpost by the Chinese communists, I discovered a clip of my on-the-spot summation of the "incident" in *The Sunday Times* of London (10 October 1958).

"Quemoy has no hope...," it said. "It has resisted a day-and-night bombardment for six weeks by the communist mainland batteries which envelop it on three sides... The enigmatic silence which has now fallen on the red soil, granite rocks and thatched villages marks at best only a first-round, ahead-on-points count for the defenders, who can neither control the duration of the contest, say when the next round shall begin, nor hope to force a decision. The enemy has been checked but not beaten. This is a lull, not a victory. Like it or not, unless the United States is prepared to wage all-out war against China, Quemoy must inevitably be re-absorbed by the mainland, less than three miles away."

True, I was not the only barefoot reporter covering the bombardment who cabled such error. All we survivors who have since returned have humbly and publicly admitted our bad judgment to our welcoming indulgent Sino-Taiwanese military commanders — no Americans now — as we revived old memories with the explosive local *kao-liang*, which makes vodka or *mao-tai* taste like lime-and-soda.

This current visit of mine — my fourth — was the happiest. The island's population is now 60,000 (45,000 in 1971) and the green-and-russet self-supporting garden estate rests safely and securely on still-expanding miles of military and communication tunnels and underground installations.

There are no traces of the damage caused by the concentrated round-the-clock shelling of 1958 (400 siege-guns, including Soviet 203s), the intensity of which surpassed by 25 times the record of 4,000 rounds per square kilometre established at the American landing on Iwo Jima.

(It is now forgotten that in 1960 the communist artillery opened a two-day encore barrage on Kinmen on 17 and 19 June, when President Eisenhower arrived and departed from Taiwan. Perhaps Kinmen's massive underground artillery should have bombarded the mainland when US Security Adviser Brzezinski — surely Soviet derivation? — arrived in Peking on the same day that Chiang Ching-kuo became President?)

The size of today's modernised garrison (80,000 in 1971) is now, of course, censored: "It is *enough*, we assure you," the Chinese commanding general (his name now a secret) said, with a placid smile and raised *kao-liang* glass. Along the coast of the mainland, 300,000 communist troops are dug in and tied down. On alternate days there is an exchange of non-explosive artillery shells, crammed with propaganda leaflets.

At Mashan loudspeaker station, a charming lady's voice transmits daily news stories and items of interest to the China mainland and the balloon deliveries of consumer-goods and welcome-invitations persist from the Kinmen launching centre. (The communists have glumly slackened their counter-deliveries, which anyway are of such abominable inferiority that samples are on contemptuous display in an exhibition hall on Kinmen.)

Defectors still arrive, bowing and weeping, from the mainland, but the only departures from Kinmen are the well-organised "frogmen" who maintain systematic contact with the KMT 007s in China.

To close, I note from my 1958 news-clip an interview with the then formidable leader of the US Military Advisory Group in Taiwan, Col Douglas H. Lane, who had reorganised the system of Taiwan-Kinmen convoy deliveries so successfully that the commies had unprecedentedly placed a US$10,000 reward on his head — dead or alive. I asked him whether the communists had conceded the ceasefire for time to regroup.

His reply has special significance today:

"What they have got is heavy enough and they can hit us anywhere they want to hit us. There are still no signs that they intend to mount an invasion. They could take the island at a price. What price would we Americans be prepared to pay to hold them off? We would need to attack the mainland and open up a world war."

July

Thirty years ago this month, I recall with a sad sigh, I failed in a selfless attempt to help a distinguished Japanese industrialist, pearl king and sportsman, Keita Goto, to introduce the democratic sport of greyhound racing into Japan. The gambling-prone Japanese, who last year spent the equivalent of 16% of the national budget betting on horses, speedboats, cycling and motor-cycle races, still can't indulge in dog-racing.

Goto approached me at the Foreign Correspondents Club in Shimbun Alley in July 1948. Then 61, he had been purged from public office by Supremo MacArthur because he had been a minister of transport during the war. But he was still the proprietor of the Tokyo Highspeed Tramway Co., owned a string of racehorses and had ¥30 million (then US$450,000), which he asked me, as an Australian reporter, to inform the Australian public that he wished to invest in Japan's first dog-racing association.

The difficulty was that he had to get permission from MacArthur and the then prime minister, Hitoshi Ashida (on the eve of arrest on charges, later found unproven, of having confused personal gifts with political subscriptions from a large electrical undertaking). Even if he succeeded, he had to recognise that the yen was not then convertible, and that he would need to exchange goods for dogs on a barter basis. He therefore proposed a unique exchange of 75 flawless pearl necklaces, valued at ¥7.5 million (then worth US$30,000 on the black market) for 20 pedigree Aussie racing greyhounds.

Also, he offered a luxurious home in Japan, substantial living expenses and a handsome salary for an Australian greyhound boss to accompany and tend the faithful animals.

The story hit the headlines in Australia. (I swear, with an angry oath, that I was offered not a single pearl in the project.) My Australian news editor cabled: DOG STORY WILDFIRING STOP OFFICE FLOODED WITH APPLICATIONS AND BLOCKADED BY GREYHOUNDS STOP GOSFORD (HEART OF NEW SOUTH WALES GREYHOUND COUNTRY) FEARS MASS MIGRATION STOP PEARL MARKET LOWEST STOP KEEP SENDING FULLEST DETAILS.

The Aussie greyhound airmail began to pour in — registered, thick and bulging with photographs of dogs which all looked the same to me but which were embellished with the most frank and explicit individual claims of their sexual potency as well as racing speeds. A total of 112 applications were received from Aussie dog-trainers — some ingratiating, some arrogant.

But Operation Honourable Greyhound faltered. The Japanese Diet was sluggish.

MacArthur: preoccupied.

By then Ashida and several of his ministers were in jail. MacArthur was preoccupied with the operations of a prim, implacable little banker, Joseph M. Dodge, who was introducing notable reforms in the original MacArthurian plans for the Japanese economy. And the severely correct Australian Embassy told me there would be formidable difficulties in clearing the personal arrival of a paid dog-sitter and that the barter operation did not come under the heading of either "cultural" or "developmental" influences prescribed under the Occupation Act.

The patience of Goto's fellow shareholders eroded. Each of the 112 dog-training applicants received a sincere and apologetic explanation, urging them not to abandon hope.

Finally, Goto — who had, not surprisingly, dumped me as a go-between — discovered a new democratic sporting trend in resurgent Japan and turned to bicycle racing, which the Diet and the Occupation jointly blessed on the plausible grounds that it would encourage the development of the local bicycle industry. I heard that Goto gave the pearl necklaces away as prizes to winning cyclists.

Still, that was three decades ago. Would the Australian greyhound boys be enterprising enough to revive the project for today's Japanese gamblers who still haven't caught on to the sport?

August

Thirty years ago this month a charming Japanese lady, Mrs Miki Sawada, a devout Catholic descendant of the Iwasaki family which founded Mitsubishi, became involved in perhaps the most humanitarian undertaking during the Occupation of Japan.

We surviving senile foreign-devil correspondents who covered the Occupation have never forgotten her. I thought she had passed on to her reward, but now I am delighted to learn from my old barefoot-spy mate, Dr Bob Horiguchi, that she is still alive and thriving, and that her devoted labours were recalled this month by Nippon TV, after six months of worldwide research.

What she did for three decades was to care for the unwanted illegitimate children spawned in Japan by triumphant *gaijin* troops. Their fathers dumped them; their mothers were ostracised. They would have had no future if Mrs Sawada had not dedicated herself to their shelter, education, upbringing and possible adoption at an institution in Oiso, opened in July 1948.

We reporters ran stories from time to time about the undertaking, but now Dr Horiguchi has sent me the first full report I have seen (based on the TV documentary and interviews in the enterprising Tokyo weekly, *Shukan Bunshun*).

Approximately 1,600 rejected "Occupation babies," it seems, were saved by Mrs Sawada at Oiso — many of mixed black and Japanese heritage. Half of them eventually quit Japan and Nippon TV tracked down some of them in the US and Brazil. It was evidently difficult to make contact with those who remained in their semi-homeland. Most of those who left Japan were adopted by US foster-parents, under an arrangement between Mrs Sawada and Pearl Buck (RIP).

One of the grimmest disclosures, I think, is that not a single deserted "Occupation baby" was adopted by Japanese foster-parents. And only one of the 1,600 wards of the Oiso refuge has ever been acknowledged by his father — in circumstances which evoke Edgar Allan Poe.

A month before he was born, his father, a corporal in the Occupation forces, was convicted of the murder of another GI, after a personal argument over the mother-to-be, and was sentenced to life imprisonment in Kansas. Mrs Sawada contacted the family in the US and the corporal's sister adopted her nephew when he was three, educated him in Little Rock, and applauded his decision to join and serve for three years in the US Army in Germany before becoming a teacher in Little Rock. His father was released in 1974 after serving 25 years and is a construction worker in Little Rock. No one, alas, seems to know what happened to the Japanese mother.

Another sad history: a little boy whose *gaijin* father was killed in the Korean War when he was four, lived in the Oiso shelter until he was 11, and was then adopted by a South Carolina family. He volunteered to fight in Vietnam. "I am going to bring peace to Asia," he wrote to his still-loving Japanese mother. He was killed in action in Vietnam in his early 20s.

Some of the foundlings, happily, have not forgotten their debt to Mummy Miki Sawada. She arranged for half a dozen to go to Brazil, where she invested US$60,000 in a three-year farming project in an area where she hoped there would be no racial discrimination. The venture flopped, except for one protege whose pepper-tree farm is now flourishing.

On his property today stands a luxurious villa, which remains vacant in the hope that Mummy Miki may decide that her Oiso connections have been terminated and that she could spend some happy days every year with one of her salvaged "sons," his Brazilian wife and their two sons.

Is there, one wonders, some honour which could be bestowed upon Mrs Sawada by Japan? By the United States? Or by the United Nations?

September

It was amusing last week to hear Ratna Sari Dewi, the one-time Tokyo "geisha"-hostess and No. 3 wife of the late president Sukarno, denouncing the CIA for complicity in the abortive 1965 communist coup in Indonesia. Living in queenly and never lonely luxury in Paris since "Bung" Karno's death in 1970, she has always liked to picture herself as having been an apolitical Evita Peron or even Jiang Qing.

She stressed that the CIA she referred to was that well-known United States body and not — as the anti-communist Indonesian press pointed out at the time of uproar — the "Chinese Intelligence Agency."

It tends to be forgotten now that the Indonesian Communist Party was the third largest in the world, with 3 million registered members and 16 million organised followers, in the mid-1960s when it was violently suppressed in the aftermath of the communist-planned, pro-Sukarno, anti-US murder of six leading Indonesian military commanders 13 years ago this week (30 September 1965).

Sukarno hung on technically as president for 18 months, though his own foreknowledge of the plot emerged at the trials of those arrested — one of whom was his foreign minister, Subandrio, who was sentenced to death but still lives on serenely under house arrest (that smooth old dog had me — a poor, harmless, barefoot reporter — declared *persona non grata* just before the coup).

Communists had infiltrated the Indone-

...emorial to the murdered generals.

sian army but its high command was predominantly anti-commie and rallied toughly and shrewdly during the 1965-67 emergency. Seven military leaders had been marked down for assassination; one, Gen. Nasution, escaped over his garden wall in the darkness, though his little daughter was murdered; three of the doomed six and Nasution's aide were trucked alive to the communist training camp at Crocodile Hole and tortured and eye-gouged before being bullet-riddled and flung into a prepared well (from which the bodies were later recovered and photographed before ceremonial burial).

One of the vicious asides of this mass murder was "Bung" Karno's complaint of the "exaggerated" press coverage of the generals' deaths: "They were executed in an orderly and graceful manner by decision of a people's court. They were blindfolded before being shot and their executioners apologised before killing them."

These old memories do provide an opportunity to pay tribute to President Suharto, who so admirably directed the reactions and counter-reactions to the 1965 crisis, controlled the students' uprising and restored the People's Consultative Congress, the original constitutional authority of which had been castrated by Sukarno. He also restrained the Indonesian army command from similarly castrating Sukarno.

My old mate and namesake, John Hughes, now editor of the *Christian Science Monitor*, superbly summed up Suharto's wise policies in *The End of Sukarno* (Angus and Robertson, 1967): "Privately Suharto told friends he wanted no Latin American–style power takeover in Indonesia. If the army simply fired Sukarno, he argued, that would set a precedent. If the president was to be dismissed, then it must be by constitutional means . . .

"Another restraint upon Suharto in his dealings with the president was his own patriotism and national pride . . . Sukarno was, after all, the father figure of the Indonesian revolution. Now Suharto sought to retire Sukarno with relative dignity and avoid humiliation of the man who had been Indonesia's voice for two decades."

Sukarno, that arrogant hypocrite, never gave Suharto credit for his characteristically Indonesian perception and generosity. Now, of course, he has been symbolically declared a "national hero" and his grave is being rebuilt. Madam Dewi is angry because her home — not as ornate as that of "Bung's" No. 2 wife — has been converted into a military museum (though she doesn't allege CIA influence).

Monique and Sihanouk.

November

As the Cambodian (Sino)–Vietnam (Soviet) showdown sharpens, Comrade Prince Norodom Sihanouk, bravely enduring his party hair-shirt in Phnom Penh, must be brooding over his accurate forecast, in the 1960s, of the future of his then dedicated kingdom. "Communism is inevitable in Asia," he told a group of us barefoot foreign-devil reporters at one of his last champagne-enlivened morning press conferences at the palace, overlooking the Mekong. "We will have to settle for the role of a Southeast Asian Albania — instead of a Southeast Asian Finland. But we will strive to maintain our name, our flag and our identity."

He always talked frankly and freely, obsessed only by selfish personal anxiety for the peace, safety and happiness of his people. (We newspapermen always received a unique, gracious personal letter from him, thanking us for our presence after we had returned to our bases.) He made no secret of the fact that he then feared and distrusted the communists and the Vietnamese — Hanoi and Saigon alike — more than the Americans and the West.

As he predicted to a visiting German professor in 1965: "When the Americans leave without guarantees of non-communism and territorial integrity for South Vietnam, Cambodia will be face to face with communism along the entire eastern border. This will be very dangerous for Cambodia. For us, of all possible communism, Vietnam communism is the worst."

When in power, he managed to defer the inevitable show down by a skilful policy of circumventing alien internal influences while exacting maximum aid offerings from all alien bidders for their share of Cambodian "neutrality." One of Phnom Penh's main thoroughfares was named Boulevard Mao Zedong. It cut across Boulevard USSR (acknowledging Soviet aid — curious today), which in turn was an extension of American Aid Highway (acknowledging US aid in those happier days).

In his current ordeal of semi-imprisonment in the old palace, Sihanouk at least has the happiness of the presence of his favourite wife (No. 4). She is Princess Monique, the still-lovely Saigon-born, Eurasian daughter of a Cambodian mother and Italian father, who once won a beauty contest in Phnom Penh.

Now 43 — "the ripe fruit is ever the sweetest," they say in Cambodia — she rejects with a shrug (and her husband with a snort) charges by Sihanouk's coup successor, former premier Lon Nol, of bribery, corruption and conspiracy — charges which would have involved the death penalty. In April 1970, when she had accompanied her husband to voluntary communist exile in Peking, she was accused of exerting an evil influence over Sihanouk, of selling ambassadorships, and of "selling land which she did not own to the Vietcong and the North Vietnamese, when the communists established

their strongholds in eastern Cambodia."

"Monique only corrupted Sihanouk with love," to quote a former minister now "reformed" in Cambodia. "Everything in his world centred and centres upon Cambodia and Monique. He wanted to travel elsewhere only to show her beauty to the world." Apparently she still hopes that he will be re-crowned King of Cambodia — he resigned in 1955 to return as chief of state — and that she will become Her Majesty. Improbable, alas.

December

It seems strange that Peking's wall-poster blast for "democracy" has not included a single nostalgic holy-watered evocation of the rosary-bead days when Roman Catholicism was tolerated — if party-adulterated — in China.

This week, coincidentally, was the 20th anniversary of Pope John XXIII's decisive pronouncement that "schism has developed in the Catholic Church in China" and his excommunication of a communist-blessed and "elected" archbishop in Hankow and a bishop in Wuchang. That action determined the Vatican's belated, defensive response to the anti-Catholic crusade which had broken out in China in 1950.

It is estimated that there were 3 million practising Catholics in China at the time of the 1949 "liberation." About 700,000 lived in rural areas. The Catholic clergy then totalled about 12,000, of whom 6,500 were Chinese. Between 1950 (when the Korean War started) and November 1953, the estimated number of foreign-devil priests and missionaries had shrunk from 5,500 to 364 through arrests, imprisonment and expulsion. The drive also proceeded against Chinese Catholic leaders, most of whom were denounced as counter-revolutionaries and spies. Among those arrested was the highly-revered Bishop of Shanghai, Dr Kung Ping-mei.

Comrade Tung Pi-wu reported to the People's Consultative Conference on 11 January 1956: "A clear distinction should be made between followers of religions who commit bad action through being misled by counter-revolutionaries, and the counter-revolutionaries themselves, who, clad in the garments of religion, purposely perpetrate sabotage . . . The Kung Ping-mei counter-revolutionary faction is an imperialist group which carried on planned training and organisation of underground espionage inside the Catholic Church."

It is amusing now to recall that when we religious foreign-devil reporters in Peking were covering the Chinese scene in the 1950s, the "counter-revolutionary" brand for Chinese Catholic priests had been changed to "rightist" and the Vatican's No. 1 listed "offence" was "collusion with imperialism to carry out reactionary policies against the Soviet Union," and then, in lower priority, "against communism, socialism and the new China" (New China News Agency, 12 December 1950).

The broad masses can now argue on Peking's walls that the irreligious Soviet Union is more counter-revolutionary than the Vatican. After all, papal infallibility has at last descended upon a Pole, and Polish support for Moscow is now being compared to party apostasy in Romania. Comrade Ceaucescu may not be a holy Roman but he is certainly closer now to the Vatican and the Forbidden City than to the Kremlin.

When I went regularly to Mass in Moscow in 1955 and early 1956, there were always far larger congregations than I ever knelt with in Peking's solitary Catholic church in 1957. There were fewer locals in the Peking pews, most of the communicants (instructively) were resident African blacks, the two confessional boxes (it seemed to me) were locked against penitents and Chairman Mao's picture hung beside the altar where the excommunicated priest was blessing us.

(I hope I will now be forgiven for recalling that in Peking a couple of non-RC newspaper mates of mine used to accompany me reverently because we could there have a Vatican-cleared background chat with some foreign diplomatic staffers of the same faith who were often evasive or inaccessible in non-worship hours.)

The party-blessed "Catholic Church Reform Movement," which was launched in Sichuan by Chinese "Catholics" in November 1950, initiated the "democratic elections" of Catholic prelates, whom Pope John excommunicated 20 years ago. But no one hears now of that movement.

As Chairman Mao said in his *Principles of New Democracy*, "Communists are permitted to create a unified anti-imperialism line with the idealists or even the religious followers as a political move, but they can never uphold their idealism or religion."

R emote Xinjiang is characteristically back in the news again, coinciding with the official death of Peking's 30-year "peace-and-friendship" alliance with Moscow, and the recent substitution of Chinese for US gunfire in Vietnam. Obviously Peking fears possible uncomradely Soviet intervention along the 2,000-km border of what was once High Tartary as well as across the Siberian border or through Outer Mongolia.

A new reinforced military command has been approved by the party's Central Committee at Turfan in the Altai mountains, northwest of the capital Urumqi and China's nuclear-testing base at Lop Nor. Also, it appears, some of its former border army outposts and Kazakh-Uygur-Tartar settlers have been withdrawn to counter possible Soviet military and espionage operations in what has now become almost a "no-man's land."

Xinjiang — China's largest and most remote province — had its own rebellion, with the creation of a then pro-Soviet East Turkestan state with its own army five years before Mao came to power in China. Peking systematically flooded it with Chinese "volunteer" migrants and hand-picked cadres after 1949, and the Chinese communists, it seemed to me on my only visit to Xinjiang in mid-1957, enjoyed and strengthened friendly relations with their non-communist Mongol counterparts, who had willingly set up one of China's first communes, "Marching Forward," in beautiful alpine country 60 miles west of Urumqi.

Here I had an accidental shadow-interview with the durable Mongol communist, Comrade Ulanfu, who, now 75, has retained his provincial authority in the party, though his senior Uygur comrade, Saifudin (63), has fallen under a cloud since the purge of the "gang of four."

It is now forgotten that in 1975 the Politburo sent — of all people — young Comrade Wang Hongwen, later denounced as one of the gang, to Urumqi, to investigate published claims by the *People's Daily* that Moscow had been "sending spies and traitors openly to incite rebellion and perpetrate armed aggression" in that Oriental Wild West. The results of Wang's investigations were never announced, and today anyway he might be branded as one of the masked leaders of non-Xinjiang treachery and espionage.

I tasted, for the first time, sour and heady mare's milk with Comrade Ulanfu, also visiting, in a *yurt* belonging to a wrinkled, energetic, intelligent, non-communist Tartar, Hasim Sasimbayu, who was headman of the "Marching Forward" commune.

Those *yurts* are precisely the same type of dwelling as those in which the red-maned Genghis Khan lived when he subjugated China, enslaved Islam and terrorised Europe. They are portable tents of thick felt, mounted on and roped to a foundation of sturdy wattle boughs. They are shaped like domes to resist the wind, with an opening in the top through which the smoke from stoves escapes.

Hasim insisted that his non-communist

Xinjiang today: almost a no man's land.

commune was better off because the alien Han communists had moved in, and Ulanfu kept nodding as Hasim paid tribute to improved breeding methods, disease and pest control and the economic advantages of divided labour under Peking's arrangements and guidance.

One speculates as to what extent the current reorganisation of Xinjiang has involved a new search for spies, who have always been a bristling problem in the province whoever is in power. One grotesque spy case, which would have bewildered even Ian Fleming or John le Carré, was the 1938 discovery by a Soviet army intelligence unit (then *persona grata* in Xinjiang and elsewhere in "unliberated" China) that the Kuomintang governor of Yarkand (southeast of Urumqi), a gross northern Chinese, was — unbelievably — a British

"double agent," spying on the Soviet setup in Yarkand. the Russkies seized, questioned, tortured, murdered and secretly buried him in their mission grounds.

Too complicated, I guess, for espionage operations and hunting in Xinjiang today.

April

As a senile ex-Australian army heavyweight boxer (1925-27; 178 lb), I am sentimentally prompted to urge that, in the current exchange of sporting, arts and other representatives between China and the West, an attempt should at last be made to provoke Peking's interest in good old Queensberry boxing. To hell with this bastardisation called *kung fu*, which, I reckon, combines the worst traits of mugging, Siamese groin-kicking, *sumo* and *karate*, and which the Kuomintang is now introducing as "a Chinese martial art" into Saudi Arabia.

I have raised this subject before, brooding over the wasted, inborn talent for heavyweight boxing among the 6 ft, 200 lb-plus Han "shadow-boxers" in north China, which has never been properly developed.

The Japanese, Siamese, Koreans and Filipinos can of course produce excellent flyweights, lightweights and welters, but no heavies. A good foreign-devil coach could train half a dozen potential Han boxers inside a year and set the stage for the appearance of the first Chinese world heavyweight champion in history. Muhammad Ali, who went to Moscow last year, would surely leap at a Peking invitation.

(Last week, my barefoot spies in Peking informed me, two former Olympic Games gold-medallists, Briton Brian Wilkie and American Don Schollander, were exchanging techniques and offering advice on swimming on a 10-day invitation tour of China.)

Peking, now adopting all world sports to defeat the decadent capitalists and hegemonic Russkies, could lead appropriately with the left with the greatest of ease and eventual success. Mao himself, in my opinion, would have made a first-rate boxer around the eve of World War I, when he was 20 and wasting his time reading Adam Smith's *Wealth of Nations*, Darwin's *The Origin of Species* and John Stuart Mill's *Logic*.

He recalled to Edgar Snow in his *Autobiography* (first published 1938) his first defiance of his father when he was 13 and threatened to commit suicide in a pond if his old man, Jen-sheng, tried to thrash him. "From that time on," he recorded, "I learned to use the method of self-resistance to protect myself." What better definition of Queensberry rules could there be? Also significant was his own later "Thought" in 1947: "Courage in combat, face to face; no fear; one step back, two steps forward."

It is now 80 years since the *I Ho Chuan*, or Society of Harmonious Fists, revived that 200-year-old semi-religious society and launched the Boxer Uprising against the resident barbarians. True, they didn't use gloves and didn't observe Queensberry boxing rules. But their uniforms, if too ornate for the PLA, were at least a bright and handsome party-line red, and they knew how to give the knuckle.

That, however, is the only historical challenge which Peking can offer to the Greek and Roman invention of *pugilatus*, and the Pommy Queensberry development in the 18th century of "the noble art of self-defence."

Comrade Plutarch has asserted that boxing was the most ancient of the three gymnic games, whose exponents were divided into the Boxers, the Wrestlers and the Runners. Comrade Homer, my literary friends tell me, justified this order of precedence in the original Olympic Games: first, the man attacks (or defends himself) with the fist; secondly, he closes or wrestles; and, finally, should fear, inferior skill or deficient strength intrude, he takes to

115

the third course and runs. Also, Comrade Plutarch described *pugilatus* as "a discipline, an exercise and an art," which sounds like another Mao thought.

And yet China, advancing from ping-pong and badminton to swimming, running and most other sports, still neglects the noble — or let us now say, comradely — art of boxing. One can only hope that their aspiring role in the Third World, into which boxing has decisively moved, will put the gloves on their formidable Han fists.

Name-dropping footnote: Jack Dempsey, whom I had the honour of knowing and lunching with on my rare visits to New York in the dear dead days when he presided over his Broadway restaurant, always insisted that, correctly trained, a giant Han who did regular "shadow-boxing" exercises could without doubt become a world heavy champ.

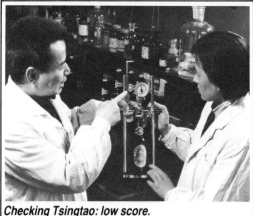

Checking Tsingtao: low score.

July

Sophisticated beer-drinkers will have been astonished by the Peking *People's Daily* claim last week that China's Tsingtao brewery has earned US$57.66 million in foreign exchange between 1971-78. The "modernised" brewery announced a direct challenge to the world sales and quality, specifically, of Carlsberg lager. There must have been smiles in Denmark at that.

The original Carlsberg Brewery had no shareholders but was directed by five professors from the Danish Academy of Sciences, who devoted the profits to art, culture and science. The brewery, uniquely, restored two ancient castles, built a national House of Honour and financed research excavations and scientific expeditions.

Tsingtao, of course, owed its beer birth to resident German foreign-devils. It is an excellent brew, but has naturally never sold well in Australia — too light and too sweetish, as well as non-Aussie — and I have always been served local beers at restaurants in New York, San Francisco, Chicago and Soho Chinatowns.

Let it also be remembered that, at the (only?) beer-tasting competition in the Far East — in Hongkong, two years ago — Tsingtao was rated seventh among the 18 different Asian (including Australian) beers sampled by seven world judges.

Singapore-Malaysia's Tiger beer scored

first place (23 points); Taiwan and Australia (Carlton Draught) dead-heated second (22 points); Japan's Asahi came in third (21 points). Tsingtao scored a mere 12 points. The last were Thailand's Amarit and Vietnam's Beer 23 (six points each). Perhaps Tsingtao should try to develop a beer market in Vietnam — but that is a jest in poor taste, even if the Chinese beer clearly tastes better.

The *People's Daily* report did not give details about China's other expanding alcoholic export — Great Wall vodka, which, one would expect, should be more rewarding than Tsingtao beer. Like the Polish product, Chinese vodka is better than the Soviet.

Beer-drinking, clearly, is becoming locally more popular in Asia. Updated figures are not generally available but, according to recent estimates, the per capita Japanese intake is 70 bottles a year. (Australia's, however, is reckoned to be 180 bottles.)

Asians, anyway, are not persecuted today by the laws of state and church which restricted beer-drinking in the earliest days of Christianity in Britain. In the fifth century, the bishops ruled: "If any monk, through drinking beer too freely, gets thick of speech so that he cannot join the psalmody, he is to be deprived of his supper." And, two centuries later, Theodore, seventh archbishop of Canterbury, decreed: "If a Christian layman should drink too much beer, he will have to do 15 days' penance." Even the "gang of four" and the Deng Xiaoping cadres would never be as severe as that about Tsingtao revolutionary toasts . . .

*He that buys land buys many
  stones;
He that buys flesh buys many
  bones;
He that buys eggs buys many
  shells;
He that buys good beer buys
  nothing else.*
    — Confucius, Mao Zedong,
    or Comrade Shakespeare?

September

The telephone rings in the Pope's Vatican chapel-study. His Holiness rises from his knees before the papal altar and lifts the phone: John Paul speaking. Who is that, pray?

Voice: Pardon me, Your Holiness. This is the Dalai Lama, calling from Gangchen Kyishong — not, alas, Lhasa.

The Pope (*dragging a praying stool under him*): Welcome, my son — (*hastily correcting himself*) — pardon me, I should not of course call you "my son" because of your belief in reincarnation.

Dalai Lama (*chuckling*): Never mind, Holiness, although you are correct. I am of course the reincarnation of Buddha and the 14th Dalai Lama. But let us forget these minor matters. I have taken the liberty of making this call for discussion of a proposal which occurred to me as I prayed this morning.

The Pope *(grasping his rosary beads)*: Pray proceed, Dalai Lama.

Dalai Lama: Like me, Holiness, you, I am sure, have been intrigued by the recent changes and alleged changes in China, and — just as suspiciously as me, I trust — have been brooding over the possibility of turning the commies' baited hooks against themselves.

The Pope *(bending forward)*: The point is made. As you know, we have been compelled again to stress that bishops cannot be nominated and appointed by the local party substitute for the Vatican. That so-called Chinese Patriotic Catholic Association clearly seeks to promote "patriotism" to "infallibility." The Vatican's reaction has naturally led to characteristic party curses which would enforce heavy penance penalties in any normal confessional box.

But we have also deemed it useful to send a couple of Jesuit Chinese priests to China, and, instructively, the party — not just the Patriotic Catholic Association — has deemed it useful to appear to welcome them.

Dalai Lama: We are in complete agreement, Holiness. As you also know, I have — until now *(voice hardens)* — refused invitations to re-visit Tibet, from where I was compelled to flee 20 years ago. But I have also approved the quiet entry into China of a Buddhist mission. They may remain there for several months, touring Tibet and cautiously awaiting Chinese party approaches.

The Pope: Yes, Dalai Lama, I read that in a recent REVIEW issue, which, I assure you, is not a Jesuit publication.

Dalai Lama: Now we know well, Holiness, the craftily propagandistic pressure which will be applied to our mission, assuring us of restored "freedom" of religion. They will be escorted, like tourists, to areas which the party would like them to see and kept away from the areas which they would want to see. We know, anyway, that there are now only about 1,000 monks in Tibet, compared with 110,000 in 1939, and 10 monasteries compared with more than 2,000.

So, Holiness, to my proposal. It occurred to me after my recent visit to the Soviet Union and Mongolia. I have noted your similar interest in increased travel abroad. May I suggest that I announce that I shall accept the invitation to visit Tibet, and that you then suggest that you accompany me, and that we travel together in China as well as Tibet. What would we have to lose? What would they have to gain?

The Pope *(startled)*: A joint mission, Dalai Lama? Buddhist-Catholic — I mean, Catholic-Buddhist? Unprecedented!

Dalai Lama: Precisely, Holiness. If they decline, they will be sorely embarrassed. If they agree, we can sorely embarrass them. You can ask simple but vital questions about Buddhist changes and hopes which I could not ask. I could ask similar questions about Catholicism.

They would have to widen our tour of mutual discovery, to double their team of misleading escorts, and to run the risk of promoting confusion and even quarrels between their alleged Buddhist and Catholic running-dogs when we asked questions which we had carefully and jointly prepared. And we would be laying the foundation of a Christian-Buddhist united front.

The Pope *(uneasily fingering his beads)*: You are very persuasive, Dalai Lama. But I must consult my cardinals. This, I repeat, would be an unprecedented decision.

Dalai Lama: We live in unprecedented times, Holiness. Pray consider, and next time you phone me. May Buddha and God bless us. *(Hangs up.)*

The Pope *(leaning back)*: A shrewd fellow . . . I wonder? *(Lifts the telephone.)* Attendant, what did that call cost him? What! It was a collect call? *(Hangs up.)* Shrewder even than I thought!

October

Last month Japan uncomfortably marked the 56th anniversary of its disastrous Kanto earthquake, which flattened Tokyo before noon on 1 September 1923, destroying nearly 750,000 houses and buildings, killing 140,000 people and injuring another 100,000.

With warning rumbles already from Indonesia and Mt Aso in Japan itself, a sincere cyclical encore of that upheaval must be expected, starting from the beginning of last month. The unruliest and most perverted earthquake areas, it appears, at least observe rhythmic uproar. World rec-

ords show that the average time between major quakes (six to seven on the Richter scale) is 69 years, but with a margin either way of 13 years. So no risks can now be taken in Tokyo.

How risks can be avoided is of course the question. Tokyo authorities, with characteristic Japanese preparedness, have already organised anti-earthquake and — more importantly — anti-fire safeguards in the threatened area. Five months ago, my Tokyo barefoot spies tell me, the government established at a cost of US$30 million "an emergency hotline network linking the main disaster control section with municipal offices, the police, self-defence forces, hospitals and broadcasting stations."

It appears, however, that they have quietly discarded the world's first model of a warning-and-action system that was under consideration in September six years ago. In theory, this invention by seismological experts in Tokyo could automatically sound street and building siren warnings, halt all street and rail traffic in and near Tokyo, cut off oil and gas pipelines, close all petrochemical complexes and raise flood-gates, in the city's canals and rivers.

The maximum warning, however, would have been only a heart-chilling 10 seconds: the time taken for a detected and computer-assessed major vertical-wave shock to travel the 70 km to the city from the Sugamo Bay–area epicentre of the 1923 catastrophe.

The flash-alarm project; which would have cost US$17 million, was shelved — but not rejected — by Prime Minister

Kakuei Tanaka, who was beset with budget difficulties. Also critics had pointed out, reasonably and respectfully, that the proposed warning set-up would operate efficiently only if the epicentre dutifully staged its encore in Sugamo Bay. If it moved irresponsibly nearer Tokyo — like the one which destroyed Edo, as Tokyo was then called, in 1855, one year earlier than the established average — the computers would of course be uninformed, clueless and useless.

But the inevitable looming quake of 1923 intensity will surely create more havoc in overbuilt, skyscrapered Tokyo and, it has been estimated, could kill 300,000. Most earthquake casualties are caused by fire or destroyed buildings and traffic pile-ups.

Also, the spectacular — some say reckless — construction of giant skyscrapers has certainly darkened the future. Formerly, no buildings higher than 12 storeys could be built in Tokyo. Now buildings rise to a height of 40 to 50 storeys because of the acceptance of alleged quake-proof technology, which hopefully uses special steel frames and "slit walls" to counter shock. The theory is that the body or mid-section of the skyscraper merely "sways gently" under impact, while the top and the base "remain relatively firm." "Like a golfer driving a ball," as one Japanese builder put it, "his derrière wobbles harmlessly, while his head and feet remain stationary."

On a 1977 visit to Tokyo, I was in a skyscraper elevator with a dozen Japanese when a minor quake hit us near the 25th floor. The so-called "swaying" was terrifying and the elevator halted. Impressed by the stoicism of the Japanese, I haggardly assumed indifference. Everyone nodded placidly and, sure enough, the swaying ceased and the elevator went into action again.

That's the point for *gaijin* to remember: you lose face if you lose calm in front of Japanese in a quake. I still recall my first error at a press conference in 1940 Tokyo, presided over by the smooth, double-crossing Yakichiro Suma, then head of Japan's Foreign Office "brains trust." A rather sharp quake — my first — shock the fourth floor of the Foreign Office and rolled the water-decanter off Suma's desk. I sprang to my feet in shock — alone.

Suma waggled his finger at me indulgently: "Do not be frightened, Hoojis-*san*. An earthquake is serious only when the ceiling falls in."

Okay, but I still don't want to be back in Tokyo for the 1923 encore.

The fate of jewellery and gold bullion worth US$200-300 million, looted by the Japanese army in Malaya and Indonesia and sunk aboard the fake hospital-ship Awa Maru off the China coast on 1 April 1945, remains a haunting mystery. More than three months have now passed since the Chinese fulfilled their May pledge to restore "the remains and belongings" of 158 (pretty precise) recovered bodies of the 2,000 fleeing Japanese aboard the 11,249-ton cargo-passenger vessel.

Welfare Minister Hashimoto led a mission, including 10 members of families of the dead, to Shanghai in July and received the bodies and "384 pieces of personal belongings, including name-tags, rusted military swords, shoes and fountain pens, in 13 boxes."

A correct half-hour Japanese ceremony was held the same week at the Welfare Ministry head office, and relatives of the deceased were allowed to "inspect and identify" the remains and belongings. Another ceremony honoured the remains when some were placed in a cenotaph at Zojoji temple in Chiba and others in the Tomb of Unknown Soldiers at a Kudan park.

All this detail was reverently reported in the Japanese press, with Hashimoto's reiterated expressions of gratitude to China and pledges of Japan's continued work for peace.

On the hard news side, China's Vice-Minister of Communications Peng Deqing told Japanese reporters that salvage operations by 700 workers in more than 10 boats had been in progress since May 1977 and that no treasure had been discovered — yet. Search for the two missing welded-steel, wardrobe-sized safes, which contain an estimated 2 tons of bullion and precious stones, would continue, if necessary, until next year.

Instructively, that news item was played down in the Japanese press coverage. The media leaders have obviously agreed to build up and polish their Japanese version of the sinking. Their news backgrounding was an explicit denunciation of Washington and the US Navy and an implicit warning of hardening misrepresentation for history.

The facts — confirmed and unchallenged by international sources at the time and fully reported by the world's No. 1 salvage authority, octogenarian Capt. W. Doust, in his classic, *The Ocean On A Plank* (1976) — were that the Awa Maru slipped out of Singapore just before Hiroshima, after having been craftily disguised as a hospital ship by Japanese army leaders, who secreted the looted treasure aboard. All Chinese labour was suddenly expelled from the passenger ship's dock and only Japanese soldiers were used for reconstruction and the loading of 7,000 tons of comandeered rubber, quicksilver and other metals — as well as the loot.

A pious application for a safe-conduct permit was granted by the International Red Cross in Geneva (which Tokyo had not previously recognised during the war) for the Awa Maru's direct return to Yokohama via the then Formosa Straits with non-existent hospital patients, doctors and nurses.

Correctly suspicious, the US despatched two submarines to shadow the ship, brilliantly illuminated and carrying the necessary Red Cross flags and markings, and — justifiably, according to international law — torpedoed it when in early morning it suddenly switched from its approved course in the direction of Shanghai (then still held by the Japanese).

Now the Japanese press suggests and repeats that the Awa Maru was a mercy ship — never a hospital-ship — which had been carrying relief goods to interned Allied prisoners of war in Southeast Asia, and which a US submarine callously torpedoed in abrogation of the Geneva permit.

There is also modest recollection that

Japan decided to waive a justifiable claim for reparations and replacement of the Awa Maru by the Americans "in gratitude for US help towards Japan's restoration and rehabilitation at the end of the war."

In retrospect, the real tragedy is that Capt. Doust, who had been informed by Rear-Adm. William Sullivan, chief of US naval salvage, of the precise location of the wreck, was denied proper support from the British Admiralty for immediate and doubtless successful recovery of the ship and the two safes. That was 30 years before the Chinese at last started to nose around the now corroded and wide-swept wreckage.

If they ever do find the treasure, they are now legally entitled to keep it — even if the Japanese finally reverse their new line and claim sincerely that the loot is theirs and far more valuable than invisible hospital beds.

November

This month is the 35th anniversary of the launching of Japan's unique long-range missile attack on the United States: Operation Flying Elephant. It was a desperate effort by the Japanese to carry the war physically to the US West Coast with huge hydrogen balloons carrying incendiary bombs. Nothing has been officially written or admitted by either Tokyo or Washington about the operation, which many of us barefoot correspondents vainly tried to investigate during the Occupation.

The originator of the Jules Verne–like attack was the eminent Japanese scientist, Sakuhei Fujiwara, who had rejected the theory that the jetstream was a seasonal wind and was convinced that it was "a current of air, with directional stability, whirling at high velocity around the globe during winter months." Operation Flying Elephant — despite the complete and abiding blackout of its results — confirmed the Fujiwara theory.

It had been conservatively estimated that, of the projected 10,000 balloon-bombs planned for the six-month jetstream period (November 1944–April 1945), at least 3,000 would make a fiery landing, hopefully against the forest-mountain regions of the northwestern US, though any that did get across the Pacific could have landed anywhere from Alaska to Mexico. The Japanese scientists and military directors apparently never discovered officially whether a single balloon hit the widespread area.

Each Flying Elephant balloon, with contents, weighed 182 kg: balloon and chassis, 52; flight apparatus, 25; sand ballast, 70; incendiary bomb, 35. The balloons were caught in the jetstream at 10,000 m and then were projected eastward at 200 km to the north, drifting slightly farther north, with the expectation of reaching, and setting fire to, the American homeland in approximately two days and two nights. Because the temperature fell to around 55°C below zero at 10,000 m, intense metal-testing was needed, which resulted in the disappearance of all dry ice in Tokyo for the six-month summer in 1944.

The balloons were inflated with 300 m³ of hydrogen — more than half their total capacity. Lifting-power at sea level was 300 kg. The balloons swelled to total capacity at 4,500 m and floated to the 10,000-m level in 40 minutes. The timing mechanisms on the bomb-releases were set at three to four days, according to weather conditions.

The only known facts of this baffling, baffled and macabre project were patiently gathered by Mitsutoshi Kondo, a tough, amiable economist-newsman, with a pilot's licence, who undertook the investigation in 1964-65 for "Tiger" Saito, then editor-in-chief of *This is Japan*. I had the honour of knocking his thorough and objective documentation into 2,000-word English shape for that now defunct annual (published by the *Asahi* newspaper).

Kondo-*san* interviewed some of the technicians who launched the balloons. At the outset, the launchings took place (from Chiba, Iburaki and Fukshun prefectures) at dawn. It was a near-noiseless operation, in which the harsh crinkling of the stout ricepaper of which the balloons were made could be heard, and then the huge balloons, in eerie procession, arose slowly and silently and soared away into the morning mists. Later there were launchings after sunset under floodlights.

"It didn't seem real," one technician recalled. "We were all silent as we worked and then stepped back and watched. There was no cheering, no demonstrations. You had the feeling that it was a dream, or that you were watching the opening of a festival, and wondered why the balloons weren't gaily coloured and trailing pennants, and why the fireworks weren't being exploded, and why there wasn't a cheering crowd."

In all, 9,300 Flying Elephants were unleashed: November (1944), 700; December, 1,200; January (1945), 2,000; February, 2,500; March, 2,500; April, 400. To repeat: to this day no one in Japan seems to know how many of the balloons completed the crossing; where, if at all, they came down in America; or the extent of any damage they may have caused.

(To pay tribute to Dr Fujiwara: I was told that he was distressed by the prostitution of his scientific research to attempted belligerence and destruction, and that he refused to participate in the exercise unless the windborne Japanese tokens of ill-will to the US were restricted to incendiary bombs and did not include germ weapons or delayed-action high explosives.)

December

Tipplers, drunkards and alcoholics-to-be should all read Dr Margaret Sargent's classic *Drinking and Alcoholism in Australia* (Longman Cheshire, Sydney). They don't have to be Australians to learn, to brood, to reform, to paddle with new restraint or to continue their self-drowning descent into the merciless sea of alcohol after perusal of this deeply researched study.

As an Australian who never tasted liquor until he was 28, and who now — 45 years later — only sips occasionally to reduce grossness and check osteoarthritis, I learned something new, surprising and encouraging in each of this study's 13 chapters.

Basically, alcoholism is non-racial. But it is instructive to discover that few Jews have alcoholic problems, and that "among Christians there are proportionately more drinkers among Catholics and fewer in the 'ascetic' sects of Seventh Day Adventists, Mormons, Baptists and Methodists. But *among drinkers* the proportion with problems seems to be higher in those sects than in Catholics and in the Church of England."

Sargent offers an interesting explanation. She argues plausibly that drinkers belonging to groups where drinking is expected learn how to drink in a moderate and controlled fashion, while drinkers in groups where drinking is not permitted are taught to believe "that controlled drinking is not possible and that all drinking is a vice."

(Myself the elder son of a happy marriage between members of a bigoted Welsh Baptist family and a bigoted Irish Catholic family, I seem to have a useful alibi regardless of whichever path I now pursue . . . No, no — I mean, of course, along the moderate path which I will continue to tread firmly.)

Sargent blames early Irish Catholic influence for the Australian habit of "shouting" rounds of drinks. The term "shout," I have learned for the first time, is a unique Aussie contribution to the English language and is defined in the *Shorter Oxford English Dictionary* as: "Australian slang — to call for drinks in order to treat the bystanders." (It should have added, "and in expectation of their reciprocity.")

"Shouting not only means giving generously but also has a strong under-current of reciprocity and so the male world of the bar is a centre for the symbolisation of equality," Sargent points out.

"By shouting, then, men assert their equality with others in the group and at the same time indicate their acceptance of the others as their equals . . . The act of taking turns to provide generously for the group makes the individual feel that he is participating in the group feeling and activity."

The Sargent theory on alcoholism is that "the production of alcohol and the social pressures on individuals to drink is closely related to the power structures operating within our society . . . We as a society have become alcoholic dependent and have built up behaviour patterns around drinking."

So politics do intrude: "It is not just a matter of people being *permitted* by social attitudes to drink in a certain way; it is rather that some groups are subjected to positive social and economic pressures to drink heavily and get drunk occasionally. Pressures to drink have received scant attention from writers and even less from politicians. Yet it is only by taking strong measures in this area that there can be a reduction in alcohol problems."

In summation, the Sargent recommendations involve community effort, legal control, personal resolution, more sympathetic treatment for alcoholics and the creation of "no-shouting" bars. She would surely have approved last week's unique decision by Irish brewers to spend £500,000 over the next three years in a campaign to induce hard boozers to drink less.

1980 February

Just for the record, the most uncivilised robbers in the Far East, in my opinion and experience, are now Cantonese rogues. The most civilised are the Japanese with the Lao as No. 2. What the hell difference does it make? Quite a lot if you are a foreign-devil victim, whose stolen passport and traveller's cheques (unusable by the robbers) must be laboriously replaced (if possible), and whose personal documents and reference-papers are ransacked and destroyed.

During my 35 years of happy travail in the Orient as a resident barefoot reporter, I have been robbed twice in Tokyo (1948-50) by individual operators, once in Laos (1961) by a gang of two, and now, with my wife in Hongkong, by a gang of three, armed with a meat cleaver and heavy sticks. The Chinese thugs, who evidently were illegal immigrants from Canton, threatened my wife with the cleaver and struck me with a stick when they quietly forced their way into our humble Mid-Levels abode at 3 a.m.

They gagged us and bound our wrists and ankles with wire while they searched the apartment, dragged out all drawers, tipped the contents on to the floor and destroyed or scrabbled all files and newspaper cuttings before they were satisfied that my passport, traveller's cheques, about HK$1,000 (US$200) in cash and my dear Chinese wife's family jewellery were all they could seize to possible advantage. Around 4:30 a.m., two of them crept upstairs — leaving the third to stand guard over us with his stick — and dragged down a neighbour couple, gagged, bound and stripped of cash, papers and jewellery. They quit around 6 a.m.

The instructive and objectively racial difference between this raid and my own earlier victimisation is, I believe, worth recording: when my celibate Tokyo home in Shibuya suburb (during the Occupation) was entered, I suddenly awoke to realise that an intruder was operating. I rushed from the bedroom to the living-room brandishing a walking-stick — too late to prevent the young Tokyo burglar from diving out of the side door and dropping 20 feet into the dark street below. He had stolen all my yen, but had considerately placed my wallet, with my essential papers and passport, on one side.

In the second raid on my next villa, behind the British Embassy, the unknown intruder stole all my yen, in my absence, but he scrupulously preserved my passport, cheques and personal cards, leaving them undisturbed beside my bed. (Good on 'im.)

In Vientiane, a decade later, I was walking back, late at night, to Maurice Cavalerie's Constellation Hotel (the rendezvous for all barefoot reporters in Laos), when an apparently infirm, elderly man asked me in broken English for a cash offering. I indulgently and stupidly produced my bulging wallet, which he grabbed as I was shoved from behind to the ground by an unseen accomplice who had sprung silently from the rear. The pair rushed up a dark lane towards the Mekong and I limped, cursing, to the hotel. An hour or so later, my wallet — minus only the money — was flung into the open public bar of the Constellation by the robbers. (Good on 'em.)

Two other *gaijin* victims of robbery in Tokyo have told me that the personal contents of their wallets — unrewarding, of course, for the thieves but vital for the owners — were quietly tossed into their gardens a night or two after similar robberies . . . "Let us not embarrass you — unless to our own advantage." Fair enough, I guess, in this evil world.

(May I, in passing, pay tribute to the swift and efficient investigation of the Hongkong police, who were on the spot within 15 minutes of our delayed telephone call from the caretaker's office after we had succeeded in unwinding ourselves. Half a dozen sought all possible evidence and helped to tidy up, while another team, with my wife, conducted a swift but fruitless car hunt in surrounding roads. They have since maintained close and patient contact.)

There is a curious time-lag — common it seems to all races — in reaction to these crimes of violence. Chinese friends, who have also been victims of robbery and violence, have told me that their rage — like mine — developed a week or so after the attack. After a once pious retreat, I have now marched furiously back into support of hanging and flogging in the Far East. If flogging were restored as correct punishment for mounting violence in Hongkong, I would happily volunteer to act as unpaid flogger of the Cantonese gang of three who gave us three hours of hell that night.

March

After more than three decades on death row, the most celebrated poisoner in Japanese history, Sadamichi Hirasawa, has just passed into his 89th year. He is still technically under the shadow of the gallows, but has been granted temporary permission to leave his Sendai death-cell — not for a birthday party but for medical treatment.

His awesome crime — indexed in Tokyo police homicide files as *Teigin Jiken* (the Teikoku Bank incident) of 1948 — was unique and as near-perfect as any planned crime can be. It could have been committed only in Japan and could not have been solved except in Japan.

A distinguished Tokyo artist with a respectable background, a happy family and two mistresses, Hirasawa had incurred dishonourable debts. So he quietly planned his mass-murder-robbery, and — unarmed and unaided — coolly conducted two rehearsals before striking the busy Teikoku suburban bank.

He presented himself on 26 January at closing time (then 3:30 p.m.) wearing a white cotton jacket with an armband marked "Sanitation" and carrying a medical kit. He bowed, presented his name card (Dr Jiro Yamaguchi) to the manager, and declared that he had come to inoculate the bank staff against an outbreak of dysentery.

Traditional Japanese respect for authority guaranteed no challenge. The 16 men and women on the staff, headed by the manager, lined up and gratefully drank the prophylactic (in fact, cyanide) which "Dr Yamaguchi" poured into their teacups. Most died in minutes. The good doctor stepped over the writhing bodies, scooped up all the yen in sight (only the equivalent then of about US$800) and quietly let himself out into the busy street. He carefully closed the door behind him.

Ten of the 16 died on the spot; two of the six lingered because they had vomited, but died in hospital. Food poisoning — not uncommon in early occupied Japan — was suspected at first and only after a lapse of three hours was cyanide diagnosed.

Hirasawa was eventualy tracked down by my friend and founding fellow member of the Baritsu Chapter of the Baker Street Irregulars, the redoubtable detective Tamigoro Igii, who checked the Clue of The Fake Namecard. Hirasawa had fatally presented another man's genuine card (Dr Shigeru Matsui) when he made a rehearsal call at another Tokyo bank.

Dr Matsui, by a prodigious effort of memory, recalled Hirasawa as one of the 96 Japanese with whom he formally exchanged cards. He remembered clearly the gentle, modest artist with whom he had swapped cards on the train ferry between Hokkaido and Honshu six months before the crime. Hirasawa-san had been carrying one of his paintings which the Crown Prince of Japan had consented to accept.

Detective Igii traced most of the Japanese who had given their cards to Dr Matsui. He noted that Hirasawa — unlike most Japanese — did not have (or said he did not have) a photograph of himself, and also

that — like many guilty men — he eagerly gave a detailed alibi for 26 January before it was requested.

Hirasawa, Igii then discovered, had financial difficulties. A telegram allegedly from a friend, in payment of "an old debt," was traced to Hirasawa himself. The alibi, under renewed examination, broke down. Then Hirasawa broke down and confessed.

He was duly sentenced to death, but successive Japanese ministers of justice have evaded signing his execution warrant, which must be carried out within five days of authorisation. Japanese ministers tend to shrink from this responsibility not because they are opposed to capital punishment but because they believe that the signing of a death warrant — "ah so?" — leads to personal misfortune.

There has been speculation that Hirasawa might be released, but this now seems unlikely. This is the second time he has been hospitalised. The first was six years ago. He is a relatively pampered inmate of his two-roomed death-cell, where he has continued drawing, painting and composing poems. He has written his own testament:

Death or Life?

It serves you right! Didn't I tell
*   you so?*
Sadamichi Hirasawa is dead.
He is really dead.
Nobody can see him any longer.
He has become ashes, for sure.

Obviously he was a better murderer than a poet.

April

History was happily made last week when two Japanese destroyers peacefully entered Pearl Harbour and their crews were welcomed ashore — in the 39th year after the Imperial navy and air attack which brought the United States into World War II. They had, of course, been participating in Pacific naval exercises in alliance with the US, Canada, Australia and New Zealand and initiating Japan's belated return to essential self-defence.

Appropriately, the reappearance of the Japanese navy in Pearl Harbour coincided with an exclusive report in the *Honolulu Advertiser* of the discovery — at long last — by a Hawaiian university professor of documents giving details of Japan's secret plan to invade and occupy Hawaii in late 1942. The researcher is Professor John J. Stephan, who is fluent in Japanese and has had access to hidden diaries of Japanese army and navy officers.

The tentative plan, Stephan told *Advertiser* writer Tom Kaser, involved "a quickie invasion of the Big Island, a submarine blockade isolating Hawaii from the United States, an all-out assault on Oahu, a disbanding of Honolulu's 'Big Five' corporations, a re-education programme for second-generation Americans of Japanese ancestry in Hawaii — and possibly a revival of the Hawaiian monarchy."

The idea, it seems, was promoted by Adm. Isoroku Yamamoto, brilliant commander-in-chief of Japan's combined fleet, who had been elated by the comfortable success of the Pearl Harbour attack and who, from the outset, had recognised that air power was the key to victory in the Pacific and that, as long as Hawaii remained under US control, the Americans could launch carrier attacks against Japan and Japanese forces anywhere in the South Pacific.

However, as the fighting spread down south, top planners in Tokyo headquarters withheld approval until Jimmy Doolittle's celebrated air raid on sacred Tokyo in April 1942 which, Prof. Stephan points out, "was a terrible psychological blow to the Japanese because it showed that carrier-based US planes could penetrate to the heart of the Japanese empire."

Three Japanese divisions were ordered to stand by for the invasion, scheduled between October 1942 and January 1943. Midway Island was to be occupied first, then Palmyra and then the Big Island. Airfields would be built and a massive submarine blockade of all the Hawaiian islands maintained.

However, the burgeoning scheme was destroyed by the battle of Midway, 5 June 1942, when the Japanese lost four aircraft carriers — and also Adm. Tamon Yamaguchi, one of the strongest advocates of the invasion. A curious sidelight is that, because the Midway disaster was not reported in Japan, the civilian planners continued their long-range programme for developing the food resources of Hawaii and reinforcing Hawaii's fishing industry with fleets of Japanese fishermen.

The Stephan research reveals that the Japanese had been diligently searching for descendants of the overthrown Hawaiian monarchy, so that restoration of a king could be "a front for a nominally independent kingdom that would have been under Japanese control." This would have been in accord with the Japanese creation of a Manchurian monarchy in 1931, when they crushed the Chinese and respectfully welcomed back a descendant of the old Qing Manchu dynasty.

There was also — correctly — concern over the possible reaction of second-generation (Nisei) Japanese residents in Hawaii, who were not expected to shout *Banzai*! to invaders from their old homeland as heartily as the Issei (first-generation) Japanese would. (That concern was certainly justified by the loyalty to their new home in the US manifested by young Nisei in California, many of whom tried to enlist in the US Army after Pearl Harbour.)

Stephen stresses the instructive point — useful to remember today, when some Japanese capitalist leaders are opposing defence spending — that the Japanese military were far more realistic than the civilian planners in dismissing the invasion project after Midway. "Japan's civilian planners still wanted to remake Hawaiian society, restructure Hawaii's economy and keep Hawaii for Japan permanently," he says.

Personal footnote: Stephan, let us hope, is still pressing for unpublished files kept by Shigeru Yoshida, the post-war Occupation prime minister who carried on as elected premier after the Americans left. We barefoot reporters tried vainly during the occupation to check rumours of the intended Hawaiian invasion plan. Yoshida once told me, off the record, when I had the honour of occasionally seeing him while he was preparing his autobiography, that he did not intend to make any reference to "that Pearl Harbour encore notion," because "it would only discredit us." At a brief exclusive interview with Gen. Hideki Tojo, on the eve of his death sentence, I also raised the subject. "I don't know what you are talking about," he said, with a bland smile.

May

Evidently, alas, the Peking Man, half-a-million years old, has not survived his lost, stolen or strayed disappearance in the Yangtse River more than 38 years ago. American millionaire-anthropologist Christopher Janus, who has selflessly spent hundreds of thousands of dollars in his volunteer search for the lost fossils since 1972, has announced in Peking that he has withdrawn his offer of a US$150,000 reward for their recovery. Over the years, he and Dr Henry Shapiro, director of the American Museum of Natural History, have fruitlessly followed more than 300 alleged leads.

On his visit to Peking this month, Janus observed coolly that "for the first time the Chinese said 'thank you' to me." The priceless bones — reminiscent of Pleistocene humans, but neither ape nor man — were unearthed by a Swede and a Canadian in 1926 at Chicken Bone Hill, 25 miles northwest of Peking, and were reverently studied for 15 years by the world's archaeologists at the Peking Union Medical

College, then administered by the United States.

When the Japanese "liberation" began to flow down from north China, it was decided, by agreement between Washington and the Nationalists in Chongqing, to sneak the Peking Man out of Shanghai under the care of US Marines evacuating on the eve of Pearl Harbour. The remains were housed briefly and secretly in the US Marine base near Tianjin and loaded aboard the President Harrison, which ran aground (foreshadowing the Iran muck-up) in the Yangtse on 8 December 1941.

Chinese river-pirates, who wouldn't have known who the hell the Peking Man was, went aboard to loot, the Japanese captured the marines, and the Peking Man vanished. In his idealistic and indefatigable search, Janus went in 1974 to the Golden Triangle — straddling Burma, Laos and Thailand — to try to contact two former Kuomintang generals, then allegedly growing opium in Burma, who were said to have hidden the relics among their poppies but still in the two once-sealed chests in which the Peking Man (really 38 men) had been loaded.

After a futile incursion to Burma, Janus vainly sought Peking's permission to be allowed to visit and inspect the Tianjin area and the old US Marine base for possible clues. The Janus-Shapiro search has attracted continuing claims by two Australian businessmen — one, who said that Manila, where he had been imprisoned in 1975, was the site; and the other, who claims to have smuggled the Peking Man (or "45 of his bones") into Australia and then re-buried him in a Tasmanian rain forest.

("Improbable, my dear Watson.")

The Australian who said he had given the Peking Man expedient sanctuary in Tasmania demanded a Janus reward of US$10 million, and the other, who had been deported from Manila, wanted a return visa but only US$3.25 million. ("Instructive, my dear Watson.")

Most Old China Hands had reckoned that the Chinese pirates, looting the President Harrison, had pro-

Peking Man: 'Deep waters, Watson.'

bably chucked the Peking Man — not photographically identifiable — into the Yangzi, or dragged him and his two coffin-chests into an old cockloft or a river-front cellar. ("No use to us, but hide it and we can sell the chests later.")

But one vital (?) new clue, which would intrigue The Master, Sherlock Holmes, is that Janus had been told by Shanghai Museum curator Hu Chengzhi — belatedly — that the Peking Man had been packed "beautifully and wrapped in velvet" before being sealed in the chests. Surely no river-pirate or Japanese invader would have chucked those contents away. Janus reward or not, couldn't the Peking Man still be alive?

June

Some curious and even embarrassing airmail is reaching my praying-stool — together with a couple of recent phone calls by transient visitors. The inquiries are from old mates and friends of old mates who are going as barefoot reporters to cover the Moscow Olympic Games and who want some suggestions on how to spend rest-and-recuperation days in the Soviet Union, and even to indulge in a possible week's Intourist extension after the games limp to a halt. Doubtless their interest will be shared by other visitors who are ignoring the boycott.

This foreign ignorance certainly reflects the swift, significant and intelligent superiority of the Chinese over the Soviet comrades in encouraging tourism. I have to remind the current inquirers that my superficial knowledge of Russia and Siberia goes back to the late 1950s and the 1960s. But, even under Marxist oppression, the Russian people were (and are) urbane, generous and warm-drinking people; their country is a wonderland, and no foreign devil — if he can sometimes escape the normal, party-line Intourist guides — can be bored rambling around Moscow.

The visiting Olympic enlisted will, of course, be marshalled into new tourist hotels, where they can be kept under surveillance and handled as a mob. But I am urging my newspaper inquirers to use the utmost pressure to have their daily meetings and personal discussions at the Hotel National, the oldest and still the best pub (I have my own contemporary advisers) for visitors in Moscow.

A rambling, Tsarist survival, from whose balcony Lenin originally harangued the populace, it stands on the corner of spacious Gorky Street and Hunters Row, facing the Kremlin, with its 65-ft crenellated red walls, its soaring towers, its flood-lit turrets and domes, and its five one-ton, ruby-red stars floating against the clouds.

This was where we resident foreign-devil reporters used to meet — either in the old bar or in the magnificent suites in which some of us were lucky enough to reside. At breakfast, we respectfully watched elderly party officials guffawing over their carafes of vodka before beginning duty at the Kremlin.

I also recommend that visitors rediscover the old champagne bar above the fruitshop window in Gorky Street, opposite the cable office. That was where the Bulganin-Khruschev newsmen met after filing their copy. (In those days we had to submit three copies of each story: one for transmission, one for the censor's files and one for belated return to the sender, indulgently showing the brutal cuts.)

The major triumph for Olympic visitors to Moscow — newsmen or not — would be successful application for a visit to Siberia. It would be difficult for Olympic visitors — with the time and resolution — to be denied at least a visit to Irkutsk (halfway between Moscow and Vladivostok) and lovely Lake Baikal — where, strangely but officially, "Siberia" ends and, absurdly, the real Siberia is called "the Soviet Far East."

Irkutsk is a gracious, 500-year-old city of log cabins and ancient buildings, trees, parks and university spires. No nuclear base and no reformatory camps — so far. Two hours away is Lake Baikal, the deepest (5,315 ft) and in many ways strangest and most beautiful lake in the world. More than 300 rivers and streams flow into the lake and only one, the Angara, flows out.

Behind Baikal's narrow, ochre beaches and russet cliffs, ridges of pine, birch, larch and cedars rise sharply to the Baikal mountains. The crystal waters freeze in the winter and the shores are regularly but safely shaken by good-natured earthquakes. There are thousands of seals in Baikal, huge sturgeon and a curious, transparent fish which is 35% oil and which literally melts away if it is left in the sun.

On my one and only unforgettable Trans-Siberian Railway trip — from Yokohama (by sea, of course), then via Nahodka, Khabarovsk and Irkutsk to Moscow — I had a simple but memorable lunch of sprats, caviar, black bread and vodka, under a blue sky mirrored in the blue waters, with a debonair Intourist interpreter, who had improbably survived Stalingrad and then marched to Vienna. The fact that his name was Lenin lent an air of historical fantasy to our conversation.

Also, he shared my reverence for The Master, Sherlock Holmes, and I later airmailed him a certificate of membership of the Baritsu Chapter of the Baker Street Irregulars. Alas, I received no acknowledgment and I sometimes brood over the possibility that I may have done him harm with the party by seeking to inveigle him into the only Far Eastern Sherlock Holmes society.

Irkutsk is still a rail and air stopover for visitors to and from Russian — I mean, independently sovereign — Mongolia. It is not on the road to Afghanistan. But visitors receive no tourist encouragement to visit Lake Baikal. If it belonged to China, tourist hotels would be under construction there.

The Russsky comrades are still fearfully parochial. Let Olympic Games visitors — with one foot in the door, at Moscow's invitation — at least embarrass Intourist by demanding caviar and vodka at Baikal.

July

It will be interesting to observe whether old-style Chinese opera or new-style reformed opera dominates the shows which will be presented to audiences on the looming first tour of the United States by a full Peking opera company. Given the new mood of Peking, the old style should be favoured. But will current actors and performers be competent or sufficiently practised to revive the old style? Consider the differences:

▶ Old-style Chinese opera: An emperor, face painted white (denoting duplicity), stalks stiff-legged in imperial yellow robes across the stage while cymbals crash, turns to the audience and announces that he is evil and resolved to achieve his will. The appalling music swells and a beautiful, bejewelled concubine (her face painted green, for passion) slinks in, accompanied by two black banners at half-mast (signifying the arrival of sweet-scented night).

▶ New-style Chinese opera (from the early 1960s): An army officer, his face unpainted (denoting honesty), and wearing the uniform of the Long March, stalks with the same stiff-kneed stride across the stage, while the same cymbals crash, turns to the audience and announces that he is good and resolved to achieve Chairman Mao Zedong's will. The same appalling music swells and a beautiful, uniformed girl commune worker slinks in, accompanied by two red banners rampant (signifying that she helped surpass Mao's production norm).

One can hardly doubt which opera style US audiences would prefer today. And the indications are that the Peking promoters of this unique detente approach on American stages share that view, because so far they have announced the choice of three old-style operas: *The Monkey King*, *The Jade Bracelet* and *The Yan Dang Mountain*.

For foreign devils, a first night at the Peking opera old-style — which had its origins in the lyrics and dances of the Shang dynasty (circa 1300 BC) can be a stupefying experience: brutal music, painted faces, absurd beards, piercing voices, stylized pantomime, blazing colours, legendary plots, and a casual intermingling of stage-hands (supposed to be invisible) with players at dramatic moments. In Western musical theatre, the players sing, dance or act in alternate bursts — not, as in Chinese opera, all the time at the same time. Speech is set to music in Peking, as are all expressions of emotion and character.

I remember one pre-reformation opera in Peking, when a Chinese friend proudly pointed out how effectively the dying coughs of an abandoned concubine, accompanied by the cough-music of scraping fiddles and tiny bells, conformed to the Chinese idea of a cough. "But it doesn't sound like real coughing," I whispered. "Of course it doesn't," my friend snapped, impatient with the gross transparency of the West. "If it did, it would be bad opera."

The only character who is supposed to sing, speak or laugh in a normal manner is the clown or comic (the *chou*), whose behaviour naturally provokes the audience to paroxysms of laughter because it is normal. The conventions of Chinese opera are more often than not something unconventional and illogical, yet strict tradition imparts a kind of logic.

The audience can immediately recognise a character's character by the paint on his face. In general, white represents deceit and cunning; red (fortunately) means loyalty and honour; green means passion and justice; black means cruelty. In case anyone is colour-blind, the actor also introduces himself and his intentions on his entrance in a high-pitched chant, accompanied by monotonous percussion and, at the end, a thunder of gongs.

If an emperor or general intends to mount his (invisible) horse, a stage-hand in the Chinese equivalent of shirtsleeves strolls out and gives him a small horsewhip or tasselled stick. To show that he is riding, the actor prances forward with raised knees, extending the whip. When he lifts it above his head, he has halted; when he casts it on the floor, his horse has been led away.

Certainly *Red Lantern* will not be considered as a possible show on the Chinese opera tour. Jiang Qing — the widow of Mao — took the byline credit for this first "super-opera," into the score of which that Western invention, the piano, was sensationally introduced. This outraged many Communist Party opera buffs, but demonstrated that the revolution could graciously adopt, and rewardingly adapt, cultural ideas from the decadent West. Although Jiang Qing cannot play the piano, it was also politely pretended that she composed "the first piano concerto to portray people's war" — *The Yellow River*.

Chinese opera, communist-style, represents a convulsion of plot and a distortion of character, still designed to harmonise — however grotesquely at times — with the classical formula of the ancient art form. The new performers continue to ape stylized traditions and declaim in the same high-pitched voices to an accompaniment of the same explosive percussion. Yet they are trying to invoke the wisdom of Mao and Karl Marx instead of the wisdom of the celestial gods. Raw wine was poured into old bottles. To repeat, let us piously hope that this first US tour will stick to the old style.

R eports of these new private cooperatives in Shanghai — as industrial extensions of individual trade in family shops — bring back memories of the old "secret factories" which were allowed to operate before the Great Leap Forward (that became the Great Flop Backward) in 1958, and then the suicidal Cultural Revolution.

These cooperatives sound more respectable than the secret factories, though by scrupulous Mao-Marxist standards they are surely deviationist. But clearly they are as necessary as private sideline production by the communalised peasants.

Vice-Premier Chen Yun himself defended Shanghai's secret factories at one of the last interviews I had with him in Peking in 1957: "They are generally doing useful work. They can do things which big plants cannot do — or are too busy to do. Some use up waste material which big plants reject."

Comrade Sa Kungliao, who was then leader of the loyal non-communist party opposition in China's parliament, also endorsed Shanghai's secret factories, as he certainly would today's cooperative factories. A lively and articulate politician and the only Chinese I interviewed in those remote days who wore a Western-style tie, he received me in the handsome quarters of the China Democratic League, a block or two from the Pavilion of Purple Light.

"We can tolerate competition in industry in this happy community just as we approve political freedom, when our non-communist opposition party can consult, discuss, suggest, consider and agree with the communist party," he told me, deadpan. "We are all working together." (I wonder where he is working today.)

So eventually I made my own non-party inspection of one of these tolerated illegal set-ups. I drove with my astute interpreter through the maze of crowded cobbled streets in changed and unchanging Shanghai to a secret factory not far from the Temple of the Jade Buddha.

The secret factory, the owner of which — in those pre-pinyin days — called himself Shin Chun-yung, was not heavily disguised. On one of the stone pillars at the gateway, a cardboard sign — on which someone had scrawled an obscene but non-political drawing — read simply and plainly:

THE SHIN FACTORY
(UNREGISTERED) FOR STRONGLY
MADE PENS.
Forward The Capitalistic Revolution
In Aid Of Socialism!

A policeman questioned my interpreter and bowed to me very politely. "He just wanted to make sure we had the correct address," my interpreter said.

Indoors, we passed some children playing pingpong in the hall, stumbled under a shadowed staircase and entered a dark kitchen where half-a-dozen people were producing the Strongly Made Shin Ballpen. I am no artisan but it seemed to me that the Shin manufacturing technique — secret or registered — was primitive. An asthmatic man in overalls and a cap was operating a wheel with pedals; two boys were compressing tiny cylinders between rolling-pins; a couple of elderly housewives with violet-stained fingers were apparently battering the ends of the completed products with hammers. Strongly Made was right.

No one had the slightest hesitation in answering my questions about the secret and illegal, but known and accepted, industrial complex. Shin, unfortunately, was absent — visiting, it was said, his sick old aunt in Suzhou. (The alibi — as my interpreter needlessly pointed out — should not be taken seriously. The most beautiful girls in China reputedly come from Suzhou.)

The housewives reported that they produced 900 dozen pens a month at a rate of Rmb 7.20 a dozen. The Shin employees totalled 13 — mostly employed on a family basis. They worked eight or nine hours a day and earned an average of from Rmb 50-60 a month. The pens were sold throughout China but chiefly in Harbin — and were not, of course, for export. Raw materials were supplied and distribution and marketing arranged by properly registered and legal party authorities.

Did they support Mao Zedong and like life better now in Shanghai than before liberation? "Of course we do!" the housewives cried. One added: "We are helping the revolution by working here as well as at home."

I asked what taxation was payable on the capitalist profits of the secret factory. "I don't think we need ask that question," the interpreter whispered. He spoke briskly to the man on the pedals and the housewives and then told me that only Shin himself could give the answer.

"He is the boss, you see," he explained as we left, carrying some gift pens. "He is the only one who would know. Capitalism is corruption — whether it is secret or out in the open."

August

A recent rambling column of mine about the non-registered but party-accepted "secret factories" of Shanghai in pre–Cultural Revolution days brought me some letters demanding to know if I had seen any normal, taipan-owned, slave-labour factories there before "liberation." Their point was well made. I have never forgotten one visit in 1940.

I had been rebuked by an Old China Hand in the historic Shanghai Club for having, no doubt arrogantly, asked a Chinese waiter to convey my compliments to the club chef on the quality of his underdone rump steak. We were standing at the so-called "longest bar in the world" (now, alas, gone with the rising east wind). My host, an elderly Pommy with pink jowls and yellow moustache — let's call him Col Marjoribanks — pushed aside my post-lunch glass of Coke (I was only 34 then).

"No, Hughes, you mustn't say that," he told me, pleasantly but sharply. "These fellows tend to get above themselves, as it is." I was taken aback. No tribute to good food and good service?

Later I met a Chinese newspaperman — Wong, we can call him — and asked him if that was typical of the attitude of local

taipans. He smiled sadly: "Col Marjoribanks, you said? I don't know him personally. But commercially he is one of the biggest employers of slave children in Shanghai. Come and see for yourself."

We plunged into a labyrinth of alleys off Bubbling Well Road, past fat moneychangers in their cages, deafening brassbands playing for advertisement at the open windows of silk stores, medicine shops that sold fish-bladders for potency, crowded restaurants with varnished ducks on the counters and legless beggars who whined and plucked at our coats.

We entered a ramshackle wooden building, stinking of sewage and sweat, clambered up a broken stairway and plunged — after a few mumbled words between Wong and a cold-eyed Chinese wearing a skull-cap — into a Turkish bath. That's what it seemed like. It was a narrow, low-roofed, corridor-like room, sweltering in the steam that rose from boiling water running down a long horse-trough in the centre of the workshop.

On each side of the trough, emerging like dwarf ghosts from the steam, were Chinese children — boys and girls of 12, 13 and 14. They were doing something complicated with what I suddenly identified as silkworm cocoons. They were twisting these cocoons in their bare hands in the boiling water. Their sleeves were rolled up. Or they didn't have sleeves. And their hands looked raw.

They didn't stop or turn to look at us. They kept plunging the cocoons in the boiling water, twisting them, flinging them with those terrible little hands into trays behind them.

"Cheaper than machinery, much cheaper," Wong said softly in my ear. "They'll work here for three years before they pay off the money their peasant parents accepted from the contractors. The hot water helps them unreel the cocoons. The foremen beat them with bamboos or slap their faces when they slow down. They get tired, you see, after 10 or 12 hours' work a day."

"Can't they at least open the windows?" I asked weakly, panting and sweating. Wong raised his hands in amazement. "Any breath of wind would spoil the silk threads," he explained. "Besides, didn't John Gunther say in *Inside Asia* that the Chinese never sweat?"

He wiped a fine bead of perspiration from his own high, smooth brow and laid a gentle hand on the shoulder of a small boy, who winced away and flicked terrified eyes in a gray, sweating, old face at us . . .

I saw Marjoribanks later at the Shanghai Country Club, in the snug bar where the double-size oil of Queen Victoria then disapproved of her surroundings. (I wonder where that painting finished up?)

"I was down at one of your workshops today, colonel," I said. He drained his double pink gin. "Not mine, Hughes, not mine," he said. "The Chinese run it for me.

Leave that to them. Very efficient. I never set foot there in my life."

I reckon that best sums up old Shanghai.

October

One of the great modest foreign-devil heroes of the Far East — (perhaps foreign saint would be more appropriate in his case) — is patiently and uncomplainingly awaiting his end in a hospital in Sydney. He is Fr Archie Bryson, who has terminal cancer and perhaps only a few weeks to live.

Now 75, he spent his life since the end of the Pacific War in Japan, Hongkong and Southeast Asia. His friends ranged from peasants to the Emperor of Japan and included Buddhists, Muslims, atheists and every brand of Protestant, as well as Micks of all races. A formidable but genial giant of a man and one-time Australian army boxing champion, he seldom wore a priest's collar, could write poetry — as well as hear confessions (with generous penances) — and was an efficient reporter-editor for the bulletin he published for the Japanese mission of the Missionaries of the Sacred Heart, which he founded.

I first met him in Occupied Japan when he was a chaplain with the United States army as well as the Australian troops and was honoured by the emperor for his services to the Japanese Catholic community and help to all Japanese who wanted to approach a *gaijin* clergyman. Although he never talked about it, he was also decorated by the Vatican.

He had not intended to become a priest. After he left school he began to work as a lawyer. "But then came the Depression," he recalled in a recent death-bed interview in the *Sunday Telegraph* (an old Sydney paper of which I was once the editor), "and I found myself like some gruesome Micawber waiting for people to get into trouble and profiting from it.

"That was the first time I thought seriously about becoming a priest. I had led a pretty worldly life. I never thought I was fitting material for the priesthood. But, thank God, they took me in."

He had founded a Catholic mission in New Guinea and was raising money in Australia for the venture when the Japanese attacked Pearl Harbour. He decided that the only way he could get back to the mission field was to join the army as a chaplain. He did, and combined front-line fighting with front-line Masses.

I had known that Fr Bryson — "Archie," as he always liked to be called (though over the years I, of course have always reverently addressed him as "Father") — had buried and blessed hundreds of Australians killed in action — including two Victoria Cross winners. But, from the *Sunday Telegraph*, I learned for the first time that he had used his boxing proficiency to promote regular Mass attendance near the frontline. It seems that every Mick who wasn't up in time in the morning — even after night raids — and had missed the dawn services in the Bryson battlefield "churches" was invited to explain himself in the ring to the good father, who always carried two pairs of boxing-gloves with him.

Archie Bryson

"I got to know Australians as they really are when I was in the infantry," Archie testified. "I discovered just how fair-minded the Australian soldier is. Maybe a bit of a larrikin when he was out on the grog but when he had a job to do he did it. He might have been a bit of a no-hoper when he was out of the action, but in it he had a morale and even a morality that few achieved.

"Even the blokes who had spent a living hell in Changi and on the Burma railway had a place in their hearts for the Japanese. Sure, the Japanese shot at me many a time but I learned through the Australian infantryman just what forgiveness is."

Let it be recalled that two Japanese whom Fr Bryson converted to the Catholic faith more than three decades ago have already travelled down from Tokyo to bid him a sad farewell and gain his blessing. "I am running out of time and it won't be long now," Archie told them. "Soon I'll be gone and forgotten." Gone, but not forgotten, Father.

Conversion footnote: I always remember Fr Bryson's tribute to converts during our early friendship in Japan, where he was holding aloft the Catholic torch with conspicuous success. "I am afraid that I am a bad Catholic, Father," I admitted. "So — a bad Catholic," he observed, with a tolerant swallow of Johnny Walker black. "Don't you remember what the great G. K. Chesterton once said? G. K. C. was a convert, of course, and therefore more dedicated and devoted than many of us born Catholic faithful. He pointed out that the Protestant always says, 'I am a good Protestant,' while most Catholics say, 'I am a bad Catholic'."

I guess Confucius, Buddha and the Dalai Lama, as well as the Pope, would have shared my approval.

December

As an Australian expatriate since 1945, I am happy to note that the old homeland is marching confidently into the Year of the Cock, with mounting Asian connections.

The Aussie-Japan link, in particular, is being logically strengthened. A scientific and technological plan has been signed between the two ends of the boomerang-judo alliance, and young Aussies and Japanese will now be able to exchange 12-month "working holidays." The youths must be between 18 and 25 — upped in some circumstances to 30. They can take temporary employment — in "a programme to promote mutual understanding between the people of Japan and Australia."

Certainly a happy and mutually rewarding advance since 1940, when I first went to Japan and when — on the eve of Pearl Harbour — there was still no Aussie ambassador in Tokyo and not a single Aussie barefoot reporter in Japan.

The old White Australia policy has now gone with the rising eastern wind. Trade relations with Asean are continuing to expand. Aussie coal is likely to provide a massive substitute for Middle East oil supplies.

Foreign Minister Tony Street, who made a recent "very productive" trip to Asean countries, said: "They need coal and we have the expertise to provide it. It is now up to the Australian private sector to seize this opportunity as well as many others which were apparent during my visit." (Which raises again the speculative query: will Australia and New Zealand ever join Asean?

As already noted, Singapore's Prime Minister Lee Kuan Yew abruptly dismissed the possibility when I saw him last month, though Deputy Prime Minister Sinnathamby Rajaratnam said that it would be a welcome "gradual insertion," and New Zealand Prime Minister Robert Muldoon told me a couple of months ago en route to Peking that New Zealand could well become an Asean member in 10 years' time.)

On the world front (East and West), the number of skilled tradesmen migrating eagerly to Australia is soaring. More than 100,000 should arrive this financial year.

"A large proportion of this increase is workers with skills in demand in Australia," says Immigration Minister Ian Macphee. "What is particularly pleasing is that the increase, including the intake of refugees and the substantial family reunion component, is occurring at a time when overall unemployment levels for both Australian-born and overseas-born are decreasing."

He stressed that the Australian Government was giving first priority to finding jobs for people already in Australia: "Training and retraining programmes are being conducted on a large scale but they do not provide a short-term solution to labour demand in all instances. Immigration complements other manpower programmes, opening up new employment opportunities especially for semi-skilled and unskilled work."

Australia is also generously relaxing immigration regulations to allow victims of the disastrous Italian earthquake to settle with relatives in Australia — a further projection of its immediate contribution to relief work in Italy.

Within 48 hours of the disaster, Aussie relief funds had topped A$700,000 (US$823,000). The Commonwealth Government is matching the states' contributions and has now weighed in with A$500,000.

Earthquake victims who have lost members of their families can join relatives who live in Australia — no selection interviews for spouses, children and parents whose accommodation and initial care are sponsored by the locals.

Special telephone links have been provided to help relatives in Australia contact survivors.

Australia's Anzus alliance with the United States also rolls steadily forward as the Cock crows in 1981. HMAS Adelaide, the first of four new guided-missile frigates being built in Seattle, will arrive in Australian waters around November. Of the other three, HMAS Canberra will complete acceptance trials in February, HMAS Sydney is due for commissioning in January, 1983 and HMAS Darwin in early 1984.

Two Nomad Searchmate aircraft, fitted with high-performance radar and navigational equipment, will also begin operating around northern Australia as part of the government's coastal surveillance programme.

Exports are booming, too. Australian-built motor vehicles and utilities worth A$3.3 million have been sold to Sumatra and Trinidad. And the historic, controversial but again logical decision has been made to allow the export of uranium. Buyer nations will be required to sign an agreement that the uranium will be used only for peaceful purposes.

"The primary objective is to prevent the spread of nuclear weapons," said Street. "Withholding supplies is not the answer. Under these nuclear-safeguard agreements, material will not be able to be diverted without being detected."

Up the Aussies!

1981 January

Ian Fleming and John le Carré would certainly be speculating over the strange return to Kuala Lumpur of Musa Ahmad, alleged chairman of the Communist Party of Malaya (CPM), together with his wife, after nearly 25 years' exile in China (REVIEW, 9 Jan.). There can, of course, be nothing but derision for his claim — endorsed deadpan by Home Minister Tan Sri Ghazali Shafie — that he "escaped by a secret operation."

Clearly his departure was cleared by Peking. But what were the reasons? How could Peking hope to benefit from his retreat home and his televised appeal to his former comrades to abandon their struggle? Ghazali pushed into the hour-long TV-and-radio show with logical support for Musa's attack on the Chinese commies and his sensible warning that Peking could not be trusted. Wouldn't Peking have expected him to take that line?

Of course, the mastermind behind the CPM is Secretary-General Chin Peng (now, like Musa, in his 60s, but, unlike him, a Malaysian Chinese). He is still inflexible and durable, though he has to spend most of his time now in Peking — not with the insurgents along the border.

He was — and apparently remains — an honest revolutionary communist. His real name is Wong Man-wa. He was born in Sitiawan (south Perak) where his father was a bicycle-repairer, and he joined the Grand Old Party when he was 18, on the eve of Pearl Harbour, and became No. 1 party boss in Perak state before he was 20. He prefers to speak Cantonese rather than Malay.

He always insisted honestly to his British imperialist allies in the jungle war against Japanese invasion forces that the wartime alliance was temporary and expedient, and that, as soon as the Japanese were driven out of Malaya, he would direct all his energy and cunning to driving out the Pommies.

Chin Peng's straight-out warning to a British leader of Force 136 in 1943 (then harassing the Japanese occupying troops) has been officially recorded: "We are fighting together now because we both have a common objective — destruction of the Japanese. But of course you understand that our ultimate objective is different from yours. We are aiming to establish a communist republic in Malaya."

Yet Comrade Chin Peng took part in the victory march past King George VI, and — correctly but incredibly — was awarded the Order of the British Empire (OBE) for his jungle services with the Malayan People's Anti-Japanese Army. (He doesn't normally wear the medal, but he has retained it.)

He is a born organiser and not normally a gunman terrorist, though Musa alleged in his TV appearance that in the early 1979s, when Chin Peng suspected that the CPM had been infiltrated, he ordered the execution of all recruits who had joined after a certain date. He plans, administers and fixes. He maintained trusted contacts in key jungle villages in northern and central Malaya, who were never tempted by the £30,000 (US$73,000 at current exchange rates) reward once placed on his head when he was moving between Peking and the jungles.

When they retreated to Peking early in the 1960s, Chin Peng and his wife left behind a son and a daughter, who must now be in their late 20s. The children had remained with their grandparents when daddy and mummy were in the jungle. No one seems to know where they are now or what they are doing.

Unlike Musa, Chin Peng could smell out treacherous party operators. He exposed, with genuine and bitter sorrow, the unprecedented treachery of the first secretary-general of the CPM, Comrade Loi Tak, who organised the party after secret consultations with the late Ho Chi Minh in Hong-kong in the 1930s.

Loi Tak warranted a role in an Ian Fleming or John le Carré adventure. He collaborated with the Japanese in Singapore, when he was allegedly leading the local commies against the invaders. Well-rewarded, he directed the arrest and execution of many party members. Several times he was personally presiding over committee meetings raided by the Japanese but providentially he managed to escape through an unguarded exit. Chin Peng unmasked him after patient, documented research.

Yet Loi Tak succeeded in absconding with the party funds before Chin Peng moved in. He is supposed to have escaped via Hongkong to Bangkok, but my barefoot spies tell me that he was eventually located there and eliminated by honest Chinese party boys.

All this confused and confusing CPM background does not help to resolve the Musa mystery. Surely the Chinese consulted Chin Peng before allowing Musa and his missus to make their "secret escape." Even if Musa, incredibly, planned that successful evasion of his Chinese protectors, after underground contact with the Malaysians, he would have had to fool Chin Peng.

Why would Chin Peng have reckoned that the CPM could gain anything from the preposterously disguised "escape?" Have the Malaysians brooded over the possibility that Musa may have come back as a double agent?

February

By unrelated coincidence, Chinese influence — certainly divided — shares responsibility for the death of historic capitalist landmarks in London and Sydney.

The more elegant victim was the 18th-century Chinese embassy in London's Portland Place, consisting of two neighbouring houses designed by the celebrated London architects, the Adam brothers, and doggedly protected by the Historic Buildings Committee of the Greater London Council until ignominious defeat last month.

According to one of my papers, the *Sunday Times* of London, the Chinese originally established a diplomatic presence in one of the buildings, No. 49, in 1870, then spread into the twin, No. 51, after World War II. After Westminster switched recognition from Chiang Kai-shek to Mao Zedong, the Chinese occupants demanded demolition of the building.

A senior official of the Greater London Council says that pressure was applied for more than a decade to induce the Chinese, under London law, to maintain the property in good repair, but "after intimate discussions between the Department of the Environment and the Foreign Office, it was decided that, in view of the diplomatic situation and the sensitive nature of the Chinese, it would be expedient not to be too hard on them."

The confrontation persisted. The Chinese continued to complain, to reject local basic safety-maintenance obligations and to demand reconstruction. The Foreign Office tried to persuade the council's authorities to surrender, raising the issue of "diplomatic immunity." So a sullen compromise was reached. It was agreed that the frontages would be retained but the interiors replaced.

Alas, it was then too late. Irresponsible Chinese lack of maintenance had undermined the ancient structure and the whole embassy has now been demolished. The question is: will the architects try to build a replica frontage on the site? Can the Pommies be as stubborn as the commies?

There is a private member's bill before the House of Commons urging stiffer penalties against owners or occupants who neglect or demolish historic London buildings. Conservative MP John Heddle has said: "There is nationwide concern at the growing number of cases involving the sudden demolition of listed historic buildings, both large and small, urban and rural. We must strengthen the penalties to protect these buildings."

Doubtless that embarrassing question of alleged "diplomatic immunity" will be reraised. The Foreign Office has already denied — with a pious cough — that it was an influence in restraining insistence on Chinese renovations and repairs.

The Sydney landmark — lost psychologically, if not physically — is a humbler casualty. It is the old Trades Hall Hotel, built at the corner of Sussex and Goulburn Streets in the 1890s. It has long been the unofficial meeting place for Labor Party MPs and trade union bosses and many important Australian policy decisions — state and federal — were made in its parlours. We barefoot reporters were often able to pick up front-page stories from relaxed drinkers at the comfortable central bar.

Then — believe it or not — Women's Lib moved in.

The Chinese takeover was indirect — though also feminine. In 1979 the building and its drinking licence were bought by Eleanor Grassby, wife of the Commissioner for Community Relations Al Grassby, and her partner, Judy Tuck — the first woman proprietors in its history. They put it up for auction a couple of months ago, and — again, believe it or not — it was bought by Hongkong's irresistible Sally Aw, who will now convert it into a presumably teetotal office for a welcome Australian edition of her newspapers for Overseas Chinese.

One wonders how long it will take for visiting unionists and Labor politicians to accustom themselves to another reliable and recommended Sydney pub for their comradely exchanges. Maybe they will go to one of the two oldest bars in Sydney (still operating, I hope): the Lord Nelson, built as a private house in 1834 — 20 years before the birth of Sherlock Holmes — and then enlarged and licensed as a pub in 1843; and The Hero of Waterloo, a three-storey, sandstone building across the road from a church, and licensed in 1845.

Just for the record, as old institutions disappear, let us recall that the oldest "continuously licensed hotel building" in Australia is Hobart's Alexandra Hotel, originally called The Hope and Anchor when it was built before 1814, but renamed after King Edward came to the throne in 1910.

Why do the Aussies, with their convict background, still nurture their Pommie links and memories?

March

This Year of the Cock is becoming the Year of the Cocked Pistol in Australia. United States President Ronald Reagan's basic policy of expanding defence expenditure is being copied by Prime Minister Malcolm Fraser. So are systematic measures against possible Soviet intrusion.

Hence the recent Canberra reaction against Soviet Ambassador Nikolai Soudarikov's undiplomatic threat that Australia could become a nuclear target if US facilities in Australia were strengthened and B52 bombers allowed to land there. There have already been demands that Soudarikov should be kicked out, and — related or not — increased surveillance of the movement of Soviet citizens in Australia will be enforced, belatedly matching the restrictions on all foreigners visiting the Soviet Union.

All Soviet citizens — not merely diplomats, officials and businessmen — will now have to supply Australian immigration authorities with a detailed itinerary before their arrival and notify any changes. (I well remember the annoyance of having to get permission even to visit Leningrad when I was first in Moscow in 1955-56 and again in 1963.)

Aussie former senior intelligence officer Bob Mathams has warned a parliamentary defence committee that the US facilities at North-West Cape and Pine Gap would certainly be Soviet nuclear targets if the superpowers went to war. Australia, of course, can stop US access if it stupidly wants to make a mockery of the Anzus (Australia, New Zealand, US) pact, but Mathams pointed out that, apart from the advantages of a US presence on Australian soil, the bases give Australia a first-hand insight into US intelligence.

Last month, Australia at last began to build a Defence Force Academy in Canberra, designed to provide an education system to enable the navy, the army and the air force to operate together as a united Australian defence system. The system had been proposed in the 1960s but we stupid Aussies take a long time to get things moving — except at two-up and horse-racing.

"The need to establish an integrated training system for the three services stems from recognition of the need to set up one concerted, committed, hard-hitting and effective defence force," said Fraser. "The responsibility for national defence and for an independent national contribution to the security of our allies and friends places new and taxing demands on the personnel of our defence forces, and particularly on its leaders." ("Taxing," I guess, is the operative word.)

Australia has also acquired its second guided-missile frigate, Canberra, from the US. The first, Adelaide, unhappily ran aground off Seattle in January on an initial trial run but has now been returned to service. A third frigate, Sydney, will be built in 1982 and a fourth, Darwin, in 1984. (Why no Melbourne? That is where I was born.)

On the happier economic — but still self-defensive and anti-Soviet — front, Australia is improving relations steadily with Asean and China. Australia has suffered undeserved criticism too long for alleged protectionism. Asean exports to Australia have been rising at an annual rate of 35%. Developing countries' share of total Australian imports rose by nearly 50% between 1973 and 1979. In that period, Australian imports of manufactured goods from the developing countries increased by more than 400%.

"On a per capita basis," Fraser has pointed out, "the US is the only developed country which imports more manufactured goods from developing countries than Australia does. No country imports as much as we do of textiles, clothing and footwear. And we are going to increase those imports." He claimed that a new system of preference for developing countries would give them a significant advantage in increasing their share of the Australian market.

"These facts and figures," he insisted, "make nonsense of the image of Australia as a country dug in behind protectionist ramparts and indifferent to the needs of its Third World neighbours."

Australia is now pushing a non–"White-Australia" and non-ideological campaign to provide China with technological advice and equipment and to train Chinese students in Australia. Agreement has been reached, the Foreign Affairs Department reports, on assistance with land development, forestry and agriculture. Other activities will include the natural sciences, civil engineering techniques, health and English-language tuition. (Shouldn't that be "Australian" language?)

Sad footnote: Alas, my personal hopes for an ultimate constitutional merger between Australia and New Zealand and under the name of Anzac (Australia–New Zealand Allied Confederation) are fading. Aussie Minister for Primary Production Peter Nixon (no relation to Richard) has told the Australian Agricultural Council that "closer economic ties with New Zealand would be unfairly disadvantageous to Australian farmers." He complained that those ties "might affect potato, bean, pea, mushroom and dairy industries." Surely parochial, when Australia is encouraging the arrival of B52 bombers?

April

On the 39th anniversary of the fall of Singapore, there has been some Fleet Street argument over the details of the surrender and the behaviour of the British commander, Lieut-Gen. A. E. Percival and his Australian partner, Lieut-Gen. H. Gordon Bennett.

These two comrades — both brave men — unhappily fell out. Bearing the shame of the disaster, they died in retirement in the 1960s. Perhaps the basic facts — now blurred and often forgotten — are worth recalling.

Gen. Percival was responsible for the initial failure to prepare defences along the northern shores of Singapore, facing Malaya, because he argued — strangely — that their construction, as the Japanese were hurtling down from Siam, would "lower morale among the garrison forces and civilian population of Singapore."

In his classic *Sinister Twilight* (Collins, 1968), Noel Barber says: "Percival seemed to combine all the opposites in human nature. He had considerable personal charm, if one met him socially, but an irritating stubbornness in front of a military map; a completely negative, colourless personality when dealing with a group of men, but a career at staff college which had been brilliant. He had an ability to work out military schemes which looked excellent on paper, but which somehow frequently got bogged down in practice."

Certainly his superior officer, Gen. Sir Archibald Wavell, commander-in-chief of ABDA (American, British, Dutch, Australian) Command, was appalled when he discovered the lack of elementary fortifications in northern Singapore on his first arrival in January 1942.

The Japanese had pushed down from Siam through Malaya in 70 days — an extraordinary average of nine miles a day. Gen. Domoyuki Yamashita was assembling three crack divisions — the Imperial Guards, the 5th and 18th divisions — with strong tank units and more than 200 aircraft against a paperstrong force of 85,000 British, Indian, Australian and Malay troops, with many of the Australians untrained and poorly armed, and only one token squadron of Hurricane fighters.

Percival also made the vital error of assuming that the Japanese would attack the northeast coast, where he dug in most of his defence force. The Japanese invasion on the northwest was crushing. Their air attacks were devastating. The Prince of Wales and the Repulse were sunk. (Churchill had insisted that they arrive, though they lacked air cover after the carrier Indomitable had gone aground.)

In a cable to Wavell, Percival hinted at possible capitulation. But Wavell ordered immediately from Java: "You must continue to inflict maximum damage on the enemy for as long as possible, by house-to-house fighting if necessary. Your action in tying down the enemy and inflicting casualties may have vital influence in other theatres."

But, despairing, Percival trudged to an interview with Yamashita, with three staff officers carrying an unfurled Union Jack and a white flag, at 4 p.m. on Sunday, 15 February. After vain attempts to secure "conciliatory terms," he signed an unconditional surrender at 6:10 p.m. His final signal to Wavell was: "Owing to losses from enemy action, water, petrol, food and ammunition practically finished. Unable therefore to continue the fight any longer. All ranks have done their best and grateful for your help."

The tough, red-headed Australian commander, Gordon Bennett, had agreed that surrender was inevitable. He had earlier privately cabled to Australian Prime Minister Curtin in Canberra that he intended to surrender "to avoid further needless loss of life." He then made secret plans to escape personal surrender and prison-camp internment and to sneak, via Sumatra, to Canberra, where, to his dismay, he was given a cold and hostile reception by the Chief of the Australian General Staff, Gen. Sturdee.

After the war, Percival wrote to the Australian Army Board, denouncing Gordon Bennett's escape and demanding a judicial inquiry. The finding was that he should have remained with his troops "until surrender was complete," but that his escape was "inspired by high patriotism and by the belief that he was acting in Australia's best interests." (He retired from the army and died of a heart attack in 1962, aged 65.)

Less fortunate was the Australian commissioner in Singapore, Henry Bowden, an elderly but tough diplomat, who was aboard a refugee ship that was seized by a Japanese patrol boat and taken to Banka Island. Correctly claiming diplomatic immunity, Bowden angrily remonstrated with his guards, two of whom punched and threatened him with bayonets. He re-

mained aggressive, and finally the guards dragged him out, made him dig his grave and then shot him.

During his camp internment, Gen. Percival admitted to Brig. Ivan Simpson, who had been director-general of civil defence, that he had been wrong in failing to build up the defences of Singapore immediately after his arrival.

Simpson wrote later: "Percival was the only one of all the senior men to admit that his decision on defences had been wrong. That goes a very long way to expiate his first error as the general who was expected to fight to the last man without any air or sea power."

Percival, lonely and broken, died in 1966, aged 79.

May

Old ghosts and old memories were happily on the march this month when the Foreign Correspondents' Club of Japan celebrated the 35th anniversary of its foundation at No. 1 Shimbun (Newspaper) Alley in May 1946. It was a crowded reception and dinner on the 20th floor of a Yurakucho building — the third location to house the cultural body after it quit its ancient four-storey brownstone building in Shimbun Alley.

I was specially grateful to be there because I had been — absurdly — the alleged "manager" of the club for nearly two years (at US$80 a week), when I had had a row with my then Sydney boss and was out of a job. Gen. Douglas MacArthur had requisitioned the dilapidated, rat- and cock-roach-infested premises, of which Mitsubishi were the owners and landlords, and helped indirectly to gouge ¥285,000 (quite a large sum in those days) from them for essential renovations.

The club now has a membership of 250 correspondents and 2,000 associates, with a patient waiting list. It is still run by Mitsubishi, who make a good profit, and is one of the best clubs I have ever known, still with some of its original staff, including the present manager, Washida-san; the unaging Chinese accountant, Mr Ling; Mary, the best bilingual telephone receptionist I have known, and a dedicated bar and waiting staff. (No one, alas, seems to know where Akimoto-san, the No. 1 bartender, has gone.)

All the Old Hand members still based in Japan were there, of course. So were British Ambassador Sir Hugh Cortazzi, and Australian Ambassador Sir James Plimsoll. United States Ambassador Mike Mansfield sent a warm message of goodwill, deploring his absence in Washington.

It was regretted that there was no one there who could play on the piano *Sioux City Sue*, which had been the theme song of the Japanese band in 1945. But a huge, blown-up photograph of No. 1 Shimbun Alley (discovered by master of ceremonies Karl Bachmeyer) towered above the top table — showing the tiny stone Shinto shrine on the roof which I managed to save from destruction by one demented correspondent who tried to tip it into the alley, and also the neighbouring building which had then been a dormitory billet for ladies working in the Soviet occupation set-up.

They never drew blinds across the large windows of their bedrooms and bathrooms. Our club's Room No. 7 on the fourth floor surveyed these windows and was always a popular gathering-place for members who, hidden by transparent curtains, preferred to breakfast there rather than in the ground-floor restaurant. (Today, there are no such carnal distractions. On a clear day — regrettably not during my visit — club members can survey Mt Fuji from the bar and reading-room windows.)

Tokyo knows how to run happy and flourishing clubs. Two other clubs which I had joined on my first visit in 1940 are flourishing: the resilient Tokyo Club (whose members are officially forbidden "to discuss business, politics or religion") and the luxurious American Club (still a neighbour of the now sky-scrapered Soviet Embassy). I paid my humble respects at both those clubs, where old members with astonishing memories are always waiting.

In the old days, all Russky FCC members were amiable and popular and we never had a political row — only brawls among drunken non-Russky members. The club now — correctly — has correspondent members from Peking as well as the Russky members. However, neither group mixes often with the capitalist boys and, of course, they are never seen together. They usually arrive in self-contained groups. The reporters from Taiwan, happily, remain there in full strength.

As an ignorant foreign devil, I once committed an egregious racial blunder by sacking two Japanese kitchen-hands when I was supposed to be manager. Roast beef was suddenly and unexpectedly "off" half-way through a crowded lunch session — so a pretty and efficient little waitress told me in apologetic surprise. I went into the kitchen and detected two servers — red-handed and greasy-handed — who had secreted three joints of beef in a large container to smuggle away. They offered no defence and remained expressionless and silent when I sacked them on the spot.

After lunch, the little waitress approached me, bowed humbly, expressed deep contrition for the affair and announced her resignation. I gave her distracted and near-apoplectic assurances that no one suspected her of the faintest complicity or even knowledge of the affair. Had she not reported the strange withdrawal of the beef to me herself?

But she left quietly and with great dignity and I could never find out where she went, or what happened to her in a city then singularly deficient in respectable employment for young women. Of course, she was right and, of course, I was wrong. I was a goddam foreigner, a *gaijin*. She was a Japanese. I had sacked two Japanese, and she, a Japanese, had been involved, however innocently.

"It would have been okay if you had told me to sack them," explained Kay Kawana, my alleged Japanese aide, who was the real manager. We reflectively recalled the incident at the 35th anniversary. He is now boss of the Miyako hotel chain in Japan.

Anyway, a toast to No. 1 Shimbun Alley's next 35 years and I hope to be there in 2016.

June

(My barefoot Aussie spies have at last smuggled to me a tape-recording of one of Prince Charles' bugged Australian telephone conversations with Lady Diana. Confidential, of course.)

Charles: G'dday, me old Sheilah. Owyer-goin, sport?

Diana: I beg your pardon? Who is that speaking, please?

Charles: Sorry about that, old bean. One rather gets carried away when one is with people who speak like that every day. But there was something special one wanted to say to you. And please, please not a word to Mater about it.

Diana *(hesitantly)*: Charles, you haven't done anything . . . foolish, have you?

Charles: Foolish? Whatever do you mean?

Diana (*brokenly*): Well, one has seen pictures in *The Times* of you with some rather, er, buxom Australian ladies and you were, um, kissing them, if you know what I mean . . .

Charles: Know wot yer mean, sport? Too right I know wot yer mean. There's Sheilahs around here that could knock yer eye out at 50 yards (*breaks off suddenly*) — no, really, old bean, there is something jolly important one wants to ask you: would you like to start married life down under, as it were?

Diana: Down under?

Charles: Yes, a little home in God's own country, in the outback, beyond the black stump. In short, Di, one would rather like to be governor-general of Australia.

Diana: But, Charles dearest, from what your father was saying before you left about "bloody cow-cockies" and from what you said about the terrible conditions in that horrible school I'd never have imagined you would want to live there — and so far away from Harrods, too.

Charles: Yeah, but that was before I'd seen the Sheilahs — I mean before one had seen the scenery. Quite beautiful, it is. And one can get a good steak and a bottle of excellent wine here. It's not all Fosters and meat-pie floaters. (*Firmly*) Besides, it's time one showed the flag around here. For too long they've been allowed to get along with native governors-general — sacking prime ministers is not good form, after all, even if the prime minister in question was a parlour-pink. Now some of them are even talking about republicanism, though who they could find here that would make a president one couldn't guess at. What they need is a touch of royalty, a bit of the old spit-and-polish, parades in full regimentals, that sort of thing.

Diana (*still unconvinced and uneasy*): Australia is so far away, dear. I had sometimes thought that, if we wanted an outside post until your mother retired, it might have been useful for you to be appointed perhaps governor of Hongkong. More important and useful, darling — involved with China, Japan, the United States, Southeast Asia.

(*Long pause while Charles ponders.*)

Charles: Dash it all, old thing. That's not a bad idea at all. One seems to remember hearing talk at home that the chap they have there at the moment . . . chap about nine feet tall . . . is about to hump the bluey back home to Scotland. And one has always fancied a touch of the chicken chop suey. Starve the lizards, Di, that idea's a cracker.

Diana: And I've seen pictures of the governor's mansion in your granny's family album. It does look lovely, Charles.

Charles: Yeah, bonzer. And one's uncle has a very good tailor there. And to cap it all, there's free membership of the Hongkong Club thrown in with the job.

Diana: But, Charles, haven't you heard? The Hongkong Club is no more. They're pulling the place down and making it into an office block.

Charles: Really? What dashed bad luck. Come to think of it, Hongkong's the sort of place where they're likely to pull down the governor's mansion and turn that into an office block. And in 16 years one would be likely to be out of a job in any case. Maybe one should stick with down under. It's better than a poke in the eye with a burnt stick.

Diana *(rallying)*: Dearest, wherever you go, there go I, as my stepmother's mummy would say. And, naturally, I won't breathe a word of this to anyone. I know now as well as you do how gossip spreads up and down Fleet Street. And you are being careful there, aren't you?

Charles: My oath, Diana! The more two-up one plays here, the more careful one becomes. No one will be able to boomerang one in the back.

Diana: And you are sure that this conversation couldn't possibly have been tapped and taped?

Charles *(laughing)*: Not at all, old thing! One can always trust the Ockers . . .

July

The problems of non-English-speaking immigrants to Australia are vividly illustrated by the story of 34-year-old Thong Souk, who came to Australia from Laos five years ago and worked happily and efficiently in a suburban factory, where his Aussie fellow-workers naturally taught him to swear in native fashion.

Then one day, confusingly and accidentally, he was ordered to do one job by his foreman and another job by his supervisor. Using some of the words he had become accustomed to hearing and repeating in normal and friendly conversation, Thong wrote in the log book a protest to the supervisor. "Many words beginning with the letters 'f' and 'c' were used," according

to the New South Wales conciliation commissioner, who heard Thong's appeal against dismissal for what was denounced by the supervisor as "an abusive and insulting message." (He could certainly have said "obscene.")

Thong's indulgent foreman argued that swearing was prevalent in the factory. He said that even the supervisor who sacked Thong "swore in a jocular manner." He said that he had been surprised at the words he had seen in the log book because "Thong was friendly to everyone and a good worker." The factory manager criticised neither Thong nor the supervisor. "It would be futile to stop swearing on an Australian factory floor," he said, "and there are no written directives for it to stop."

In a civilised judgment, the commissioner recommended that the firm should take Thong back on a three-month trial after he had submitted a written — and non-obscene — apology to the supervisor. Both the manager and Thong happily accepted the ruling and Thong is back in the factory — talking and not writing. (The Lao are always reasonable and adaptable — at least under non-communist rule.)

The unique case concluded with an ethnic and immigration studies conference at the University of New South Wales, which discussed an appeal by the Australian Council of Trade Unions for non-English-speaking migrants to be given a programme of tuition. The migrants asked that they be given 900 hours of English (Australian?) instruction in the first two years of their arrival. This would consist of 300 hours in the first 10 weeks and 600 hours in the following 21 months.

151

Meanwhile, there are still an estimated 400,000 migrants in Australia who cannot speak English. The chairman of Australia's Ethnic Affairs Commission, Dr Paolo Totaro — an Italian who came to Australia 18 years ago — says that there was then "no tolerance whatever and in-built Australian dislike of foreign food, foreign neighbours, and hearing a foreign language spoken in a public place."

He believes there has been a marked improvement — as "White Australia" parochialism was discarded. "Sydney is one of the most cosmopolitan cities in the world and we are definitely moving in the right direction," he told the conference. "There is an amount of soul-searching among Australians that would have been unthinkable 20 years ago."

Community Relations Commissioner Al Grassby agrees and says that recent surveys show that "80% of the population reject any form of racial discrimination." He believes that the communities still subject to "intolerance and bigotry" by the Australian majority are Jews, Asians, Irish, Italians and Greeks.

Grassby made a point which I had forgotten: "The Australia of 1981 — with the sole exception of Israel — is the world's most diversified country. Its people come from 140 different ethnic backgrounds, speak 90 languages at home and practise 80 religions."

Neither he nor Totaro objects seriously to ethnic jokes — exchanged by friends of related by stage comedians. "The ethnic joke is usually harmless," says Totaro. "It's in-built in language and traditions and you have to take it with a sense of humour."

"Tell them to your friends with a smile," Mr Grassby recommends. "The difference is between genuine jokes and those simply to degrade others . . ."

Holt

As for myself, as a lazy, ignorant Aussie who has lived and worked in Asia for 36 years, I have the safest defence whenever anyone asks me how many Asian languages I have learned. "Why, I don't speak any," I reply with Australian cockiness. "As an Australian, I haven't yet learned to speak English."

Still on English (Australian?), when the late Harold Holt, then prime minister of Australia, visited Aussie troops in Vietnam, an elaborate — if highly irreverent — welcome was prepared for him. As he passed along a double line of Vietnamese workers, soldiers and tradesmen associated with the camp, these worthies shouted what they had been taught to believe were loyal addresses but which in fact, if listened to, urged the Almighty to bestow blessings on Holt which would certainly never be ordained by heaven.

Holt blanched at such blasphemies and, turning to his escorting general, said crisply: "I need a drink after that." So into the officers' mess they went, only to be greeted by the Vietnamese barman (standing stiffly to attention) who shouted out:

"Good morning, prime minister. How are they hanging?"

Holt — no spoilsport — replied: "Like a well-packed suitcase, thank you, barman." Then he turned to the officer with him and said ominously: "I'll have a word with you later, brigadier."

November

When and where was the world's first daily newspaper published? Alas, my own honourable and venerated — if, alas-ser, still not profit-making — paper, *The Times*, is not in the running. The contest, surprisingly, is between West and East: Europe or Korea.

There is, not unnaturally, some confusion about who produced the first newspaper in Europe and where. As early as 1513 a news pamphlet appeared in England giving stop-the-presses news of the battle of Flodden Field. But it is generally agreed that the first regular newspapers did not appear until the beginning of the 17th century. According to the Encyclopaedia Britannica, possibly the earliest was the *Nieuwe Tijdingen* (an early example of newspaper tautology: who would print old tidings?). This was published in Antwerp from about 1605 onward. There were also several early German newspapers, among them no fewer than three called the *Avisa Relation oder Zeitung*, published in 1609.

Up to now, the claim to the first daily newspaper has been firmly in Europe, my own belief being that German capitalists

The Times *of 1805: not in the running.*

were the first with the *Leipziger Zeitung* published in 1660.

Again, according to the Britannica, Japanese newspapers began early, the first known being in 1615, describing the battle of Abeno Osaka between the forces of Tokugawa Ieyasu and Toyotomi Hideyori. Interestingly, these early broadsheets were called *yomiuri kawara-ban* — *yomiuri* meaning "selling by reading out loud" — which has an echo today in one of Japan's biggest journals, *Yomiuri Shimbun*. However, there is no evidence that these Asian efforts were in any way regular newspapers.

But the German claim is under respectful challenge by South Korean scholars, whose rival daily entrant allegedly beat Germany's on to the streets by nearly a century, but was selling for only three months in 1577. Its brief survival was not due to poor sales but to regal suppression. It had an executive staff of more than 30 and His Majesty's basic anger against its "reportage of official court gazettes from Korea and China" was obviously spurred by its popular interest and sales.

The Korean case is based on *Chronicles of the Yi Dynasty*, which described the publication as "a printed daily newspaper" and indicated that it was "a private commercial enterprise," because the king's accusations included profiteering by the unnamed bosses who were sentenced to execution. There were no charges of pornographic reporting or anti-monarchy propaganda, but presumably there were advertisements, which would make interesting reading today.

Some court officials appealed against the royal sentence — which smacks of Kim Il Sung's comradely rule today — and sought exile rather than execution. No one seems to know whether the petition — improbably — was successful. But the paper was certainly killed.

A recent edition of the periodical *New Korean Glimpses* gives an unprejudiced report of the Korean case, which also evokes a precedent of German and Korean competition in first printing with movable metal type. For years, Herr Johannes Gutenberg had been given the credit for initiating that method when he printed family Bibles in the 15th century.

Again there were unsubstantiated Korean claims that a 50-volume anthology on past (and then-present) social life and religious rites had been printed in 1230 during the Koryo Dynasty by movable metal type. Maybe that was too early. But in 1972, a Korean book entitled *Abstruse Principles of Zen* was discovered in the French national library; it had been printed with movable metal type in 1377. A French bibliographer, who had been serving in the French Embassy in Seoul in the early 1900s, had brought the volume back with him to Paris and placed it in the national library, where it lay hidden for seven decades.

Before the creation of the "modernised" metal type, Korea also beat Japan in the production of woodblock prints. The oldest printed material in the world was believed to have been a Japanese *sutra* (verse) called *One Million Pagodas*, printed in 770. But then — again inadvertently — in 1966, a roll of 12 sheets of Korean paper, inscribed with prints of a sutra written in Chinese characters, was found in a Buddhist temple at Kyongju, built in 751 during the Silla dynasty. Specialists reckoned that the writing on Korean tree-bark paper had been printed at least a generation ahead of the Japanese scroll.

Those remarkable Koreans never gloat about their achievements in what they call "the world's culture of letters." But they remain confident that their publication of the first daily newspaper about a century before *The Leipziger Zeitung* will be proven, as were the other printing successes. Who really cares, anyway, except perhaps senile newspapermen, who usually can't remember when their own papers were born.

1982 March

The honoured ghost of Col Masanobu Tsuji, Japan's Imperial Army Academy genius who vanished inexplicably in Laos or Vietnam (or China?) 18 years ago, must be stirring now that Japan and China are considering military ties. Tsuji — who should have been a general — was born in Ishikawa and graduated brilliantly from the Imperial Army Academy in 1931, when he was only 29. He was top staff planner of the invasion of Malaya and the capture of Singapore. He personally directed the field and jungle training on Hainan of the numerically inferior but militarily superior Japanese forces which outflanked and overran the British in Malaya. He also served in the field in Guadalcanal and Burma.

He once told me: "I was wounded seven times by the bullets of the Chinese, the bombs of the Americans, the shells of the British and even bullets from Japanese-made machine-guns supplied to the Burmese, who later fought against the Japanese."

I got to know him tolerably well in Tokyo in 1955-59. He was an engaging man with a shaven, gleaming skull, large eyes, large nose, large spectacles and — occasionally and disarmingly — a large grin. He despised Gen. Hideki Tojo, revered Gen. Tomoyuki Yamashita and blamed the Japanese navy for the loss of the war.

He hated communists generally but admired Ho Chi Minh personally and believed that the Japanese could come to terms with the Chinese. (His ghost undoubtedly would be promoting the drive for stronger Japanese defences and approving the current contacts with Peking — the more so because he utterly distrusted the Soviets.)

He first won a seat in the Diet in 1952, but his outspoken criticism of the American-dictated plans for Japanese self-defence led to his expulsion from the Liberal Democratic Party. He easily won immediate re-election to the upper house of the Japanese parliament as an independent.

I had the honour of helping him prepare the English version of two articles which he wrote promulgating his independent views on defence expansion (three decades ago): "We must defend neutrality by our own hands . . . Let us equip ourselves with the latest American missiles and spend our defence budget on reorganising the Self-Defence Force into a nuclear-equipped military force.

"If there is to be a showdown, the government must obviously overcome the people's opposition to nuclear weapons. Laws must be created for the protection of military secrets. This is admittedly a difficult task but a responsible politician should have the willpower and courage to accomplish it."

At 62, he was an established if independent political figure in Japan and a respected, if unofficial, military authority. It was then that he suddenly departed on his vague "mission of inspection" to Bangkok and Saigon, ostensibly of his volition and with no known governmental or military sponsorship, official or unofficial. He disappeared on the night of 24 April 1964 from his Saigon hotel, taking his luggage and leaving money for his bill. The Japanese Government sent a top-level intelligence group to Saigon to try to trace him but made no official comment.

It was later painstakingly discovered that he had travelled under escort to Vientiane in Buddhist monk's robes, presented letters of introduction to a Pathet Lao unit, been guided to an airstrip near the Plain of Jars and flown in a Soviet aircraft to Hanoi to meet again Ho and Vo Nguyen Giap.

The known trail ends there and then, Radio Peking announced bluntly, briefly and amazingly, that he had been executed by — of all people — the CIA. Washington denied the announcement with derision and Peking has never mentioned Tsuji since.

Early in 1965 a ransom demand was delivered by a Chinese to the Japanese Consulate-General in Hongkong. The demand contained a signed and dated identification by Tsuji — accepted as genuine by his family in Tokyo — but the demand was not followed up. Next year there was another demand — but without identification and again no follow-up.

Tsuji would never have demeaned himself by aping the spy. But on his personal mission — rash and irresponsible — he could still have persuaded himself that he was humbly but honourably serving the emperor, even if he expediently changed his monk's robes for the uniform of a military "observer" with the North Vietnamese and Viet Cong forces.

Of course Tsuji is dead. But his record and patriotism still demand a solution to the mystery of his disappearance. Let the Japanese now use pressure on Peking. We must find out what happened to him. (I think I can see his ghost grinning.)

No one surely can have been surprised at the uncovering and deporting of Soviet spies in the Singapore, Kuala Lumpur and Jakarta embassies — eight in the past seven months. As the Soviet Union seeks to expand its influence in the Far East, there can be no doubt that similar counter-espionage surveillance must be deepening in Bangkok and Tokyo.

Even ignorant barefoot reporters like myself knew that in Tokyo during and after the occupation, rival bands of Soviet spies from the KGB and Soviet military intelligence (then the 4th Bureau of the Red Army, now the GRU) were operating from the massive, capitalist-style embassy. The United States and Japanese observers regarded the 4th Bureau as more efficient than the KGB.

One of the 4th Bureau agents was a regular drinker at the old Foreign Correspondents Club — an amiable "cultural attaché" called "Ivan The Chain-Puller" because, whenever he visited resident gaijin reporters, he insisted on sitting in the bathroom and pulling the primitive dunny-chain while he talked off the record. "You can't trust the Japs or the Yanks," he would insist. "They've got all these rooms bugged. They can record everything you are saying unless you make this noise." (Another needless rustle of toilet-paper and clanging of the chain.)

In the 1960s, Bangkok was believed to be a central base for the Soviet Southeast

Asian espionage network. Perhaps the absence of deportations there means that current surveillance is helpful and informative. Let us hope so.

Right or wrong, we reporters who had been based in both Moscow and Peking believed that the Russkies kept a far tighter and more suspicious ear and eye on our humble and honest activities. None of us who were housed in the old days in Moscow's Hotel National ever talked indiscreetly in our comfortable suites facing the Kremlin and Gorky Street corner.

Some of us in Asia — I recall enviously — took non-innocent counter-action. I remember two who had crafty success in strike-backs (both, alas, now RIP). One skilfully and ruthlessly organised the abrupt recall of a top party observer at pre–Korean War negotiations on the border by brushing close to him with conspicuous inadvertence on two separate occasions, under the suspicious eyes of other party representatives, and whispering in his ear: "Good-day, comrade; how are you?"

The other counter-plot was more devious and complicated. I won't say where or when it happened — though the context will show that it was after the Soviet army had rescued Czechoslovakia from the tyranny of the Czech people.

A large mob of us correspondents were covering a regional party summit conference and had learned to our disgust that an agreeable drunken old embassy party hack, Comrade Y, whom we all liked, had been back-stabbed by a KGB or GRU colleague, Comrade X (whom we all detested), and recalled to Siberia. My tough old friend, Dudley, who clearly should have had CIA connections, reacted ferociously. "We know now that Comrade X is a bigger bastard than we thought," he snarled. "I shall have him recalled! Leave it to me."

Rumours spread among foreign diplomats at the conference that Comrade X was now in trouble himself — as Comrade Y had been. We pressmen were asked what we knew. Comrade X, a gross scoundrel with a con-man's laugh, had learned of the rumours that he had incautiously and publicly denounced the Prague takeover and was clearly ill at ease. But I could not believe that Dudley's undercover operations could do more than discomfit him. Then the conference ended and we correspondent birds-of-passage sought our home perches. Comrade X was still there.

A month later, Dudley and I met in Jack Conder's old Hongkong bar. "Well met, Richard," he said, with uncharacteristic self-satisfaction. "The bastard X has been recalled. Whimpering, I assure you." I was astounded. Then the cunning details came. Dudley had first arranged for a friend who spoke the language of the country to call the embassy, allegedly from "Overseas Telephone Calls," to seek the private number of Comrade X for a booked incoming call from Washington. Then, under instructions, old and trusted friends of Dudley at widely separated Western capitals had airmailed straight-forward postcard messages of goodwill to Comrade X, each brief message incorporating a stipulated numeral as a needless date or an obscure reference — obviously a code.

"Dear X was already under dark surmise because known 'advisers' in certain embassies were constantly rolling their eyes and nodding their heads whenever they glimpsed him in public," Dudley said. "You don't seem to realise that, for every Comrade X who can eliminate a Comrade Y, there is always a Comrade Z, who is waiting in the wings to eliminate Comrade X in the name of party loyalty."

Frightening, I still reckon — apolitically, of course.

May

North Korean President Kim Il Sung's son and chosen heir-apparent, Kim Jong Il, is still certain to be his manic daddy's successor. Kim Il Sung's 70th birthday celebrations last month endlessly repeated his titles — National Hero, Great Leader of the International Communist Movement and World Revolution, and Saviour of Humanity.

He had returned to his fatherland to rule the northern half in 1945 as a Soviet army major. There, from 1948 onwards, with the support of the Russkies — and, let it not be forgotten, of the Chinese People's Liberation Army at the vital stage of the Korean War — he established what many people now call a socialist monarchy, with himself as "king" and his son (who celebrated his 40th birthday this year) as "crown prince." As South Korean University professor Kim Gahb Chol (no relation) observes: "Because of the absence of revolutionary achievements, it was necessary for him to glorify his family line falsely, fabricate symbols for a shamanistic personality cult, strengthen nepotism and establish a royal succession system to maintain Kimilsungism without Kim Il Sung."

All the evidence surely shows that Kim Jr's delayed appointment as one of North Korea's three vice-presidents reflects discretion rather than denigration or even uncertainty. Reports from Japan and Seoul and a public statement by the president of the (North) Korea–Japan Friendship Association, Comrade Hyon Jan Guk, stress that he is "the only one" to succeed Kim Il Sung. The "crown prince" was made organisation chief of the North Korean Workers Party (KWP), which rules the government, in 1973, and No. 2 in the KWP in 1980. "Kim Jong Il is in charge of policies on behalf of the party and the government," Hyon told the Japanese press. "He is policy aide to his father in every domain, including diplomacy and national defence. He is gifted with outstanding leadership and lofty character."

"King" Kim's birthday also coincided with the first detailed revelations of the operations of eight concentration camps in which an estimated 105,000 "ideological criminals" are imprisoned for life in North Korea (REVIEW, 16 Apr.). This staggering information is based on on-the-spot reports by horrified recent defectors from the North — who are identified and quoted.

After a preliminary survey in 1958-65, it is revealed, "an extensive, four-year-long examination of the loyalty of the North Korean people was initiated in 1966, dividing the people into three classes: the core class, the unstable class and the hostile class." The core class was those on whom the regime could rely in time of emergency; the unstable class was those whom the regime could not depend upon and the hostile class those who were "considered likely to take sides with South Korea in emergency or who were subject to group resettlement and special surveillance."

According to the report, the core class was estimated to total 5.06 million (28% of the population); the unstable 8.14 million (45%), and the hostile 4.88 million (27%).

Those classified as "especially dangerous" in the hostile class were interned in the concentration camps, where they now have to work for more than 12 hours a day without pay and to attend at night a two-hour ideological re-education session, based on self-criticism. Undercover agents are planted in the camps to detect "doubly dangerous" (and obviously indiscreet) prisoners, who are often publicly flogged.

The prison camps — surrounded by barbed wire and electric fences and minefields — are based in remote mountainous districts in the far north over an area of about 1,000 km^2, and the prisoners — all on life sentences — live in spartan dormitories, tiny log huts or caves dug in the hillsides, and usually work as miners or loggers or reclaim land. They must surrender their citizenship cards on arrival and forfeit all basic rights. New arrivals obtain potato and corn seeds from old-time prisoners and plant them to grow their own food. Relatives and friends are not permitted to visit them or even to correspond. The death rate — not surprisingly — is said to be very high.

The three North Korean defector-informants responsible for this information are two former intelligence agents and a trained spy who was despatched to Japan (before defecting to Seoul). Once faithful party members and supporters of "King" Kim and "Crown Prince" Jong Il, they were outraged when they first visited the camps. They urge that the United Nations demand an inspection of the "living hells."

June

Because I will be on an all-too-brief visit to my Aussie homeland this week, I have been checking on under-reported parochial events there. Alas, the emphasis seems to remain parochial — though I had had an earlier impression that liberalised immigration was widening the Australian horizon, to the West as well as the East.

Believe it or not, Prime Minister Malcolm Fraser is apparently losing votes because he travels abroad so often. His latest visit to the United States was his 26th absence from Australia since he became prime minister — an average of more than four a year. And he is supposed to be planning two or three more trips before the end of the year. All the better, I should have reckoned, because he was showing the Aussie flag overseas and strengthening international ties.

But my astute Canberra colleague and informant, Peter Costigan, takes the opposite view. So — as he points out — does Labor opposition leader Bill Hayden, who is hesitating to accept an invitation to visit the US during the next four months. As opposition leader he is entitled, under the Australian Constitution, to make a round-the-world tour every year. He has made trips to the Middle East and Europe, but has visited the US only once since he became top Labor man four years ago.

Hayden is convinced that Fraser's travel is on Labor's side as the next election looms and he will apparently soon make an open pledge that he will never travel abroad more than once a year if he becomes prime minister.

(It is interesting to recall that former Australian conservative prime minister Sir Robert Menzies travelled frequently but that Labor prime ministers Jack Curtin and Ben Chifley seldom left Australia. Surely Menzies will be remembered in Australia long after Curtin and Chifley are forgotten?)

Hayden is more interested in Asean than Anzus and maybe would move to have Australia join Asean if he toppled Fraser. Of course, he is not really anti-American but he argues that Australia is too dependent on the US. If he risks a trip abroad before the next election, he will certainly travel through the Far East on his way to the US. He must be prepared to defend himself against charges of anti-Americanism as he seeks to lessen Australia's so-called dependence on the US — vital, of course — in any revision of the Anzus pact. Probably he will stay home.

Of course I will visit Canberra on my visit to the homeland. Alas, I will not be there for the 35th national conference of the Australian Labor Party in July. Previously, this conference, which tries to close ranks and unify an election offensive, met in Sydney and Melbourne — more convenient and more economical.

This will be the first Labor meeting of an expanded delegation of 99 members — including, astonishingly, about 25% lady members. (Are we Aussies going women's-lib-crazy?) These lady delegates intend to make a non-political proposal that Labor policy will in future favour "abortion by demand." This move could split Labor because many of its supporters are Catholic religious groups.

(Democratic politics are so often vulnerable to morality and religion and the influence or compliance of the ladies. After all, President Zia-ul Haq of Pakistan, in his recent campaign for "women's liberation," has aroused controversy by arguing that "the ideal woman in an Islamic society must combine dignity and service, and [Muslims] must give them respect and dignity but emphasise their roles as housewives.")

And so we move to another minor but prickly Australian issue: a dispute over whether women — married or single — who apply to join the police force should have a compulsory pregnancy test. The New South Wales police department made this mandatory when a recent recruit admitted, after acceptance, that she was pregnant and so must have a relaxation of her 12-week initial training.

The New South Wales Police Association denounced the decision as discriminatory: "Supposedly, it is not all right to be pregnant the day before you start in a training class, but it must be all right if a female member becomes pregnant after the first day's training." (Interesting implication?)

Believe it or not, on the six random taxi trips which I had reluctantly to pay for during my last week's bludger visit to Sydney, after one year's absence, all the affable drivers were migrants — from Greece, Italy, Turkey, Cyprus, Egypt and Lebanon. They had been Aussie residents for the past six years and clearly and warmly regarded Sydney as their home. Three said they had married since their arrival and the other three winked at me when I asked. They provided individual evidence that my initial fears that Australia — or Sydney anyway — was still parochial were completely unfounded.

Alas, I didn't have time to visit Canberra or Melbourne but the old mates who phoned me from those cities stressed that the flow of immigrants was continuing.

For the record, Australia's population passed the 15 million mark at the end of 1981. The gain through overseas migration last year contributed 53.5% — 67,800. Approximately 100,000 migrants and refugees — no White Australia racism now — will have arrived in 1981-82 and will climb about another 4% the next year. Austra-

lia's population growth increased by 1.64% in 1980-81 — the highest for any industrialised country in the world.

Cuts in fares for migrants travelling by air from Britain will range from 20-40%, and will be extended eventually to East Asia, the United States, Canada, Greece, Italy and India.

Enough dull figures. The other encouraging evidence was Sydney's dominant interest in Asia in general, and Southeast Asia in particular. Apart from reunions with old friends, I had to dance for my supper on four TV and eight radio interviews during the week. (Don't laugh — I was helping to promote an undeserved biography of myself, written by former Reuter and AAP reporter and now author Norman Macswan.*) To my satisfaction, independent questions at the 12 harangues manifested special interest in possible Australian membership of Asean. Among items of interest were whether Australians were popular in Asia and if Asians were aware:

▶ that they are always welcome as visitors to — or residents in — Australia; and

▶ that Australia stands firmly behind them in cooperative military defence — when needed — against the hegemonists.

Another matter of interest was that Australian defence scientists have invented a flying decoy, which "put Australia in the forefront in the world search for more effective protection against guided missiles launched against ships." (So it was said — top secret.) Also that three satellites for domestic communications will be built at a

---

*The Man Who Read The East Wind by Norman Macswan. *Kangaroo Press*, Sydney. US$10.30.

cost of A\$650 million (US\$677 million) to haul all widely separated Australians together for instant contact. (The satellites will have as profound an effect on Australian life as completion of the overland telegraph line between Adelaide and Darwin over a century ago.)

As a humble, grateful and devoted worshipper of the ladies everywhere, I was delighted to discover that my eager but all-too-rushed visit coincided with the centenary celebration of the admittance for the first time of women students to the hallowed Sydney University in June 1882. To my astonishment, I learned that the first women — Isola Thompson and Mary Brown — forced their way literally into the university three decades after it was opened, despite the continuing objections of some professors, who persisted in addressing them as "gentlemen" at student gatherings. During World War I, one professor, confronted with a class of young women, refused to lecture because there were no "real students" present.

At the celebration, the present chancellor, white-haired Sir Herman Black, sat happily on the ground outside the university with graduates Dulcie Barr and Edna Brown, and they toasted absent lady graduates who included the New South Wales solicitor-general (Mary Gaudron), the chief judge of the Family Court (Elizabeth Evatt) and Germaine Greer.

Most of my Aussie mates — aging now, alas — have been to the Far East and want to go back or to greet more friends from what should now be called the "Near North." So does the younger generation — far smarter than the old 'uns.

July

All foreign-devil correspondents who have worked in Korea will applaud the appointment of Foreign Minister Lee Bum Suk. He is one of the great survivors of the fallen Syngman Rhee (rather, Rhee Syngman) entourage. Many of us had known him before he led the South Korean Red Cross mission to Pyongyang in 1972. Since then, he has served for more than four years as ambassador in India — wasted talent, I reckon — before being wisely recalled by President Chun Doo Hwan as minister of national unification in late 1980. (In India, it was learned by some of us, he encouraged unofficial discussions with North Korean representatives — never disclosed at the time.)

Shrewd and urbane, he always gave us a good story at a news conference and knew — with a sophisticated smile — how his name could provoke a chaste blush or a vulgar guffaw from ignorant foreigners. "Shall I tell you how to spell the name?" he would sometimes ask newly arrived reporters. "There is no 'c' in Suk."

When I first met him in the Korean War days, my puritanical chief sub-editor in Australia decided to use initials instead of spelling his name in full, but stupidly thought his last name must be the family name so Lee Bum Suk became L. B. Suk. The mistake puzzled the hell out of Koreans in Australia: had a strange Mr Suk ousted Mr Lee in a secret purge? (Let it be remembered that there are now three Lees in the new South Korean Government following 24 changes in the first six months of this year. The others are Culture and Information Minister Lee Chin Hi and Science and Technology Minister Lee Chung Oh.)

The Chinese and the Lao have, of course, the same confusion over names. I remember how an earnest American colleague in Vientiane a decade or so ago was staggered to note that a sub-editor who smugly believed he had mastered the tricky Oriental substitution of first and family names had christened the then Lao prime minister "Ma Phou." He cabled: "The prime minister is not the mother of Prince Souvanna Phouma."

As the new foreign minister and the former reunification minister, Lee will certainly be advising behind the scenes in Seoul and promoting the South Korean cause on the international horizon as manic Kim Il Sung and his crown prince son and heir continue to refuse talks on peaceful reunification.

This month, ironically, was the 10th anniversary of the historic South-North Joint Communique, which had then given, alas, a misleading impression that healthy Koreanism would at last prevail over the alien communist disease (appropriately, 4 July 1972). Now Kim has scrapped the communique and tries to argue that there had been no South-North coordinating committee.

The last — but always futile — approaches by Lee to North Korea proposed an exchange of visits between the leaders of the South and North (5 January 1981), and a formula for "achieving unification through national reconciliation and democratic processes" (22 January this year).

Blessed by the new foreign minister, this year's 4 July message to the North said: "We once more urge the North to stop turning a blind eye to the wishes of the people, to regain reason and reopen the Seoul-Pyongyang telephone line, and to come forward to a form of dialogue in keeping with the spirit of the joint communique for frank and open-minded discussions of the pending questions and the future of the Korean people."

There is a deafening silence — naturally — from the North as Kim builds up his "defences" and his crown prince gets rid of possible rivals and trains agents to enter the South via Tokyo.

For the record, the new commander of United States and United Nations forces in South Korea, Gen. Robert Sennewald, estimates North Korean military strength to be 720,000 (640,000 army, 30,000 navy and 50,000 air force) and paramilitary forces 2.69 million. North Korea spends 24% of its gross national product on "defence" — the highest of any nation in the world. South Korea spends about 6%. US Defence Secretary Caspar Weinberger has warned that North Korea has "a decided advantage in numbers of combat divisions, tanks, artillery and armoured personnel carriers." He also pointed out that the existing force of 24 submarines and 20 missile boats, still being expanded; "would be useful only in an attack role." In the air, North Korea also has a two-to-one numerical superiority in fighter aircraft.

● **Lee Bum Suk was one of 17 South Koreans killed in a bomb blast in Rangoon on 9 October 1983.**

August

The British Defence Ministry's honours and awards committee is currently examining field reports and recommendations on acts of bravery during the Falklands conflict. It is understood that six men are being considered for the Victoria Cross.

Queen Victoria decreed that "neither rank nor long service nor wounds, nor any other circumstances or condition whatsoever, save the merit of conspicuous bravery" would entitle anyone to the VC. In World War I, 634 VCs were awarded; in World War II, 182. The biggest number for one action — 11 — went to the (mostly Welsh) defenders of Rorke's Drift in the Zulu War in 1879.

To my surprise, I learn that only one VC-holder is now serving in the British army — not surprisingly, a Gurkha, Rambahadur Limbu, who won it in the jungle war against Indonesia in the mid-1960s. Sadly, there is no Gurkha among the six men now being considered; unusually, the Gurkhas arrived in the Falklands with the second wave of troops rather than the first.

I had the honour of covering front-line operations by the Gurkhas in North Africa during the campaign against Rommel in World War II and in Borneo during the 1964-65 Confrontation. The kindest killers in the world (their favourite weapon being their curved knife, the kukri), the little, brown Gurkha tribesmen come from the flowery foothills of Himalayan Nepal and are the most popular garrison troops in Hongkong.

They have served a foreign cause with unquestioning loyalty, instinctive discipline and deadly heroism for nearly 170 years. Happy family men and happier warriors, they have fought against every British foe since 1815. Their first battle honour in partnership with the British was the capture of the great fortress of Bhurtpore — or Bharatpur — in 1825. They raced the British grenadiers to the breached gates. The British cheered them. The Gurkha reply became immortal: "The English are as brave as lions; they are splendid sepoys, and very nearly equal to us."

Gurkhas are gently homicidal, warm-hearted and hot-blooded. Unlike many Asians, they have a rich appreciation of irony. They find it almost impossible to lie, but delight in misleading stupid or condescending foreigners. I once heard an arrogant new foreign-devil arrival ask a Gurkha officer in Hongkong's New Territories whether he beat his wife. "Of course," the major replied, "and with my kukri, you can be sure."

They like strong liquor and they can carry it. Duty-free rum is their army ration; at home they have a grain beer called janr and an explosive spirit called raksi. They would as soon gamble as eat — if their panchayat, or stern battalion council of five

Gurkha and kukri: gently homicidal.

senior officers, would permit them to do so.

At the battle of Wadi Skarit in Tunisia, I had the grisly experience of following the 1943 descendants of the original Gurkha Rifles after the blood-curdling night assault on the towering Rassez-Zouai rampart. Several startled-looking Teutonic heads littered the rocky defiles beside recumbent headless bodies, apparently wearing crimson barber's neck-towels for haircuts and shaves which would never again be necessary. But the Gurkhas, relaxed, spotless, hospitable and smiling, had supplemented their orthodox tea-rum-rice-fish breakfast with hard-to-get eggs for us sahib guests. And the only unsheathed kukri I saw was being used deftly to peel potatoes. (The legend that a Gurkha must draw blood whenever he unsheathes his kukri, and so ceremoniously nicks his finger if he has unaccountably failed to nick or decapitate an enemy, is untrue.)

I celebrated my 58th birthday at a Gurkha outpost in Borneo in 1964 with some old friends from the 8th Army of 1943. I accompanied an Aussie major, serving with the Gurkhas, on a night inspection of a forward post, hidden among swamp mangroves on the Tawau front. A young Gurkha, evidently ill, was lying on the earth floor of a dark, rain-soaked hut. We carried him to our Land-rover and drove him to a hospital, where he was received with stony silence by three other sick Gurkhas in a whitewashed ward. The major explained to me that the silence was eloquent evidence of the suppressed fury of the four men: "They are all furious. No Gurkha will ever admit he is sick."

I asked if there was ever resentment when a Gurkha suspected of being sick was sent to hospital — resentment either on his part because he did not believe he was sick, or among others of his unit who might feel that treatment was unnecessary. "Good God, no!" the Aussie major replied, goggling. "Every Gurkha knows that whatever his officer — Gurkha or British — decides and orders must be best for the unit and himself. No Gurkha would ever doubt an officer's order."

"*Ayo Gorkhali!*" remains the war-cry: "The Gurkhas are upon you!"

September

After 29 years, Peking, through its Washington embassy, has at last acknowledged in writing the seizure by a Chinese gunboat of a Hongkong yacht on 21 March 1953, but claims that the seizure was inside Chinese territorial waters and denies responsibility for illegal action.

The yacht was the classy, Shanghai-built, 20-year-old, 42-ft cutter Kert, which my correspondent-mate from the Korean War, Dick Applegate (RIP), had bought from its builder, who had moved to Hongkong, for US$50,000 in 1953. He had then resigned from United Press and, with two American friends (Don Dixon and Ben Kraser, a merchant marine skipper), planned to sail around the world on a TV-filming mission for his new boss, NBC.

On its maiden cruise to Macau, Kert was seized by the Chinese gunboat and Dick and his companions were dragged into a

Canton prison for 18 months, with eight months in solitary confinement.

Dick has recorded — and his charming widow, Barbara, has reiterated in the prolonged but still-frustrated appeal to the United States Foreign Claims Settlement Commission (FCSC) in Washington — how the Chinese tried to force him to admit that Kert had trespassed into Chinese waters, indicating a near-coast location on their charts as the point of seizure (which proved that they then accepted the three-mile limit).

Dick, Dixon and Kraser stuck stubbornly to their case that the point of seizure was in international waters. At last released, they crossed the border into Hongkong in September 1954. But the Chinese kept Kert in Canton, where it was regularly operated (maybe not now) as a customs launch.

Since then and since Dick's death in February 1979, Barbara and her lawyers have maintained a claim for the initial cost of the yacht plus annual compound interest at 6%, now representing a total of US$227,500. Let it be stressed here that the Applegate legal claim was given immediate and sympathetic audience by Zhou Enlai, then China's foreign minister, when, aboard Prince Norodom Sihanouk's yacht on the Tonle Sap river in Cambodia on 27 November 1956, he was told details of the piracy by foreign-devil correspondents. Zhou admitted that he had not been informed of the incident and characteristically promised that Kert would be returned to any Asian port of Dick's choice.

But nothing happened. Dick went to live in retirement in Spain in 1966 and, alas, did not learn that the FCSC was then accepting claims for property taken by the Chinese. When he returned to New York in 1968, he was told that the application should have been made earlier. Dick shrugged.

But Barbara — good luck to her! — has kept on fighting. With top legal advisers, she wrote to the Chinese Embassy in Washington, and personally also to Deng Xiaoping (apostle of honest non-Maoist justice) and Madame Zhou (who should surely have tried to implement her husband's pledge).

Now, at long last, Barbara has been granted a response, unsigned, from the Chinese Embassy in Washington: "Dear Mrs Applegate: . . . The yacht was confiscated because it entered the territorial waters of China in times of the Korean War. Therefore, we cannot give consideration to returning it. Your understanding would be greatly appreciated. With kind regards."

No acknowledgment from Deng or Madame Zhou. So what can Barbara Applegate do? She won't give up. There could perhaps be a "lobbying" venture for an Act of Congress "for the relief of the estate of Richard Applegate," which could appeal to both Democrats and Republicans in a non-party move to correct the technicality of the FCSC refusal to accept a delayed application. Surely the more publicity the case gets, the more pressure — direct and indirect — there would be on the FCSC, which already has a fat file on the unprecedented claim.

Another alternative — seeking direct US action through a federal district court —

could take years of argument and involve a fortune in legal fees.

Anyway, Zhou must be now spinning in his grave over the non-fulfilment of his 1956 pledge. And Deng could certainly use the Applegate case to demonstrate his honest and judicial "correction" of past errors. Perhaps he never got that letter from Barbara . . .

October

September 1839 marked the opening of the Anglo-Chinese war which led, first, to the ceding of Hongkong to Britain "in perpetuity" (the Treaty of Nanking, 1842), then to the similar seizure of the Kowloon peninsula (Treaty of Tianjin, 1860), and finally to the 99-year lease of the New Territories (Convention of Peking, 1898).

However protracted, the negotiations which have now started on the future of Hongkong will certainly not be as troublesome and bloody as its seizure. Nor could the British repeat the initial surprise victory which Trade Superintendent Capt. Charles Elliot, the founder of the colony, brilliantly achieved on 5 September when his two frigates ran along the Chinese line of 29 anchored men-of-war off Chuenpi Point, gave them a starboard broadside at a distance of only 50 yd, turned and let them have the larboard broadside on the return tack. The Chinese cannon on the Kowloon shore were sighted for a longer range and damaged only the frigates' rigging, wounding one seaman. In 45 minutes, four of the Chinese men-of-war had been

sunk and the remainder badly damaged. Elliot, never bloody-minded, called off the action.

Then Hongkong Island first became a British naval base, when a Royal Navy expedition of 16 men-of-war and 31 vessels carrying 4,000 Irish, Scottish and Indian troops arrived in June 1840. The commander was Rear-Adm. George Elliot, a cousin of Capt. Elliot, and a coincidental appointment which must have persuaded many Chinese that nepotism was not confined to the Land of the Dragon.

The British ships moved up the China coast, seized the Chusan Islands at the entrance to the Yangtze and boldly entered the Peiho river approach to Peking. The astonished emperor was confronted with Western cannon. The foreign devil, literally, was at the gate. But the emperor manifested the same scruples, fairness, logic and discipline that marked the behaviour of both sides from the start of the Opium War. He gave a Manchu mandarin, Kishen, the task of persuading the foreign devils to return to Canton, where he would pretend to consider and accept their demands, while his troops were assembled for a sudden counter-attack.

Capt. Elliot had succeeded his cousin the admiral — invalided home — and he soon discovered that he was being given the honourable run-around. After six weeks, he captured the Chinese forts but refrained from seizing Canton when Kishen came mincing to heel. Elliot settled for cession of Hongkong as the new, independent and invulnerable centre of British trade in China, and also for a large indemnity payable by annual instalments over six years.

167

However, the emperor repudiated the agreement and the second instalment of the war broke out in March 1841. Elliot, who was stupidly reckoned to have made a bad bargain over Hongkong, was replaced by a Sir Henry Pottinger in August. The war continued and fierce fighting took place near Nanjing, where the Manchu army was destroyed and the emperor submitted.

So in 1842 Hongkong became a British colony, a treaty was accepted for free trade with China at Canton, Amoy, Foochow, Ningpo and Shanghai, and the Chinese paid the demanded indemnity — described with chaste hypocrisy as "property surrendered on ransom," though actually it was the overestimated value of 20,000 chests of illegal opium, which had been surrendered to the Chinese in Canton in 1839.

Britain and China agreed to end the opium traffic in 1907, on condition that the Chinese curtailed their widespread production of the drug and that the British reduced by one-tenth each year the exports from India. The agreement ended satisfactorily in 1917 but by 1921 Chinese warlords had revived the cultivation of poppies to pay their troops from an opium tax. The Pommies were very angry and threatened to approach the League of Nations. There was then no emperor to approach and there was no place to send gunboats. But the commies took over and abolished opium in 1949 — three years after the Pommies had decreed opium-smoking illegal in Hongkong, which owed its birth to the poppies.

If criticised for weakness in the negotiations over the sovereignty of Hongkong, Britain's Prime Minister Margaret Thatcher should remember that both Queen Victoria and her foreign secretary, Lord Palmerston, upbraided and later exiled Capt. Elliot for accepting "the lowest terms" in his settlement with the Chinese, stressing especially the "absurd" cession of Hongkong — "a barren island with hardly a house upon it."

Let it also be remembered that, immediately after the foreign devils accepted sovereignty, Chinese from the mainland began pouring in — though they had to live in tents, shanties and huts. Would they remain at "home" or be allowed to continue crossing the old border if the Union Jack is now hauled down over the skyscrapered landscape?

● **Twenty-three months after this article was written, British and Chinese negotiators initialled a historic document transferring the governance of Hongkong from Britain as a colony to China as a special administrative region, an event commemorated by Morgan Chua in a** REVIEW **cover depicting the modern personalities involved** — such as China's Deng Xiaoping and Britain's Margaret Thatcher — as the signatories of the Nanking Treaty.

1983 January

One of Australia's great newspapermen has just retired at the age of 75 after 58 years in the trade: Reg Leonard, chairman of Queensland Press, which publishes the *Courier-Mail*, the *Telegraph* and the *Sunday Mail* in Brisbane, and owns three other papers and the Brisbane TV station 4BK-AK.

Reg and I went to school in Melbourne together at the Christian Brothers' College, St Kilda (he is a year younger than I). In 1920 he won one of the eight much-prized state scholarships available annually — which I failed to do — and then four years later, when I was (don't laugh) a railway timetable clerk, he started work as a lineage-paid junior reporter.

He was a parliamentary reporter in Canberra from 1926 to 1939. Like me, he didn't have much affection for the then prime minister, Sir Robert Menzies, but Menzies told one of his press-gallery companions that "the sun shines out of Reg Leonard because he is so honest."

Reg left Canberra to become a war correspondent in World War II — first in Britain, then in New Guinea during the Japanese invasion. And it was in wartime New Guinea that he was first re-sponsible for launching a daily newspaper.

He suggested to the grumpy Aussie commander-in-chief that a daily newspaper with home news would make Aussie troops happier. And so *Guinea Gold* was published — to the satisfaction of American as well as Aussie soldiers. It was Reg's first venture into the publishing field.

Reg never worked in the Far East — to his deep regret — but his Queensland papers are noted for their detailed coverage of Asian news. I believe that — like me — he reckons Australia should try to join Asean.

In London in 1952 he attended and reported the funeral of King George VI. As a humble Aussie, he hadn't come sartorially prepared for the ceremony, but at the last minute, with Leonard resourcefulness, scissored black silk out of his waistcoat to disguise his boomerang-throwing tie and substituted hotel black slippers for his brown shoes.

He made newspaper history in Australia when his name was splashed over street-posters by *The Herald* in Melbourne because he had become the first Australian to get into Moscow after Stalin's death (in 1955, again beating me by a year). The unprecedented poster read: "LEONARD SHOPS IN MOSCOW."

Although he always regards himself as a journalist, Reg also had a lively time on TV in Brisbane, when

Leonard: honesty is the thing.

from 1960 to 1970 he chaired a popular programme, *Meet the Press*, once a week. He could be a tough questioner of the visiting peers and prime ministers, film beauties and archbishops, actors and top athletes who were lured on to the show.

Once a surly boxing coach threatened him: "I'll pull your nose! It might be a first time on TV, but I'll do it!" Reg grinned and repeated the question. I don't doubt that he could have defended himself physically.

During his 24 years in Brisbane, Reg-the-administrator climbed on the shoulders of Reg-the-journalist. In 1958 he became managing director of the Telegraph Newspaper Co., then managing director of Queensland Press in 1970 and chairman in 1971. During his 11 years as chairman, the company's profits rose from A$3 million (US$2.94 million) to A$7 million. (Perhaps he is as good a capitalist as he is a journalist.)

He also founded the Queensland Children's Hospital Appeal body in 1971 to improve hospital conditions. In the past 11 years that appeal has raised more than A$3 million. Reg was named "Father of the Year" in 1972 and will remain as chairman of the appeal, despite his press retirement. He himself has one daughter and two grand-daughters. (For once I have beaten him: I have one son and three grand-daughters.)

In 1971 he was awarded the OBE for services to journalism and in 1972 the CMG. I hope he hangs on long enough to get the KCMG, so he will become deservedly Sir Reg Leonard.

(CMG, of course, means "Call Me God"; KCMG, "Kindly Call Me God," and GCMG, "God Calls Me God.")

In an interview on his retirement, Reg admitted that, while always a journalist, he was "a believer in helping the underdog" and thought that "honesty is the most important thing in life." I demand that he write his memoirs.

(Reg and I are sometimes in touch, but I haven't seen him for years and I am indebted for many of the facts related here — some previously unknown because of Reg's modesty — to colleague Peter Trundle.)

March

Old spy Donald Maclean, dead on the approach of his 69th birthday, was not allowed the public funeral that his mate, Guy Burgess, was granted after he also died in Moscow 20 years ago.

Having had the good luck to gouge Burgess and Maclean out of hiding when I was first in Moscow in 1956 — five years after they quietly fled from London on Maclean's 38th birthday — I had the bizarre coincidence of returning to Moscow, via the Siberian railway, on the day that Burgess died, seven years later.

I went with other foreign newsmen to his funeral, where Maclean, already looking tired and much older, uttered a brief and hollow eulogy beside a red-draped casket with an artificial orchid atop. Madame Maclean, also dowdy and coarsening, listened wearily and a conscripted round-up of bored party "mourners" slumped and fidgeted, yawned and whispered.

We pressmen had been told that we couldn't speak to Maclean — maybe because, again by strange coincidence, Kim Philby, the leader of the Gang of Three, who had hung on in London, had just scuttled across the Middle East border into the Soviet Union.

Philby, unlike Maclean, usually remains out of sight in Moscow, and anyway there should be no surprise at his absence from the Maclean funeral because he pinched Maclean's wife from him on his arrival in Moscow. (She and Maclean's children now live in the United States.)

Maclean's funeral: no ceremony.

Guy — or "Gay" — Burgess meanwhile was provided with a Moscow boyfriend, a guitar-playing electrician, in his comfortable suburban apartment. (The puritanical Chinese comrades would never have tolerated that.)

Burgess and Maclean seemed to be good friends when I first met them in Room 101 in the Hotel National, overlooking the snowswept Kremlin and Red Square, on the evening of 11 February 1956. (I had had the good luck to get through a written message to Bulganin and Khruschev at an interview earlier that week with the then foreign minister, Vyacheslav Molotov, warning them that their coming visit to London would be a farce if they persisted in keeping Burgess and Maclean under cover and saying that they didn't know where they were.)

Maclean, a tall handsome man in a blue suit and red bow-tie, shook hands first and said with a wooden smile: "I am Donald Maclean." But he clearly wanted Burgess, a shorter, fatter man in a blue suit and an Old Etonian tie, with a bubbling smile, to be their spokesman.

With a flourish, Burgess gave Sidney Weiland (Reuters) and me copies of their historic, three-page, 1,000-word statement. Maclean silently puffed a long cigarette while Burgess forcibly rejected our requests to be allowed to read the statement and ask questions. The interview last only five minutes.

Naturally, the jointly signed statement carried no surprises. It said that they had never been secret agents. They had merely discovered that their "information and opinion about the political situation and the danger of war were in agreement in 1950" (when they were trusted British Foreign Office men). So, as patriots of probity and integrity, the only honourable course of action left open to them was to escape to the Soviet Union, "where alone there appeared to both of us to be some chance of putting into practice in some form the convictions we have always held."

Pravda had the story out in full at 10 p.m. — but only on page three.

It would be instructive to discover what sort of a statement Philby would make today if he was similarly approached. I tried — vainly, of course — to wangle an interview with him after the Burgess funeral. He hadn't yet come up from the deep south of Russia. But I made approaches — similar to the message via Molotov to Bulganin and Khruschev — and pointed out that he had been reporting for one of my London papers, *The Economist*, after he had retired from the intelligence job which he had held for more than 20 years. (Ignorant Downing Street and the British Government had publicly exonerated him from any association with Burgess and Maclean.)

Alexei Adzhubie, son-in-law of Khruschev, editor-in-chief of *Izvestia* and likely foreign minister if Khruschev had not fallen downstairs the following year, told me he would try to fix my interview. But after a couple of days I was firmly told that there was no hope. Curiously, I was advised ("off-the-record" then) that there had been "no real reason for him to run away at that time."

June

Denis Warner and his wife Peggy, distinguished Australian authors, have written the first definitive book on Japan's mass-suicide war effort in 1944-45 — the deadly kamikaze campaign that only the Japanese could have launched and that only the atom bomb was able to crush. (Kamikaze, the wind of the gods, was the typhoon in the late 13th century which saved Japan from the attempted invasion of Kublai Khan by destroying his armada.)

Warner was personally involved as a war correspondent in the kamikaze conflict (a suicide plane hit his ship off Okinawa in May 1945). And after the war he and his wife, living in Japan, researched for years the records of kamikaze volunteers and the archives of the War History Office of Japan, and interviewed scores of Japanese survivors.

Japan began to train its suicide units in mid-1944 as defeat loomed after naval battles in the Pacific. "Japan, in desperation," say the Warners, "turned men into bombs, torpedoes and bullets, sacrificing their lives in a final attempt to snatch victory."

There are harrowing eye-witness descriptions of well-aimed death dives by the kamikaze pilots on American, Australian and British ships and attacks by piloted torpedoes (kaiten); personal close-ups of the leaders of the death-for-all offensives; details of the special training of the volunteers, and moving reports of last-minute farewells and messages to families and friends.

The first four special-attack units were called Sikishima (an old name for Japan), Asahi (Morning Sun), Yamazakura (Wild Cherries) and Yamato (another old name for Japan). Then other air force units were organised, including the Ten Thousand Petals, the Cherry Blossoms, the Divine Thunderbolts and the Floating Chrysanthemums — some carrying doomed crews of three and four.

Vice-Adm. Takejiro Onishi, Japanese authority on naval aviation, who had helped to plan the attack on Pearl Harbour, took command of the Japanese 1st Air Fleet in the Philippines after having directed the operation that destroyed the United States Air Force base at Clark Field. One of Japan's aviation pioneers, he spent two years studying in Britain, practised stunt flying and — both careful and daring as a flier — became a tough, hard-drinking, hard-wenching air force pilot. He always argued that Japan should put more emphasis on air power and less on naval power and widened the breach between Japanese naval and air force commanders.

Kamikaze pilot: no victory, no defeat.

Initially, he did not support the kamikaze project: "No matter what happens, I cannot kill young men like this," he told his wife. But later he conceded that the proposed suicide tactics should be adopted: "Even if we do not win, we will not be defeated."

Then he realised that Japan faced defeat, after withdrawing his air fleet (with a handful of new suicide aircraft) from the Philippines to Taiwan. His operations depended on the supply of more kamikaze aircraft. He tried to rationalise his actions by arguing that he was helping to save Japan's internal spirit: "Nations that win wars are not always the victors. One flower opens the spring to the world. A wave moves all the seas. So long as men die for the country, the nation will never perish."

In May 1945, Onishi became vice-chief of the navy general staff in Tokyo. On 16 August, the day after the emperor's surrender broadcast, he committed formal hara kiri — or seppuku — a decision which he deemed appropriate after his reluctant acceptance of kamikaze.

The Warners give a well-checked assessment of the kamikaze campaign: "At least 56 ships were sunk and 107 lost to the Allied war effort as a result of kamikaze air attacks. A further 85 suffered either heavy structural damage or heavy casualties, or both, and at least another 221 received lesser damage. But the results achieved by the other kamikaze operations — okas (piloted missiles), kaitens and shinyos (small explosive boats) — were not so serious.

"The succession of suicide campaigns did not prevent, and could not have prevented, the American advance," the Warners conclude. "They did add to the ill-informed notion that the Japanese were inhuman fanatics, and that in fighting them the end justified the means."

It was interesting to learn that Chinese dissident Wei Jingsheng, who had been jailed for 15 years in 1979, is now being held "in solitary confinement" in Peking's model No. 1 Prison. He is allowed out for exercise only once a month, may read but gets no writing materials.

In 1957, as a resident barefoot reporter, I was allowed to visit that prison, in which

1,200 men and 40 women were serving sentences of between three and 10 years — with a few "lifers." Stone walls and armed sentries surrounded three-storey buildings. However, I was told that there were no locks on cell doors except for the lifers; that prisoners shared dormitories; that none wore prison uniform, and that corporal punishment was officially forbidden. A difficult "normal" prisoner was — believe it or not — punished by not being allowed to work. At that time there were no dissidents in the prison, which incorporated a textile mill and a weaving plant.

"We aim to correct the prisoner, to reason with him, to reform him, to teach him to think correctly," I was told by Comrade Gi Donghan — tall, young and intelligent — who had been introduced to me as secretary of the prison.

"We re-educate him — patiently and thoroughly. He learns the truth and seriousness of his offences against the people. He works nine hours a day and studies two hours a day.

"There are regular group meetings of prisoners for self-examination, self-reflection and self-criticism, at which the older prisoners help the younger ones."

Gi conceded that sometimes there were stubborn and rebellious inmates. "But they must never be beaten or scolded," he insisted, deadpan. "Compulsion changes no man's mind. We persuade. We teach. There is no hurry.

"If a man is perverse or stubborn, we may decline to allow him the right to work at the spinning and weaving machines. He can idle in his cell or dormitory, stroll around the grounds, sit by himself. But he

Wei on trial.

knows that he is being disobedient. He suffers the silent disapproval of his comrades. Sooner or later, he will recognise his errors and testify to them voluntarily and openly. There is sincerity and penitence in every offender's heart, if we seek reasonably and earnestly and patiently enough."

Most prisoners whom I saw walking around looked relaxed, but I was allowed to talk to only one of them. Perhaps his commentary was the explanation.

He was a dignified, good-looking giant of a man, wearing blue pants and coat and jaunty white sporting cap. He was serving a 12-year sentence — not in solitary confinement and already reduced to nine years for his frank self-criticism — for espionage, sabotage and terrorism.

"I was the son of a Peking landlord," he confessed. "I frittered away money in self-indulgence. I never cared for other people . . ."

"Your wife?" I interposed.

He hesitated, then said "She is dead," and swiftly resumed his recital: "I never helped the state. I engaged in terrorism of the people. I have always lived a selfish life. When I am released I shall seek profitable work at weaving which I have been taught here. If I am asked to remain in prison to help others I shall do so."

He said he had a son aged 12 but naturally never saw or heard from him. His son would rightly be ashamed of him. His landlord father had died in 1950 after "liberation." I refrained from asking him *how* he died. I was afraid that he would reply, briskly and happily, that his father had been executed.

Anyway, he doubtless got another year struck off his sentence because of his frank, self-critical "confession," of which Gi, listening silently, clearly approved . . .

Later I saw 200 girls in blue dungarees, alert, docile and dignified, working silently at long rows of buzzing sewing machines in a Shanghai model No. 1 Prison. Their homely, venerable supervisor, comrade Yang, was astonished when I inquired about the circumstances of their arrests and sentences.

They were never "arrested," she explained patiently. They had "fallen into bad habits" and had "volunteered" to enter the No. 1 Prison after neighbours and friends had reported their delinquency. Blowing her nose delicately without a handkerchief, she reckoned they would have been reformed in about 18 months. Perhaps dissident Wei will learn how to cut back his sentence — though conditions in the model prisons must have changed in the past 20 years.

July

R eligion — not war, trade or politics — perpetrated the first real "confrontation" between China and the West, John D. Young (teacher of modern Chinese intellectual history and contemporary Chinese politics at the University of Hongkong) points out in his thorough study of the first attempt by Christian missionaries to infiltrate Confucianism, four centuries ago (*Confucianism and Christianity: the First Encounter*. Hongkong University Press).

In fact, this was not the first attempt of all. Nestorians were already actively seeking converts to their particular brand of Christianity in the fifth century.

The Jesuits, however, were led first to the Chinese border in 1552 by Francis Xavier, and later into China in 1583 by Matteo Ricci. The mission was finally terminated by the Qing emperor, K'ang-hsi, who banned Christianity from China in 1721 after a wrangle over traditional Chinese religious rites.

Ricci was a crafty — or should I say inspired? — Jesuit and soon converted a number of leading Confucianists, including Hsu Kuang-chi, an eminent scientist, administrator and writer with palace connections, who believed that Christianity would transform Confucianism and abolish Buddhism and Taoism, and "combine Confucian morality with Christian salvation."

He said: "I believe in Heaven for the good and Hell for the evil." He is an admirable choice from the several witnesses whose evidence Young examines in his study of the Christian-Confucian confrontation.

"Many of Hsu's ideas on practical statesmanship and socio-economic reforms had already been formed when he embraced the Christian faith at the age of 41," Young records. "But this does not mean that Hsu accepted Christianity merely for the sake of acquiring Western technology and science. He seemed to have produced scientific and technical treatises and translations after his conversion. Nevertheless, almost all his scientific writings were prefaced with a profession of his Christian faith. His interest in science was actually part of his social concern, which in turn grew out of his commitment to self-realisation."

Young points out that Hsu's open acceptance of Christianity never brought him any political or even personal difficulties — "not even during the height of the Nanking anti-Christian movement in 1616-17. His position in the intellectual and political environment of the late Ming period was never adversely affected by his open advocacy of Christianity . . .

"His writings showed no tension between his Christian and Confucian moral beliefs. The reforms he envisaged were inspired by both. He regarded it as possible to be 'loyal' to the Ming emperor while believing in the existence of an almighty deity. This is not to suggest, however, that Hsu was necessarily conscious that he was 'syncretist,' choosing the best from two cultures. He could simply have been pursuing what seemed to him true and rewarding, not in terms of contrasting culture but in terms of self-realisation."

However, Christianity was finally kicked out. In retrospect, the Vatican also seems to have behaved stupidly by arguing that Christianity had approved too many compromises to Confucianism. "Confucianism and Christianity [never mind communism] cannot be reconciled without a fatal compromise," Young concludes.

It is amusing to recall that St Francis Xavier would have been subject to arrest in Hongkong today had he attempted an encore of his first approach to China. He had been frustrated by the Christian mission's failure to reform India; had visited Japan, where he converted only a limited number of locals, and then turned his attention to China.

He landed on an island six miles off the mainland and 100 miles southwest of Canton, which was a smuggling base for the Portuguese and Chinese. He tried — with a bow, to the Vatican (rather than the Jesuits) — to bribe the Portuguese to take him into China without a visa, but they were too frightened.

Finally, the saint-to-be paid 200 golden pieces to a Canton merchant, who agreed to land him there. In his last letter to the

Society of Jesus, he prayed that after his visit "the Millennial Kingdom would soon come." But then he fell ill and died.

As a happy and appropriate introduction to his book, discerning Young quotes from both Confucius and the Bible:

Confucian Analects: To give oneself earnestly to the duties due to men, and, while respecting ghosts and spirits, to keep aloof from them, may be called wisdom.

St John (Ch. V, vs 24): Verily, verily, I say unto you, he that heareth my word and believeth in Him that sent me, hath everlasting life and shall not come into condemnation, but is passed from death unto life.

Australia has now joined New Zealand in increased export of live animals to South Korea. But while the Kiwis are exporting antlered deer for production of aphrodisiacs and other "medicines," the Aussies are selling thoroughbred racehorses and horses for hired trotting in private clubs and equestrian parks.

South Korea, in fact, seems to be relaxing into the English weakness for horse racing and riding. The Korean Horse Affairs Association (KHAA) has now established equestrian parks in each of Korea's six major cities — Seoul, Pusan, Taegu, Inchon, Kwangju and Changju. The Seoul Horse Riding Club has also opened another park in the Seoul stadium. (The sport might encourage more non-military defections from the North, where the only known sport is digging secret tunnels under the demilitarised zone.)

The KHAA park in Seoul, which is the oldest and largest riding course in the country, covers 6,600 m^2. Club membership costs Won 330,000 (US$430) and members can ride for Won 88,000 a month. Instructively, fees are reduced to Won 110,000 and riding charges to Won 33,000 for students, police, the army and junior government employees. In the equestrian parks, it costs Won 5,500 for a 45-minute trot, canter or gallop. The KHAA is training about 800 imported horses from Japan, the United States and Australia, but only 70 are now being used for leisure-riding and Australia is the main source of racehorses.

Last year South Korea bought 112 horses from Australia, and already this year another 168, including 56 which were air-freighted from Sydney on 26 May. With air transport charges, each horse cost about A$3,000 (US$2,600). One of the Australian exporters, John Atwood of Sydney, said that South Korea was clearly planning horse racing as a new attraction for tourists and certainly preparing for the 1986 Asian Games and 1988 Olympic Games in Seoul. "The horses were bought from breeders throughout Australia and this could become a new and major export venture for us," Atwood predicted.

The Koreans themselves are talking more about the sport of riding than racing. The KHAA now holds free lecture sessions for anyone interested in leisure-riding. One of the park chiefs pointed out that horses past their racing best are being used for riding. "It takes about one week to learn how to mount a horse and control it while it is walking, and then one month before galloping is safe," he said.

With typical Korean shrewdness, riders

are urged to buy special boots, jodhpurs and helmets, all of course being manufactured domestically.

A 52-year-old KHAA executive, who has been horse riding since he was a boy, also explained deadpan at a press conference that "the sport is good for stomachaches and other diseases and will help the flow of blood." (He made it clear, however, that he meant an internal flow of blood and strongly advised young riders to "check the condition of the saddle and bridle before mounting and to approach the horse from the front left side.")

Concurrently, South Korea is also expanding interest in golf. But there would seem to be a need literally to expand the size of the golf courses. KHAA now has the largest golf course in South Korea (next to the equestrian park and racecourse), but it still has only nine holes on its 132,000 m^2. Until 1971 it had only the customary Korean three holes. However, the golfers will now be able to watch horse-racing as they play.

The current jest among US residents, who now ride daily in the park in the early morning, is that the CIA should help finance the cheap export of reckless, untrained Aussie horses to North Korea. Such a conspiracy might help to get rid of President Kim Il Sung's son Kim Jong Il (who will be 43 next February). He would surely be a reckless horse-galloper, trying to impress his entrapped subjects with his spectacular prowess in the saddle. Let it be remembered that, when he was a graduate at the Mangyondae Revolutionary School in the late 1950s, he drove daddy's non-communist Mercedes-Benz, after having wrecked no fewer that 10 other vehicles while learning to drive. In late 1977, he was injured when he collided with a military truck.

Perhaps, happily, he might break his neck galloping on an untrained Aussie stallion.

August

So New Zealand — to this Australian's regret — has again rejected a proposal that its North and South islands should become the seventh and eighth states of Australia.

The union — or rather "reunion" — suggestion was made by an Australian judge, Justice Michael Kirby, at a recent conference on the closer economic relations agreement between Australia and New Zealand, organised in Auckland by the New Zealand Legal Association. It would be a reunion as, Kirby recalled, New Zealand had originally been a dependency of the state of New South Wales until separation in 1841.

"Provincial attitudes, petty jealousies and a fear of bold ideas have prevented reunion," said the judge. "The first 'lost opportunity' was the Federal Council for Australia, established in 1885, which New South Wales never joined. The second opportunity was the round of conferences in the 1890s, when an Australian constitution was framed and when a New Zealand representative, Sir Henry Parker, said: 'The crimson thread of kinship runs through us all'."

(It was to my surprise that I learned the Australian Constitution, in its final form, contemplated political union between Australia and New Zealand, which was specifically named as "a potential state.")

As an Aussie expatriate of four decades — with many New Zealand friends around the world — I have always argued that any union of the neighbours should not be named Australasia but Australia–New Zealand Allied Confederation, or Anzac — a peaceful evocation of the historic wartime title of the Australian–New Zealand Army Corps.

Alas, both New Zealand Attorney-General Jim McLay and his opposition counterpart Geoffrey Palmer trampled on Kirby's proposal at the Auckland conference. Grinning, McLay said: "The only notable results would be that New Zealand would get a good rugby team, Australia would get a good cricket team and it would be an Australian — not a New Zealand — horse that would win the Melbourne Cup."

More seriously, Palmer said: "I predict it will not happen — despite the generous and charitable instincts of the Australians. It will not happen because New Zealanders will continue to cherish their independence."

McLay was emphatic: "I want to lay to rest any suggestion of a political reunion between New Zealand and Australia. It doesn't really matter what happened 80 or 100 years ago. The political reality in New Zealand is such that it is not going to happen. There is no balance of advantage for New Zealand in union, even if it did eliminate some trade problems and enable New Zealand to make use of a modern High Court of Australasia as an independent court of justice."

Palmer was just as emphatic: "My distaste for the Australian federal system is shared by New Zealanders. The only chance of Australia merging with New Zealand would be if we faced a further 20 years of sustained economic adversity. We could be driven to it by the poverty of our economic performance." (That was a frank admission, surely.)

I have seen no Australian comment on this united New Zealand political reaction against the reunion proposal. I am indebted to John Slee, legal correspondent of *The Sydney Morning Herald*, for information on the under-played reports of the New Zealand conference which coincided with Australian Foreign Minister Bill Hayden's visit to Asean, followed by trips to Hanoi and Peking. Hayden's influence might have been stronger if he had been representing New Zealand as well as Australia — through Anzac.

Old Thai political, diplomatic and press contacts I met again last month in Bangkok assumed that Australian and New Zealand policy towards Asean was in firm accord. The Thai friends I talked with made it clear that they would welcome an Anzac approach for Asean membership — a possibility which Hayden's discussions and press conferences did not discourage. But they admitted that Singapore and Indonesia might not agree with them — whether Australia and New Zealand made their approach individually or as an Anzac union. To quote Palmer again: "Trade-sharing or political institutions will have to come first. It is a political task, not a legal one."

September

Last month's refuted reports of an alleged smuggling trade in panda skins from China via Taiwan provided a useful spur for panda welfare. The World Wildlife Fund (WWF), the world's largest private animal-conservation organisation, lost no time in whipping up world reaction and pushing for increased support for China's protection of these rare and beautiful mammals.

This year — the Year of the Pig — China, in cooperation with the WWF, should complete its 10th and largest reserve for protected pandas in Wolong, Sichuan province. China, which now regards the panda as a national treasure, has spent US$3 million and the WWF US$1 million on the 500,000-acre project, which will become a world headquarters for panda research. An estimated 1,000 giant pandas (protected from hunting and capture since the early 1950s) are still alive and well in the Sichuan, Gansu and Shaanxi provinces of central China.

The panda lives mainly on bamboo and because of this vegetation's poor nutritional value eats up to 20 kg over a 10-hour period. The problem of the pandas' survival is that vast areas of bamboo are now blossoming and going back to seed which takes a long time to germinate: in the past three years 150 pandas have been found dead from starvation.

The Chinese and the WWF are now planning to shift pandas to new bamboo areas, and — improbably — wean them onto alternative fare. They seldom eat meat but,

Wolong panda: legends abound.

in emergencies, will settle for birds, small mammals or fish. However, they are usually too slow to be efficient predators.

Having an average life span of 25-30 years, pandas are normally solitary creatures meeting once a year, in late spring or early summer, to mate.

The mother nurses her cub in a cave or a hollow tree-trunk, carrying it around for the first three months until it can crawl. The cub often stays with the mother for two or three years. Seemingly, the father is forgotten. Ancient Chinese legends surrounding the panda and its origins abound. One from Sichuan holds that the panda acquired its black markings because it mourned the death of a "human friend." Tang dynasty (618-907) records claim that the panda had magical powers and in those days screens bearing paintings of crouched pandas were placed in front of doors and gates.

Nancy Nash, Hongkong resident consultant of the WWF, accompanied the first foreign-devil group, led by WWF chairman Sir Peter Scott, invited to the Wolong reserve in 1980. Since then, she has visited Wolong and other panda areas several times. She tells me that back in AD 685, the emperor of China sent two live pandas and 70 skins to the emperor of Japan. And in the late 1200s, the Venetian traveller Marco Polo studied the skins of "black and white bears" in the Imperial Palace in Peking.

However, not until 1869 was the existence of the panda recorded in scientific textbooks in the West after a French missionary (Jesuit, of course) found a black-and-white animal skin on a farm in Sichuan and sent it to Paris. The French, with customary precision, registered it as a racoon.

Then in the 1900s the West waged a "scientific war" on the amiable pandas, seeking their remains and coats. For instance, Kermit and Theodore Roosevelt Jr (sons of former United States president, Theodore Roosevelt), on an expedition sponsored by Chicago's Field Museum of Natural History, shot a giant panda in Sichuan and sent the coat back home. It seemed to be the signal for hunters to start killing and capturing the animals wholesale. They were greatly sought after in the West — headline words such as "Panda-monium" became familiar.

But today the Chinese are resolved — with, they hope, foreign-devil support — to preserve the panda or da xiong mao (literally: giant bear cat). They will capture baby pandas and raise them in captivity. "A world without pandas," said Prof. Hu Jinchu, who is in command of China's preservation operation, "would be a much less colourful and happy home for all of us."

After 30 years, new facts have emerged on the Occupation of Japan in a detailed study by an American professor, Roger Buckley, now based in Japan with a Japanese wife, who has had access to recently released official documents from British, American and Japanese sources.

In *Occupation Diplomacy — Britain, United States and Japan*, Buckley reveals that Britain and Australia had far more influence on Occupation policy than had been suspected and that Britain and the US launched the trial of the Japanese "war criminals" as a sequel to the Nuremburg trial of the Nazis. Curiously, the Soviet Union lurched in belatedly to support the Tokyo trial but then wanted to have everyone hanged.

According to Buckley, the US proposed approximately 100 "criminals" while Britain originally nominated 11 (an appropriate cricket-team total) but reached agreement on 28. "Britain succeeded in beating back the United States attempt to add what the British defined as 'intermediate' war criminals to those indicted,"

Buckley records. "Any trial for this category, comprising bankers and journalists, was strongly opposed by Foreign Secretary [Ernest] Bevin, who said: 'The intermediate group are probably not war criminals in the widest sense of the word'." Britain also strongly and decisively opposed the US wish to prosecute Emperor Hirohito.

Of the 28 who were eventually arraigned, Prince Konoye escaped trial and certain hanging by poisoning himself at home the night before his arrest. Former foreign minister Yosuke Matsuoka and Adm. Osami Nagano, the naval chief of staff who approved the Pearl Harbour attack, also eluded the rope by dying.

So 25 prisoners lasted the distance, confronting the black-robed team of 11 judges. After two-and-a-half years of confused and boring trial, seven were hanged, 16 sentenced to life imprisonment, one sentenced to 20 years, and — the grossest miscarriage of justice — Mamoru Shigemitsu, the foreign minister who signed Japan's surrender to Gen. Douglas MacArthur after the lost war which he had vainly opposed, sentenced to seven years. The marathon trial could have lasted much longer had it not been for the impatience of the forceful Australian judge, Sir William Webb, who was chairman of the divided tribunal and a good friend to us pressmen.

Buckley, I reckon, should have given more detail about the scandal of Shigemitsu's sentence. The Russkies were after him because they disapproved of his record as ambassador to Moscow in 1936-38. It was also known that, as ambassador to London in 1940, he had vainly, if then secretly, cooperated with the British Foreign Office in the hope of keeping Japan out of the war.

A mass of evidence, supported by voluntary testimony from British and US leaders, was presented to the tribunal to establish that Shigemitsu increasingly opposed the initial military plotting and that his influence as a cabinet member was devoted to ending the war. The prosecution made no attempt to contest this evidence.

George Furness, Shigemitsu's able Boston counsel (still engaged in legal operations in Japan), petitioned MacArthur for Shigemitsu's release, arguing that his sentence, with all its implications, made it a crime for an advocate of peace to join a cabinet during a war in order, openly or covertly, to end the war which he had failed to prevent.

Shigemitsu, who limped on a wooden leg after having been the victim of an assassin's bomb in Shanghai in 1932, was released on parole after five years in Sugamo prison. His first request was to be driven to the Double Entrance of the Imperial Palace, where he alighted and bowed deeply in reverence to the emperor.

His family villa, with most of his treasured belongings was mysteriously burned to the ground the day before his release. The police never discovered whether the terrorist hands that destroyed his home belonged to old Japanese militarist foes or new Japanese communist foes. Shigemitsu accepted the new disaster with a shrug. He had not changed. He became the leader of a new opposition conservative party, practically indistinguishable from the existing ruling Liberal Democratic Party.

December

As the farce about former Australian prime minister Harold Holt's "espionage" and his submarine escape to China 16 years ago drags on, it becomes less amusing. He was an MP and a patriotic Aussie, and — no name-dropping — I knew him well from his old debating days in Melbourne and after he was elected to parliament in 1935. We remained old and close friends.

He was a great debater and we both belonged in our youth to a unique body known as The Debating Parliament of Melbourne, when I was a railway PR halfwit and Holt was still at Melbourne University. That was when he allegedly and impossibly became involved in espionage (1931) with Kuomintang agents in Australia and then politely switched to similar operations for substitute commie-dog agents in 1957 — eight years after their move to Taiwan. Preposterous!

Before and after he was prime minister, Holt showed no special personal interest in China. I saw him regularly on return visits to Aussie, when I was covering the Far East — with periods in China — but he never sought information, even when his alleged cunning switch to the Peking boys coincided with my six-month vigil there in 1956-57.

To my surprise, Anthony Grey, former Reuter correspondent (imprisoned by the Red Guards for two years during the Cultural Revolution) and now a distinguished author, is responsible for the tenuous work, *The Prime Minister Was a Spy*. He admits that he did little personal research, and investigations by *The Age* of Melbourne have tracked down the mastermind who — again curiously — is an Australian businessman and a former Australian naval officer named Ronald Titcombe.

No explanation has been offered in the book over the silence of the KMT when Holt is supposed to have preferred to become a running-dog for the commies. Would not Holt then have feared revelations by the Nationalists?

He is supposed to have become alarmed when he was prime minister. According to Titcombe, via Grey, he learned that the Australian Security Intelligence Organisation (ASIO) was at last on his tail. It is said that he visited ASIO headquarters personally to make discreet inquiries.

He then asked his Chinese contacts to smuggle him to China, and on the fateful day in December 1967, when he vanished in stormy waters, he is now alleged to have been "rescued" by two Chinese frogmen off the beach at Portsea in Victoria and safely hoisted into a waiting Chinese submarine — alas, without visa papers.

I have a personal and far more plausible report on his disappearance — though it does not tally with the official version — which I got from his chauffeur whom I knew, when I returned to Aussie from Hongkong a couple of months later. (I am sure his widow and family, infuriated by the grotesque report, know the facts.)

Holt, a strong swimmer and scuba diver,

went down to the beach for his daily swim, and discovered the "No Swimming" warning flag aloft over a virtually empty beach and rough waves. He was about to turn back and return home when a pretty young girl with two male companions, lying together on the beach, saw him and cried out: "Look, there's the prime minister!" Holt, always a lady's man, couldn't resist the temptation to demonstrate that he was a better swimmer than the younger men, and plunged into the waves from which he never reappeared — and which the two invisible frogmen would have found difficult to endure.

Meanwhile, Australian Attorney-General Sen. Gareth Evans has said: "On the basis of assurances given to me by the director-general of ASIO, which I accept, I can deny categorically that Harold Holt was ever investigated by ASIO. I am also assured that Mr Holt did not visit ASIO in 1967, or at any other time when he was prime minister, so that part of the story is equally without foundation . . . The whole tale seems to be straight out of fruit-cake land."

And the leader of the conservative opposition, Andrew Peacock, said: "On the basis of what I have been told, I would regard the book as outrageous and to be treated with contempt. Harold Holt was a highly respected prime minister, not only in Australia but throughout the Western world and by our friends in Asia."

Hear, hear!

The last column, published on 15 December 1983 — and submitted the day Richard Hughes went into hospital for his final illness.